Freedom on the Border

D1319196

Kentucky Remembered
An Oral History Series

James C. Klotter
Terry L. Birdwhistell
and
Doug Boyd,
General Editors

Barry Bingham
Barry Bingham

Bert Combs the Politician
George W. Robinson

Conversations with Kentucky Writers
edited by L. Elisabeth Beattie

Conversations with Kentucky Writers II
edited by L. Elisabeth Beattie

Tobacco Culture: Farming Kentucky's Burley Belt
John van Willigen and Susan C. Eastwood

Food and Everyday Life on Kentucky Family Farms, 1920–1950
John van Willigen and Anne van Willigen

This Is Home Now: Kentucky's Holocaust Survivors Speak
Arwen Donahue and Rebecca Gayle Howell

FREEDOM
ON THE
BORDER

*An Oral History of the
Civil Rights Movement
in Kentucky*

Catherine Fosl

and

Tracy E. K'Meyer

THE UNIVERSITY PRESS OF KENTUCKY

Copyright © 2009 by The University Press of Kentucky
Paperback edition 2010

Scholarly publisher for the Commonwealth,
serving Bellarmine University, Berea College, Centre College of Kentucky, Eastern Kentucky University, The Filson Historical Society, Georgetown College, Kentucky Historical Society, Kentucky State University, Morehead State University, Murray State University, Northern Kentucky University, Transylvania University, University of Kentucky, University of Louisville, and Western Kentucky University.
All rights reserved.

Editorial and Sales Offices: The University Press of Kentucky
663 South Limestone Street, Lexington, Kentucky 40508-4008
www.kentuckypress.com

The Library of Congress has cataloged the hardcover edition as follows:

Freedom on the border : an oral history of the civil rights movement in Kentucky / [compiled and edited by] Catherine Fosl and Tracy E. K'Meyer.
    p. cm. — (Kentucky remembered, an oral history series)
    Includes bibliographical references and index.
    ISBN 978-0-8131-2549-7 (hardcover : alk. paper)
    1. African Americans—Civil rights—Kentucky—History—20th century. 2. Civil rights movements—Kentucky—History—20th century. 3. Kentucky—Race relations—History—20th century. 4. African Americans—Kentucky—Politics and government—20th century. 5. Kentucky—Politics and government—20th century. 6. African American civil rights workers—Kentucky—Interviews. 7. Civil rights workers—Kentucky—Interviews. 8. African American civil rights workers—Kentucky—Biography. 9. Civil rights workers—Kentucky— Biography. I. Fosl, Catherine. II. K'Meyer, Tracy Elaine.
    E185.93.K3F74 2009
    323.1196'0730769—dc22   2009000989
    ISBN 978-0-8131-2606-7 (pbk. : alk. paper)

This book is printed on acid-free recycled paper meeting the requirements of the American National Standard for Permanence in Paper for Printed Library Materials.

Manufactured in the United States of America.

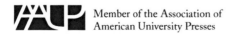 Member of the Association of
American University Presses

To the memory of my Kentucky grandmother,
Carolyn Anna Mae Bohn Sullivan
C.F.

To Colin and Norah
T.E.K.

Contents

Illustrations follow page 120

Series Foreword

In the field of oral history, Kentucky is a national leader. Over the past several decades, tens of thousands of its citizens have been interviewed. The Kentucky Remembered series brings into print the most important of those collections, with each volume focusing on a particular subject.

Oral history is, of course, only one type of source material. Yet by the very nature of recollection, hidden aspects of history are often disclosed. Oral sources provide a vital thread in the rich fabric that is Kentucky's history.

This work is the seventh volume in the series. For all too long, the African American experience in Kentucky stood mired in a second-class historical status. Over time that has gradually changed. But much remains to be done to fill in the gaps in the pages of that story, especially in regard to the years of the civil rights era. Catherine Fosl and Tracy E. K'Meyer have now allowed us to hear, once again, the voices of the people who stood up for their rights in an epic struggle. Theirs is a story of accommodation and anger, of heartbreak and heroism, of commitment and courage, of sorrow and success.

The Kentucky story of race relations has often been passed over in national historical analyses. Yet here in this middle ground between North and Deep South, significant events transpired and crucial battles occurred. This study of the civil rights movement in a southern border state provides important new insights into the march toward desegregation, its leadership, and the personal sacrifices and stories of those on the front lines as well as those in support. *Freedom on the Border* helps us understand the process—and the costs—of change, and highlights again the human element in history.

James C. Klotter
Terry L. Birdwhistell
Doug Boyd

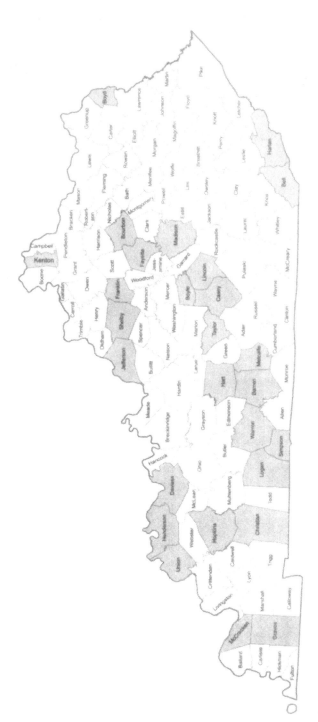

This map shows Kentucky's 120 counties. The shaded counties are the ones that activists discuss in this book, reflecting all of the state's quadrants but with greater concentrations in urban and central Kentucky. (Map courtesy of Kentucky State Data Center)

Chronology

1863   The Emancipation Proclamation frees the slaves in Confederate-
controlled territory, but does not affect Kentucky.

1865   Ratification of the Thirteenth Amendment to the U.S.
Constitution ends slavery in Kentucky.

1866   Due to widespread violence against African Americans, General
Clinton B. Fisk places Kentucky under the jurisdiction of the
Freedmen's Bureau.

1866   Kentucky General Assembly revises the 1798 "Slave Code" to
create a subordinate legal status for African Americans and lay the
foundation for legal segregation.

1868   Ratification of the Fourteenth Amendment defines citizenship rights.

1870   Ratification of the Fifteenth Amendment guarantees the right to
vote regardless of race. African Americans in Kentucky vote for the
first time in August 1870 local and county elections.

1870   Black community protest ends segregation on streetcars in
Louisville.

1879   Kentucky Normal and Theological Institute opens in Louisville.
Becomes State University in 1882 and is renamed Simmons
University in 1919.

1882   U.S. circuit court rules in *Commonwealth of Kentucky v. Jesse Ellis*
that state funds collected for educational purposes must be equally
distributed among white and black schools.

1883   U.S. circuit court rules in *Claybrook v. Owensboro* against the use of
separate tax funds for white and black schools.

1886   State Normal School for Colored Persons, later Kentucky State
College and then Kentucky State University, opens in Frankfort.

1896   Supreme Court rules in *Plessy v. Ferguson* that policies requiring
"separate" but "equal" facilities for the races are constitutional.

1897   First African Americans are elected to local offices in Kentucky.
They are: Edward W. Glass, city council of Hopkinsville; James
L. Allensworth, county coroner in Christian County; John W.
Knight, constable in North Hopkinsville.

1904   Legislature adopts the Day Law, which requires separation of blacks and whites in all educational facilities in the state.

1908   Louisville's Western Branch Library opens, becoming one of the nation's first expressly for African Americans.

1914   First NAACP branch in the state opens in Louisville.

1914   Louisville Board of Aldermen adopts housing segregation ordinance.

1917   Supreme Court rules in *Buchanan v. Warley,* a case brought by the Louisville NAACP, that city ordinances requiring residential segregation are unconstitutional.

1919   Walter White, leader of the national NAACP, travels through Kentucky, leading to the founding of branches in over a dozen communities across the commonwealth.

1919   Race riot forces entire black population of Corbin to leave the city.

1921   Lincoln Independent Party unsuccessfully runs slate of candidates for office in Louisville.

1923   Louisville creates first African American fire unit and hires first African American police officers.

1931   Louisville Municipal College, the branch of University of Louisville for African American students, opens.

1935   Republican Charles W. Anderson of Louisville is elected to the Kentucky General Assembly, the first African American elected to a state legislature in the South since Reconstruction.

1941   Two-year legal effort by Louisville NAACP results in equalization of black and white teacher salaries.

1948   Legislature amends the Day Law to allow integration of nursing schools and postgraduate physicians' training.

1948   Supreme Court rules in *Shelley v. Kramer* that residential restrictive covenants are unenforceable.

1949   U.S. district court orders the University of Kentucky to admit Lyman T. Johnson to its graduate program, forcing the desegregation of the university's graduate and professional schools.

1949   Paducah NAACP files suit to force the desegregation of Paducah Junior College. The case is decided in 1953 in favor of the plaintiff, opening the school to African Americans.

1950   Legislature amends the Day Law to allow colleges and universities to make their own decisions regarding segregation.

1950   Bellarmine, Nazareth, and Ursuline Colleges admit African American students.

1951   Interracial Hospital Movement successfully lobbies Governor Lawrence Wetherby to open tax-supported hospitals to African Americans.

1951   University of Louisville opens its doors to African Americans, leading to the closure of Louisville Municipal College.

1951   Dr. Charles H. Parrish Jr. becomes the first black faculty member on the main campus of the University of Louisville, and the first African American appointed to the faculty of a historically white institution in the South.

1952   Desegregation of Louisville neighborhood branch libraries.

1954   Supreme Court rules in *Brown v. Board of Education* that segregation in public schools is unconstitutional.

1954   Unknown assailants dynamite the home of Andrew and Charlotte Wade, who had moved to a formerly white neighborhood in the Louisville suburbs.

1955   Supreme Court in a follow-up decision known as *Brown II* urges school districts to integrate "with all deliberate speed."

1955   One African American student enrolls in summer school in the previously all-white Lafayette High School in Lexington.

1955   First regular term desegregation of public schools begins in Wayne County without incident in August.

1955   In September, Lexington and Fayette County schools welcome black and white students to register at the school of their choice. Five black teachers are assigned to noninstructional staff duties in previously all-white schools.

1955   Black students in Russellville are assigned to previously white Russellville High School.

1955   Partial desegregation of public schools goes into effect in Prestonsburg and Owensboro.

1955   An NAACP lawsuit results in the desegregation of the Louisville Municipal Housing Projects.

1955   After a nearly decade-long campaign, an NAACP lawsuit results in the desegregation of Louisville's public parks.

1956   Seventy-five percent of the state's school systems begin some form of desegregation plan.

1956   Public schools begin to desegregate without incident in Louisville.

1956   White opposition at schools in Henderson, Clay, and Sturgis stalls desegregation efforts.

1957   Lyman Johnson leads NAACP Youth Council in Louisville in drug store sit-ins.

1957   Sixth Circuit Court of Appeals orders the Louisville Municipal Housing Commission to desegregate its public housing projects.

1959   Louisville NAACP Youth Council holds stand-in demonstrations at Brown Theater.

1959   Congress of Racial Equality (CORE) branch forms in Lexington.

1960   Greensboro sit-ins trigger new mass movement across the South.
1960   Mass student demonstrations begin in Frankfort and Lexington.
1960   CORE units form in Frankfort and Louisville.
1960   Legislature passes ban on racial or ethnic discrimination in employment under new State Merit System.
1960   Legislature creates the Kentucky Commission on Human Rights.
1961   Demonstrations for an open accommodations ordinance begin in Louisville.
1961   Lexington theaters desegregate after stand-in demonstrations.
1962   President John F. Kennedy issues executive order prohibiting discrimination in federally funded housing.
1963   Louisville Board of Aldermen passes an open accommodations ordinance, the first such law in any southern city.
1963   Governor Bert Combs issues fair employment executive order banning discrimination in businesses licensed by the state.
1964   March on Frankfort sponsored by the Allied Organizations for Civil Rights brings Martin Luther King Jr. and Jackie Robinson to the capital to lobby for a state civil rights bill.
1964   U.S. Congress adopts the Civil Rights Act, prohibiting segregation in accommodations and employment, and ordering public schools to complete desegregation within ten years.
1966   Legislature passes the Kentucky Civil Rights Act banning discrimination in employment and public accommodations.
1966   Bardstown-Nelson County adopts the Kentucky Commission on Human Rights model open housing ordinance, the first local government in the state to pass open housing legislation.
1967   Mass demonstrations for open housing ordinance begin in Louisville.
1967   Louisville, Covington, Kenton County, and Fayette County adopt open housing legislation.
1967   Georgia Davis Powers of Louisville becomes the first woman and first African American elected to the Kentucky Senate.
1968   Luska J. Twyman of Glasgow becomes the first African American elected mayor in the state.
1968   Legislature adopts the Kentucky Fair Housing Act, the first state open housing legislation in the South.
1968   Rash of racial violence breaks out across the state, including confrontations between whites and blacks in Lexington, Louisville, Owensboro, and Berea and bombings of black-owned property in Bullitt County, Bowling Green, Lexington, Hart County, and Jefferson County.
1968   Trial of the Black Six, African Americans in Louisville accused of conspiracy to cause a riot and blow up West End oil refineries,

begins in Louisville. It ends in 1970 when the judge directs a
verdict of not guilty.

1968   Black Student Union organizations form at the University of
Kentucky and University of Louisville.

1969   Black Student Union members at the University of Louisville take
over the administration building in protest over the lack of progress
on a recruitment and curriculum proposal.

1972   *Robert Jefferson et al. v. Fayette County Board of Education*
finds Fayette County schools in violation of the Fourteenth
Amendment: district closes five inner-city schools and assigns
black majority to predominantly white suburban schools.

1973   Sixth Circuit Court of Appeals rules that the Louisville and
Jefferson County Public Schools must desegregate, leading to
merger and system-wide busing.

1975   Antibusing demonstrations and riots rock Louisville and Jefferson
County in protest of the inauguration of the school integration
plan; busing supporters organize in response.

Introduction

Popular images of the movement for African American civil rights center mostly on the Deep South: from the Mississippi delta to the smokestacks of the industrial Alabama city African Americans called "Bombingham." Kentucky, situated at the region's northern border and once central to the struggle for African American freedom as the escape route from slavery across the Ohio River, is little more than a footnote in most histories of the modern civil rights movement. Yet the movement for racial justice swept through the commonwealth just as it did the Deep South, changing irrevocably the lives of post–World War II Kentuckians, both black and white. This book aims to introduce readers to some of the activists across Kentucky who helped to make that change and to usher in legal equality for African Americans during the second half of the twentieth century. In this volume, over one hundred Kentuckians who opposed the existing racial hierarchy and took risks to break it down share stories of life under segregation, individual acts of resistance, mass demonstrations, and political, economic, and cultural strategies for fighting racism. In doing so, they offer a hint of the varied experiences of African Americans across the commonwealth.

Southern in many respects in its culture and politics, Kentucky has several features that distinguish it from much of the rest of the region, especially the eleven former Confederate states. First and perhaps foremost is the fact of Kentucky's relatively small African American population, which after emancipation became concentrated in a few mostly urban areas of the state, making statewide race relations somewhat less charged and threatening, from whites' perspectives, but also less susceptible to collective economic or political pressure by African Americans. The other, related characteristic of the commonwealth that has played a significant role in the experience of its African American citizens has to do with geography: the state is divided into six distinctive regions whose topography and customs provide considerable internal variation. Whereas parts of western and central Kentucky were firmly entrenched in slaveholding, the mountainous southern and eastern portions of the state had less of a stake in southern racial politics. Louisville's river location connected it to midwestern centers of industry and commerce and their immigration patterns, making it a "gateway to the South." But while the border position along the Ohio River gave some Kentuckians access to commerce, the natural boundary of the Appalachian mountains to the east created a sense of isolation. This cultural and economic diversity produced contradictions that contributed to economic instability and inequality across the state. Citizens of Kentucky have often therefore—more so than in many states and not only according to race—been disinclined to speak with one voice on any social issue.

What would the history of Kentucky look like from the perspectives of its African American citizens? This book gives us only a few glimpses, but the story that unfolds is one of frustration, protest, and accommodation. For most of the commonwealth's past, African Americans lived a marginalized existence, first denied even the most nominal freedoms and, later, full citizenship. Although slave labor was an essential element in the state's settlement and in the creation of a stable society, blacks were visible in the historical record primarily as a collective problem (what the historian Kenneth Stampp has called "troublesome property").[1] Because of its strategic yet tenuous position in relation to the Civil War, as a slaveholding state that did not secede, Kentucky was not bound by the Emancipation Proclamation of 1863, and it became one of the last two states in the nation to end enslavement. Slavery officially ended only in December 1865 with the adoption of the Thirteenth Amendment (which the Kentucky legislature had refused to ratify).

The end of slavery did not guarantee freedom or opportunity for black Kentuckians. Racial violence in the form of beatings, expulsions from the land, or—in the words of Kentucky historian George Wright—"cold-blooded murder . . . at the hands of lynch mobs" posed an ever-present threat for African Americans in Kentucky during this period, just as it did farther south.[2] Although African American Kentuckians were never stripped of the right to vote as they were throughout the former Confederacy, segregation of the races was the custom in almost every Kentucky community, and after the turn of the century it also became law in many avenues of life. In legislating racial separation, Kentucky was generally in alignment with trends across the region, but the laws were somewhat more inconsistent and partial than was true in the Deep South. Indeed, generalizations about the quality of life under segregation for African Americans in Kentucky remain difficult because of the tremendous variation in laws and practices, depending on such matters as region of the state, black-white ratio in the local population, and community size. Still, racial segregation always carried with it discrimination and a corresponding white supremacy undergirded by assumptions of black inferiority.

In the late nineteenth and early twentieth centuries, in response to ever more repressive antiblack measures that made this period the nadir of race relations in Kentucky as in the South, African Americans fled the state, especially its rural areas, en masse. Although they comprised more than 20 percent of the state's residents on the eve of the Civil War, by 1950 African Americans constituted a mere 6.9 percent of the population.[3] Those who stayed tended to migrate internally to Louisville, the state's largest and most industrial city, where they built a vibrant black community in the face of "polite racism" that nonetheless rendered them second-class citizens.[4] To a lesser extent, African Americans gravitated after the Civil War to Lexington, Hopkinsville, or Elizabethtown, where they also established their own businesses and communities within a framework of segregation. All four of these Kentucky localities to which blacks immigrated were both urban and situated in what were once highly populous slaveholding areas. There have been some local variations from this migration pattern within portions of the state. For example, between 1910 and the 1930s, parts of eastern Kentucky drew African American in-migration because of recruitment efforts by coal operators. By the 1950s, however, when major challenges to legal segregation took shape, African Americans were on their way out of eastern Kentucky because mine closings and mechanization had dried up employment opportunities there.[5]

The flood of African American departure from the commonwealth as a whole slowed after midcentury, partly because of the improvements in quality of life that the gathering civil rights movement effected. Yet as the twenty-first century arrived, African Americans still constituted only 7.3 percent of Kentucky's population.[6] The result, today, is a state whose population is more than 90 percent white, with almost a third of its 120 counties (36) more than 99 percent white. Nearly two-thirds of all African Americans live in Jefferson, Fayette, Christian, or Hardin County. The former two comprise the state's principal metropolitan areas, while the latter two are home to military bases that have attracted sizable black populations. Most African Americans live in the same Kentucky cities—Louisville, Lexington, Hopkinsville, and Elizabethtown—where they had found the state most welcoming at slavery's end. Even the results of the movement chronicled in these pages—an end to segregation laws and the achievement of legal rights—have not made the Bluegrass State a thoroughly hospitable place for African Americans.

The Kentucky Civil Rights Oral History Project

Contemporary race relations in Kentucky and across the United States remain charged, rooted in a complex and only partially documented past. Especially in a state like Kentucky, in which nonwhites constitute a relatively small portion of the population, neither the texture of blacks' lives nor the enormous changes connected to the modern African American experience are widely represented in textbooks or conveyed well in history lessons. In this situation, oral history can be a vital tool for redressing the incompleteness in Kentucky history. Many of the African Americans who share their stories in these pages had never before been asked to speak publicly or in detail about their experiences of race in their home state. Particularly outside the state's urban centers, most of the stories they tell have never before been written in any source other than perhaps a private diary.

In this book, over one hundred Kentucky civil rights crusaders who were active between World War II and the 1970s—the years during which legal segregation was dismantled—speak. Many although not all of the oral histories that comprise this volume were collected between 1998 and 2001 as part of the Kentucky Civil Rights Oral History Project (KCROHP), an initiative of a unique state agency, the Kentucky Oral History Commission (KOHC). The Oral History Commission, a subsidiary of the state's Historical Society, is dedicated to preserving the histories of Kentuckians who may not have had the opportunity to document their experiences in writing. In 1998 the commission put a longstanding vision into practice by creating a project to gather civil rights memories from participants while they were still alive to share them. Over the next few years KCROHP collected the memoirs of more than a hundred civil rights activists across the state. Project director Betsy Brinson and an advisory board of academic and public historians worked with various university and public scholars across the state to identify narrators. African American elected officials, community organizations, churches, existing scholarship, journalists' accounts, and simple word of mouth provided leads to potential interviewees. In addition to conducting its own interviews, the commission brought together relevant ones from existing oral history collections around the state. Results of the KCROHP included a symposium ("The Civil Rights Movement in Kentucky: Voices of Protest, 1930–1970," 2000) and an award-winning documentary film (*Living the Story*, 2001).

In choosing narrators, the project sought to document a diverse range of experiences and perspectives. To do so, we set out to identify activists for racial change at all levels in Kentucky: from protesters to federal judges to state and local policymakers to journalists to high school and college students and teachers. Because a flowering of regional histories in the past few years has revealed the extent of women's contributions to the movement, especially in grassroots organizing, the project sought out women activists, resulting in an almost even gender mix among the narrators.[7] Finally, while most of those interviewed are African American, not all are. Dating back to the nineteenth-century abolitionist movement, white allies in the commonwealth played key support roles in facilitating the African American struggle for freedom, either by joining the movement themselves or by enacting supportive policies from their elected or judicial offices. White voices are thus included among these narratives—disproportionately so, at some points—as in journalists' memories of the movement, for instance, since many more Kentucky news reporters were and are white.

The nature of the project constrained the range of interviewees and thus introduced into the results certain biases and limitations about which readers should be aware. The KCROHP was not intended to be solely about the stories of grassroots social change—what the civil rights scholar Charles Payne calls "the view from the trenches."[8] The process by which initial contacts were made led to a disproportionate representation of well-known leaders, participants, or observers of the movement, thus producing what some might argue is a rather "top-down" version of the story of the movement. Specifically, interviewees were identified by having been quoted in major Kentucky newspapers or having served in elected office or as local heads of nationally known organizations, such as the National Association for the Advancement of Colored People (NAACP). Those active in small local civil rights initiatives that received little publicity, consequently, are less well-represented in the KCROHP study.

In addition, one aspect of the story of the civil rights movement in Kentucky that we opted *not* to document was the voices of white pro-segregation activists who were key opponents of it. Although white supremacy was the governing ideology in the U.S. South through the first half of the twentieth century—and that includes Kentucky in terms of its laws and customs—that ideology is reflected in these pages mostly in terms of African American resistance to it, and is evident among the white narrators only passively and even unconsciously. Like many of its southern neighbors, Kentucky has had a white supremacist movement in the form of the Ku Klux Klan and—during the mid- to late 1950s in the years immediately following the Supreme Court's *Brown v. Board of Education* decision of 1954—White Citizens' Council groups that led a movement of "massive resistance" to school desegregation. Such massive resisters never obtained the stranglehold on Kentucky politics that they did farther south, however, making them a more marginal voice in state and local political affairs. There is perhaps a place for a compilation of such voices, but this project was not it, we concluded.

Despite the fact that Louisville and Lexington produced the most visible civil rights upsurges, the KCROHP attempted to capture experiences of the movement from many parts of the state and from various generations of the twentieth century. We have tried to make the selections included in this volume as geographically representative as possible of the diverse experiences around the state. While the majority of African American Kentuckians have found a better quality of life in urban areas, a civil rights history of merely Louisville and Lexington would not be true to the experiences of those African Americans who opted for the pleasures and travails of rural Kentucky. In some cases, that search for balance meant seeking out stories from small communities and leaving out some from areas of larger African American population. Throughout the book we have tried to strike a balance between geographic coverage and documenting the significant activities in the areas where most African Americans lived.

The content of these chapters is also shaped by the decision of the KCROHP team to highlight the period from 1954/55—when the U.S. Supreme Court ruling in *Brown v. Board of Education* condemned school segregation and generated both a new wave of reaction and a new generation of mass movement exemplified by the Montgomery Bus Boycott—to the assassination of Martin Luther King Jr. in 1968. In this choice we intended to focus on the mass phase of the movement identified popularly with the nonviolent leadership of Reverend King, and to follow the chronology of what some historians call the "grand narrative" of the civil rights movement, with the exception of including some material about school desegregation in the 1970s. Our interviewees fortunately thwarted this approach by raising their own important flashpoints that both predate and outlast that period of mass activism, inadvertently connecting their stories to a much larger debate among historians about how to periodize the civil rights movement. Many of the narrators here reflect on the importance of the Great Depression and World War II in their own consciousness of the limitations segregation imposed, for instance, and a significant number of them describe civil rights activism that persisted into the 1970s and 1980s, connecting that era to contemporary antiracist campaigns. Thus, while much of the material contained in these chapters centers on the period traditionally understood as the peak years of the African American freedom struggle, there are hints of what scholars call the "Long Civil Rights Movement."[9]

One final disclaimer relates to the race of those involved in the civil rights oral history project. In the view of some, it may have been a handicap to the project—and by association, to this book—that all of the interviewers but one, the KOHC staff, and this volume's authors are white, whereas most of the narrators are African American. This is a matter not easily resolved, and one that has triggered a variety of socio-intellectual debates over the past few years in fields such as women's studies, African American studies, and postcolonial studies. These discussions revolve around the question of how well a writer/researcher can capture the experiences of any group that has faced discrimination if she is not a member of that population.[10] We have attempted to do so here, and the value of our effort is ultimately up to the reader to decide.

Given the constraints of time and staff, and the factors described here (which we explore further in the concluding essay), the KCROHP was not, and this book does not claim to be, a comprehensive study of the civil rights movement in Kentucky. Many readers themselves will remember events and experiences not recounted here. Our goal is to offer an overview of the movement and to bring some of its protagonists into focus through letting their voices speak, thereby generating provocative new questions for further study of this compelling, still incomplete chapter in Kentucky history.

Editorial Method

As scholars of southern civil rights history, longtime oral historians, and advisers to this project who conducted a few of its interviews, we inherited the task of crafting an oral history reader from the KCROHP research when project director and primary interviewer Betsy Brinson left Kentucky in 2003. We began with her basic idea for a reader and ended with a more hybrid approach that combines voices from the civil rights oral histories with contextual materials, historiography, and a discussion of methodological issues raised by using oral history to document this story. To organize the story and thus the chapters, we reviewed the interviews in the KCROHP collection to identify themes, then edited selected oral histories and arranged excerpts from them to create a coherent narrative flow, expanding a few biographies and adding edited excerpts from other related interviews we or others had conducted.

In editing the lengthy transcripts into passages suitable for these chapters, we made at-times-difficult editorial decisions related to both condensation and use of language. To render the material into a brief, accessible form, we sometimes had to cut material and on rarer occasions combine comments from different parts of an interview. We tried to minimize this practice, however, and were conscious of trying not to alter the meaning or context of the story. Some oral historians may consider our decision to use short excerpts from a large number of interviews an interruption of the narratives' integrity, but we chose to err in favor of a larger array of voices. We then balanced that decision by interspersing four longer, more autobiographical oral histories among the chapters. Regarding awkward or grammatically problematic uses of language by narrators, our practice has been to follow a common model in editing oral history by omitting redundant phrases or words, including uses of "uh" and most instances of "But," "And," "Then," or "you know," especially when they were numerous and when removing them did not alter meaning. Otherwise we left most language usage intact, even when there was subject-verb disagreement or idiosyncratic phrasing or choice of words.[11]

In order to facilitate understanding and put the narrators' words in context, we have written fairly substantial introductory material to open and contextualize each chapter, and have added transitions between some narratives. This material is specially formatted to allow the reader easy visual identification of shifts between our voice and those of the narrators. When necessary to complete a thought in the narrative, we occasionally added a few words, bracketing them so that the reader can distinguish them. Finally, at the end of each narrative is an identification of the speaker and the location of the primary story in the excerpt. More information about the narrators, the names of interviewers, and dates of the interviews are available in the appendix. Although only our names appear on the cover, we owe thanks to many people who assisted us, especially Betsy Brinson in conceptualizing and instigating the book and the rest of the Oral History Commission staff in helping to format the interviews to make them more accessible, identifying powerful stories from their vast collection, and providing consultation of many kinds. Former University of Louisville students Mandy McIlwain and Jardana Peacock also deserve thanks for helping to organize transcripts and chapter materials. Our appreciation also goes to Eric Schneider of the Kentucky State Data Center for providing us with a map. Finally, we would like to thank Lee Keeling of the University of Louisville Department of History for her kind assistance of many sorts with the manuscript.

This book traces the mid-twentieth-century civil rights movement in Kentucky topically as well as chronologically. Each of seven topical chapters begins with a few pages of introduction to the subject under examination. These introductions are lengthier where the oral histories offered less of an overview of the subject. Then the lion's share of every chapter is a collection of individuals' voices: one or two dozen edited oral history excerpts through which narrators reflect in mostly chronological sequences on the topic under examination. The opening chapter, "Life under Segregation," sets forth a sampling of the varied experiences African American Kentuckians underwent in the years when racial segregation was both the law and established

custom. Chapter 2 documents the phenomenon of school desegregation in all its phases and at all levels of schooling. This chapter examines chronologically the process of school desegregation in Kentucky,
both at the collegiate level (which took place earlier, beginning in the
late 1940s) and subsequently in K–12, which began only after the
Supreme Court's *Brown* decision in May of 1954, and then in 1969
entered a new phase with more active federal intervention in search
of a racial mix within schools. The third chapter explores the emergence of the mass civil rights movement via the new regional wave of
direct-action sit-ins to end segregation in public accommodations.
Historians continue to debate the movement's starting point(s), but
the focus here is on the early 1960s, when student sit-ins and other
forms of nonviolent direct action swept the South. Chapters 4 and
5 foreground housing and employment, two central arenas in which
African American Kentuckians fought (and continue to fight) for
their rights. Chapter 6 examines the blossoming of black consciousness as a phenomenon that in some cases drove "black power" political upsurges and in other cases remained largely cultural. The final
chapter, "Black Politics," looks at the evolution of African American
political power in the state as blacks began to attain elected office
but also faced the challenge of being a small minority in many parts
of the commonwealth. This chapter illuminates how voting rights
campaigns have differed in Kentucky from those of states farther
south, where widespread disfranchisement was the primary obstacle
to greater representation.

In addition to these chapters, this book contains a number of other materials intended to aid the reader—including a map of the state,
a chronology of Kentucky's civil rights movement, and a list of the
narrators. There are also four autobiographical oral history narratives
that highlight the activism of four of the book's many protagonists: Julia Cowans of Bell County in eastern Kentucky; Representative Jesse
Crenshaw of Lexington, originally from a tobacco farm in the southern part of the state; Helen Fisher Frye, a Danville schoolteacher; and
J. Blaine Hudson, a native Louisvillian and student-radical turned
scholar. These four profiles allow readers greater insight not only into
four important personalities, but also into some of the most important themes from Kentucky's movement that were introduced in more
general terms in the chapters: education, the Appalachian experience,
politics, law, black power, connections to other social movements, or-

ganizational dynamics, and women's leadership. The book's conclusion reflects on oral history methodology and on our findings in relation to other scholarship on the movement.

The following pages offer an overview of Kentucky's civil rights past and some insights into what that past has meant and still means to those who lived it. Part of the value of oral history in a study like this one lies in allowing activists to reflect on their work and, in doing so, to reveal some of the subtler dynamics of social change to others less familiar with what it takes to make it happen. Especially, perhaps, in a majority-white state like Kentucky that lies outside the former Confederate South, there is a need for wider understanding of the life-changing importance of the civil rights movement for the 1960s generation and those before and since. We need to know more about how and to what extent racial hierarchy and separation mutated outside the "Black-Belt" South. It is also vital in achieving a full history of the modern U.S. civil rights movement to make visible the African Americans who experienced and challenged segregation from the vantage point of being a relatively small minority of their state's citizens. Not all Kentuckians think of their state as "southern," but in its racial history, the commonwealth differs from the Deep South more in degree than in kind—with a few glaring exceptions, such as wholesale disfranchisement. Either way, as the Reverend Martin Luther King Jr. once observed, "The racial issue that we confront in America is not a sectional but a national problem." These Kentucky voices elaborate on some of the ways that the history of that problem reverberates today.[12]

Chapter 1

Life under Segregation

ALTHOUGH the ratification of the Thirteenth Amendment in December 1865 ended slavery in Kentucky, by the end of the century a new system segregated African Americans in nearly every aspect of public space and relegated them to second-class status in the economy, education, and social life. "Jim Crow," as racial segregation became known informally, got its nickname from a minstrel character created by Thomas Rice, a white performer from Louisville.[1] Blacks in Kentucky as elsewhere around the region built their own separate communities, culture, and institutions in response to Jim Crow. But while they taught their children how to navigate the complex rules that governed and restricted their lives, African Americans also demonstrated, often through example, how to stand up against those rules with individual acts of resistance. The history of the civil rights movement in Kentucky is grounded in the experiences of generations of African Americans' lives spent "behind the veil," in the words of historian George C. Wright, the most prolific commentator on Kentucky's African American experiences.[2]

Immediately after the Civil War, during the period known as Reconstruction (1865–1877), African Americans had momentary hopes of equal citizenship through the passage of the Fourteenth and Fifteenth Amendments, and the Civil Rights Act of 1875, which prohibited racial discrimination in jury selection, public transportation, and public accommodation. But while those legal guarantees were never overturned, they began to be blatantly denied all through the former slaveholding states. In the closing decades of the nineteenth century, white supremacy became more entrenched, and the paternalism that had accompanied slavery turned to a defensive hostility toward the now-free black masses. Gradually city and state governments began adopting policies—and white citizens began enforcing even informal restrictions—that limited African American access to public spaces, including schools, cemeteries, and hospitals.

Then, in 1896, the *Plessy v. Ferguson* ruling by the U.S. Supreme Court paved the way for racial segregation to become law (de jure) instead of just practice (de facto), establishing the legal principle of "separate but equal," a concept that prevailed across the South for the next half century. A Kentuckian—John Marshall Harlan, a native of Harlan Station, near Danville—was the only justice who dissented in that decision, and he wrote a strong counter-opinion, arguing that to force African Americans into separate accommodations conferred on them "a badge of servitude wholly inconsistent with the civil freedom and equality before the law established by the Constitution."[3] By 1900, a host of laws mandated racial segregation in all of the eleven former states of the Confederacy and in the border states.[4] The logic popular among whites was that "separate" could still be "equal." In reality, however, just as Harlan had predicted, that was almost never the case. Segregation kept African Americans from the best jobs, residences, and facilities, and it reinforced whites' notions of superiority even as it allowed them to ignore the inequities African Americans routinely faced.

The Kentucky mythology is that segregation in the commonwealth tended to be less rigid than was the case farther south. There is some evidence for this popular belief. As a result of black community protests against discriminatory policies in public transportation in the late nineteenth century, most local bus systems did not remain segregated in Kentucky, for instance. Moreover, African Americans in the Bluegrass State were never stripped of the right to vote as they were in the Deep South. In Louisville, which contained the largest share of the commonwealth's African American population, while segregation was very much a way of life, it was a more "polite racism," in the words of one historian of the city, than out in the state or in comparable communities farther south.[5] A thriving black business and cultural district centered on Walnut Street yielded a politically active black community in Louisville that won some victories against Jim Crow, thus providing some haven from the surrounding racism. This also occurred to a lesser extent in smaller cities and in larger towns containing sizable black populations throughout the commonwealth.

But this popular image of Kentucky as better than its southern neighbors and these few examples of relative openness should not mask the fact that in their day-to-day lives, and for nearly a hundred years after emancipation, African Americans in the state faced barriers to their full and equal participation in public life. Despite local and state policies, for example, African Americans continued to experience unequal treatment on trains in the state as late as the 1950s. While blacks held the franchise, the commonwealth's voting rolls were kept strictly segregated and access to real political power was limited. Even in communities with sufficient African American presence to demand better opportunities, they came with doses of humiliation: in Lexington, for example, from 1866 until well into the twentieth century an annual "Colored Fair" offered summertime amusement not only to black Lexingtonians but to many African Americans from all over central Kentucky. Yet it came only as a concession to the barring of blacks from a simultaneous (and still ongoing today) "Bluegrass Fair."[6] These and other restrictions narrowed horizons, shaped life expectations, and limited opportunities for African Americans in the commonwealth, much as they did throughout Dixie. Finally, while black residents of urban areas such as Louisville might be able to negotiate around some of these barriers, in many rural areas and villages a tiny African American minority might be—at best—ignored and somewhat accepted, or—at worst—subject to the whim of whites who could effect violence without fear of retribution. The voices that follow reflect that wide range of experiences.

African American parents could sometimes shelter their children from experiencing racial discrimination at its harshest, but there would typically come a moment as they grew up when young blacks would see racism fully exposed. The first narratives below describe that dawning awareness of the barriers racial discrimination posed and detail some personal encounters with racism. The second set of narratives gives voice to how thoroughly segregation shaped African American life by permeating community institutions. Not all of what evolved was negative, of course. Although forced into their own communities, African Americans made lemonade from lemons, so to speak, as revealed in Louis Mudd's memories of segregated Louisville and Taylor Seals's recollections of black neighborhoods surrounding Lexington.

Narratives in these two sections of the chapter also suggest the range of reactions to the sense of confinement that racial segregation imparted. Historians such as Robin Kelley and Tera Hunter have unearthed a host of individual insurgencies that situate the post–World War II mass civil rights movement more as a progression than as an uprising.[7] Stories of collective rebellion appear mostly in later chapters of this volume. Yet memories of segregated life also invariably tell of individual acts of resistance. Those acts range from covert forms, such as Anne Butler's reclaiming of language in her childhood insistence that she was not "colored" but "brown," to more overt forms, such as Ricardo Sisney's drive to establish a "Jackie Robinson league" to give African American youth in Bowling Green a chance to play baseball. Some resistance—especially in children—might be ignored, but it could also be met with white institutional power in the form of the police beatings Lyman Johnson describes at the edges of Louisville's black community. The narratives collectively reflect a great deal of resiliency, but also quite a lot of resentment, understandably, suggesting that Kentucky experiences of racism were indeed more a difference of degree than of kind from what African Americans found farther south.

The final set of narratives in this chapter consists of the voices of whites, who were aware of their own racial privilege in varying degrees, depending on their place, time, and social standing. Because segregation truly did create two distinct societies, white Kentuckians frequently had the luxury of remaining oblivious to the most harmful outcomes of racial discrimination. Especially in the years prior to the 1930s rise of fascism in Europe—the racial ideology of which provided an uncomfortable comparison with American racism—young whites tended, with rare exceptions, to see African Americans instrumentally, as people who were "different" and useful mainly for the service or amusement they might provide. For example, for African Americans, the most urgent threat from whites was always racial violence, but as Morton Holbrook's memoir of the public hanging of convicted African American murderer Rainey Bethea in 1936 Owensboro chillingly illustrates, whites could distance themselves from blacks' experiences so thoroughly that they could see antiblack violence as merely a form of ritualistic mass entertainment. Even when it did not produce violence outright, the psychology of segregation could yield bizarre or contradictory ways of thinking, as in the story of the blackface minstrel show put on by whites in Hopkinsville to raise funds for a segregated pool. Sometimes, as the closing narrative from the 1950s illustrates, it took an outsider's perspective to prompt a Kentucky native to finally "see" racial injustices that had been there all her life.

I Knew Something Was Wrong . . .

There was an amusement park not far from where we lived. We didn't have air conditioning when I was growing up. Not many people did then in my neighborhood. My dad would pile us in the car and take us for rides sometimes on really hot evenings. We would ride near the river where the air was a little cooler, and he would always stop and get us ice cream. But the experience that just stands out more than anything is riding past that amusement park and hearing the sounds of children laughing and screaming on the roller coaster and smelling the cotton candy and the hot dogs and the popcorn. It's strange because I remember over and over my sisters and I, and sometimes my brother would be with us, whenever we passed that amusement park, we would see the lights, the big Ferris wheel that had green lights on it. We would always ask the same question: "Can we go?" My mother and father would almost simultaneously say, "No, you can't go." We'd kind of sit there and then as we passed it, we'd say, "Well, why can't we go?" That's when there was just this deafening silence in the car. My mother's eyes would always fill up with tears, and my father would just kind of look away, and we knew something was wrong. Eventually she'd turn around and she'd say, "Well, one day we'll be able to go." We didn't understand why, at least I didn't, but I knew something was wrong. I knew something was wrong when my mother used to take me to the shoe store, and we had to go around to the back. We had to enter through the alley and sit in this little room. I could see white children in there trying on shoes, but when I would get my shoes they would pretty much be brought to us [without being able to try them on.]

Eleanor Jordan, Louisville

There were sections of the community that were designated where white folks lived. The railroad tracks, as is often the case, was a dividing line. Our school was right across the railroad tracks from the white school. I just always seemed to have been aware that there were some real differences. You would hear parents mumbling and being disappointed or frustrated about the quality of books that were available to the teachers to use with us, as well as space.

I remember my father one afternoon told me that after school I could come to this place that he was doing some paperhanging. He was going to give me some money for something. I was to get it after school. I must have been eight or nine years old. So I went to this house where he was and knocked on the front door. A little elderly woman, gray-haired, very motherly, frail-looking woman came to the door, and I told her that I was here to see my father. She stood in the door and yelled, "Lucian, Lucian, there's a little colored girl here asking for you. I'm going to send her around to the back door." And she told me, "The next time you come here, you go to the back door." I remember just steaming. When I got to the back door and saw my father, I was just shaking. What I said to him was, "I'm not a colored girl. I'm brown."

Anne Butler, Stanford

One evening, we had gone to the movie, we being my mother and my father. At that time we had to sit in the balcony. I was playing. We were coming down State Street, and I got in front of my parents. I might have been ten, fifteen feet out in front of them, and a car came around with some whites in it, and they hit me in the back with a brick. I was a kid. I might have been eight, I might have been younger than that, I might have been six or seven. But anyway, getting home and hearing the voices, hearing the conversation, made me then realize that people who were white didn't like me. Now, if my family said it, and my grandmother said it, and my grandfather said it, and my mom and dad said it, then it's gotta be true for me, because that's kind of the way it is. That is why they hit me, because there was no other reason for them to hit me. So that was one of the earliest incidents that I remember.

Don Offutt, Bowling Green

My mother and my father were very proud people. They were very independent people. They never talked about my being inferior, or our being inferior. I mean, it just didn't come up. I never knew that they had black and white bathrooms in Kentucky, because I had never been to one. My mother used to say to me, "Oh, we don't use public bathrooms." So it was like I never had to encounter seeing "colored" and "white" on them. I didn't even think they had them in Kentucky. I mean, there were certain ways that she navigated me through this minefield, that I didn't have to deal with the fact that you are black, therefore you are inferior and you can't do this and you can't do that. She would just say, "Oh you don't want to do that. You're not interested in that." And I'd just slack off. She'd give me a justifiable reason. We depended on them. I made sure that I could take care of myself. My father owned his business. We owned our home. My father had a seventh-grade education, but a very bright man.

Joyce Hamilton Berry, Lexington

When do you become aware of being black? I don't really know. I can remember my first lesson in segregated society. We were still living in Louisville, but my father was pastoring at that point in Henderson County. Because he had a job in Louisville, he'd catch the train, usually late [Saturday night] or early Sunday morning. I think he'd get on the train a little after midnight and end up in Henderson about four or five hours later, and then he'd preach that Sunday and go back that night. Well, that seemed like high drama to me, and on an occasion . . . I must have been five years old . . . he agreed to take me on the train to Henderson. I was so excited that sleep was not easy. And you know, I got a little hungry too. He said, "Well, when we get to Henderson, there's this place that has absolutely the best egg sandwich you could ever imagine." He described how you put onion on it and it was on a hot roll and how great it was. So we got off in Henderson and [were] on the way to the church where he'd probably sleep a little bit before the service. At any rate, I remember this diner. You got a block within the diner, you could smell how good it was. Egg, onion, and a slice of bacon. That day the man said, "You can't come in this door, you have to go to the back." And [my father] said, "We're not that hungry." He said, "You know, I been buying egg sandwiches there for months now, but today he had a white man in there, so he was being white." He went on to say that [for] personal dignity, and I don't know what words he used, but for things that you don't absolutely have to do, you don't go to back doors, you don't segregate yourself. Although I was starving, I kind of understood it, and we endured until the town came to life, which was hours later. That was the first lesson in Race 101.

I guess the second time that it had a rather profound impact was right at the beginning of World War II, which might have been 1941. There's a place down in Henderson County, Smith Mills, [that] had a prisoner of war camp. Corydon was not much of a town. Maybe it had one restaurant, maybe two. On the radio at that point, they were talking about how low down and dirty the Germans were. On and on and on. These, you know, scum of the earth. Everybody seemed to agree that, yes, they are. Then the word got out in the community, and it was true, that German prisoners had gone to the restaurant and been served, taken in by guards, and that was just totally confusing because black men were going off to fight for this country, to fight these dirty scum people, and they could eat in the restaurant, and blacks couldn't. And even at [age] twelve, that was heavy. How do you explain that? It was so contradictory. So I guess just in terms of [my] thinking in early life, those were two very profound, hard-hitting kinds of realizations.

John Wesley Hatch, Henderson

I was always aware of it. I was always aware because everything was separated when I grew up. I grew up as a small child in the 1930s and as a teenager in the 1940s. Separate schools, separate but unequal. I later in history learned of the 189[6] decision by the Supreme Court, *Plessy vs. Ferguson,* that established the separate but equal, as being acceptable, but in truth it was separate and very, very unequal. I was always aware of this and it was almost inhumane. But we were not as sensitive to it as we became later on, as these walls began to fall, and we realized some of the things that we had been denied. Actually when I look back over it, it was a very, very uneven playing field. Very, very severely handicapped young people growing up. I can testify to that now because when I look back and look at the facilities of the segregated schools that I attended, compared to the schools that the white people were able to attend, and the privileges that they enjoyed, I can see how it really hampered the African American population for years and years to come. The railroad was the primary mode of long transportation across a considerable number of miles, and there were segregated waiting rooms even in the railroad station. Because of my age, I didn't look at it as I look at if I had been an adult. We would even go into restrooms marked "white," until someone would run us out. Yes, we did those things, because we were fully aware that something wasn't right.

Robert A. Coleman, Paducah

I was first aware of that when I was five years of age. I didn't know what it was, but I knew whites and blacks went separate ways. Even though we perhaps grew up in neighborhoods that were intertwined somewhat and we oft time had white playmates and vice versa, we knew at a certain time [that] we stayed in this area of town, [and] whites stayed in the other area of town. I knew then there was something wrong. At least I thought it wrong.

Sanford T. Roach, Danville

[Segregation] was all around us. We could go in the drugstore and buy a fountain coke or a sandwich or cone of ice cream, and then we had to come back out on the street and eat it. In the theaters we were relegated to up in the balcony area in the little dark corner. We couldn't go in any of the restaurants like at the bus station. Some of them you could go to the back door and they would fix your sandwich and reach it to you out the back door. Then some of them, you could go in and stand to the side of the counter and order and then bring it out. We grew up with it so from the time we were just small children, we always knew.

School—we walked. We had to walk to Rosenwald, so we're talking about over a mile. But the white kids had a school here in Baxter. When we would be coming home from school sometimes, the white kids would take all of the sidewalk. Then they would push us off the sidewalks, and so fights would erupt because of that. Finally, the two schools, Harlan city schools and Rosenwald, they got together to work out a plan. The plan they worked out was that the white kids would get out first, and so that would give them time to clear the sidewalks. Then they'd let us out. We were always aware that we always had to make allowances for white people. So from the time we were just little kids, we always knew that it was different.

I used to tell people, I said, "In some ways they had it better in Mississippi than we did here in Harlan." For example, in Woolworth's, they had two lunch counters. I couldn't tell any difference between the ones for the blacks and the ones for the whites, and I said, "Well, at least we can go inside and sit down." You know, but we couldn't here. In Harlan they would have the nice water fountains for the whites, and then they'd have little fountains some place else for blacks.

Nancy Johnson, Baxter

Segregation of Institutions

Here in Covington, there was nothing for black people but the home, the church, and the school. There were movies [but] you could not go to the movies. There was a Y [MCA but] you couldn't go to the Y. We had to walk to Cincinnati for any activities of that nature. Nothing separates us except the Ohio River and you can walk across the bridge. The suspension bridge was a toll bridge and you had to pay two cents or something. We would walk all the way down [*small laugh*] to where the interstate is now and cross the bridge there because it was free.

We would walk to Cincinnati for typing lessons. Educationally we were discriminated against because we did not have any business courses in our school. So those of us who wanted to learn typing and shorthand would walk to Cincinnati and go to night school. The Holmes High School, which was the only high school here—I mean, other than our high school—it was the white high school. Holmes High School had a business program. We had domestic arts and domestic science. In our building was a furnished apartment where girls were supposed to learn how to keep house, [*small laugh*] how to be maids. We also had a big laundry. The girls at our school—in exchange for Holmes High School printing programs and things like that for us—they had to wash the football uniforms for the folk at Holmes High School. I don't know how it worked because I escaped that, but we have pictures of girls—I mean, people who were in school at the same time that I was—in the laundry, and they had these big commercial-size washers, washing these clothes.

Mary Northington, Covington

Middlesboro was a unique community. One could say it was somewhat integrated . . . as a community of, at that time, probably about 12–13,000 people with African Americans living in three different sections of the community. I say that that was different because in most southern towns you had all the African Americans living in one section of the town, but in Middlesboro there were four different African American neighborhoods. They all touched and were intertwined with white neighborhoods.

We had a very unique situation as a little coal-mining town in the mountains because the kids knew one another. I lived in the middle of a block in my neighborhood and directly across the street and two doors down from me were white families. You could go another block where my grandmother and aunt lived and they both had white families that lived on either side of them. So as kids we grew up knowing one another. Every now and then there would be an altercation or we might call each other a name or two, but the next day we'd be out in the street—playing ball again with one another. So, yes, we were racially conscious and realized that there were differences, but not compared to what I've seen in other communities.

Even though we lived intermingled and intertwined in the neighborhood, they went to one school, we going to another. White kids were picked up on the bus and bused to school; we walked or your parents had to take you to school. There was no bus system for black kids. As it was in our case, we walked past the white school to get a mile further down the road to get to the black school. It would have been much more convenient for us to have walked three blocks to the white high school. The textbooks and materials—we got the white schools' hand-me-downs. We could always tell when they had gotten new books because the custodial staff at their school would bring pickup trucks with textbooks in them and drop them off at our school. When I say "drop them off," I can remember that occasionally they would shovel the books out of the pickup trucks with coal shovels and just literally dump them on the ground outside of the school building. Our teachers and principals would go out and gather them up and tape up the books that were in real bad shape and clean them up. They would bring them over in pickup trucks that had had an assortment of things, including coal dust, in them sometime. So our material was always pretty suspect and limited.

We saw racial discrimination among police officers. In the sixth grade I was with a group of kids. We had come in contact with some white kids that lived in a section of town where there were no blacks. As I said, blacks lived in four different sections of town but they [the white kids] lived in the outskirts. We encountered them on a railroad track one afternoon and somebody called us a nigger. It was four or five boys. There ended up being a pretty good rock fight. Well, the police came to our school the next day and came to the door of the sixth grade to our classroom. The teacher went out and came back and said, "Howard, you need to come out in the hallway." When I went out into the hallway—I'm in sixth grade—a great big, robust police officer grabbed me and put his handcuffs on me. I stand in the sixth grade handcuffed and then he starts questioning me. He has these two white kids with him to identify if I was the one that had thrown the rock. Well, they said no, I wasn't the one, but in the meantime I'm in the hallway of the coatroom handcuffed in the sixth grade for something I didn't do. They said, "No, he's not the one." They opened the classroom door and let them stand in the door and look to see if they saw the one that they were looking for that had hit them. Only because the white kids said, no, it's not him, that they took the cuffs off of me. Of course, I was frightened to death. Looking back, I would question whether that police officer would have dealt with a white kid that way.

There were two movie theaters in the community at that time, and I'm trying to remember when they were integrated. I know you're aware of what was usually done with movie theaters—that the black people had to sit in the balcony. The largest of two theaters had two balconies. So we had to sit in the upper balcony and the mid-balcony was only used if the theater got overcrowded. . . . Of course, we many times would go from one balcony to the other, as teenage boys, and purposely sit where we were not supposed to just to wait and wait for the ushers to come and tell us to leave and cause commotion. And they'd call the police and then we'd leave, we'd go back to the upper balcony. . . . Let me go back and say something I do remember about the theater. My mother is not African American. My mother is a Melungeon and that's a whole other story.[8] [*Laughs.*] So we, as what was then called "mixed" kids, would now be looked upon as "biracial." I can remember as a small child when I couldn't even see up to the ticket window, and my mother would carry my sister and I to the movies. Of course, our prices were cheaper but we couldn't go through the theater. The Negro balcony, you bought your ticket and went around the side of the building and went up a long flight of steps that was adjacent to the fire escape. We went up the steps to get to that upper balcony. I can remember my mother walking up to the counter, the ticket window, and she would ask for one adult, two children's tickets. They would sell her tickets to the white section. Then the ticket-window person, when we would walk away, would then notice that she had brown children and would call her back and would be very short with her and make her give them the tickets back. Then they would charge us less, of course, but would issue us "black" tickets. So when they saw the color of her kids, they would then make her give those tickets back and make sure that we knew that we had to go outside the theater and around the back and up the stairwell.

Howard Bailey, Middlesboro

I was lucky enough to get [Louisville's] old Walnut Street experience. I mean, I could name you the stores from block to block. That represents a very memorable aspect of my life. . . . There were night clubs. No denying it. But there were grocery stores, there were drug stores, there were restaurants. There was an aura, a flavor, a way of life. It was a gathering point. It was a community—it was almost like a pivotal point within the central area of the city. Sometime during the day, if you were a black person living in Louisville and you lived anywhere within a stone's throw of Walnut Street, you would end up on Walnut Street. . . . It's something that I feel so sorry for our present kids, from the standpoint that I just don't see any mechanism that can begin to duplicate it. The camaraderie and the closeness and the fraternization that took place on Walnut Street is something that you had to experience. . . . There were three movies, the Palace was at 13th and the Lyric and Grand were at 6th. I lived very close to the Palace and it wasn't uncommon for a group of us to get together and go over to the movies. There was our version of the White Castle Hamburger, which was called Little Palace. It was a little hamburger shop and we used to go over. When I was younger, no, I did not cross Walnut Street [alone]. But there was always somebody that was going that way that you kind of hitched a hand with. So you ended up going across the street and so many of the shopkeepers—it was basically a Jewish-controlled, Jewish-owned area. There were some black businesses. But a lot of the businesses were owned by Jews. But it was a case where they were all employing people of color. They were always employing black people. It was like—oh, man, it was just a totally different kind of experience than almost anything else I've experienced in life. Unless you manage to go into a community that had something like that, and so very few do.

Louis Mudd, Louisville

Muhammad Ali used to be called Walnut Street. 8th and Walnut. From 8th up to 6th Street, for just two blocks [there were] little Negro business places, little shops, all sorts of shops all along Walnut Street. When you got up to 6th Street it kind of spread north and south on 6th . . . but there was a kind of unwritten law, a definite understanding that Negro businesses didn't go beyond 6th Street. Because after you passed 6th Street, here comes 5th and 4th. At that time we didn't have any shopping centers in the suburbs and the main commercial thoroughfare for Louisville was up and down 4th Street. Negro businesses had gone up as far as 6th Street and on either side of 6th Street were two imposing buildings. One is still standing called Mammoth Life Insurance Company. Now across the street was Domestic Insurance Company. Both of them were Negro businesses. . . and they were doing a big business. They were a credit, not only to the black community but to the city to have those two big establishments, right at 6th and Walnut. Two blocks from the main thoroughfare. But the general understanding is no further. Okay, but no further.

There were establishments all along there [that] created what we used to call Little Harlem. On Saturday nights, the Negroes used to let their hair down. They would dress in their nice clothes and strut up and down the avenue and drop in. After 5:30, 6:00 in the evening, from then on until 1 or 2:00 the little joints would just be jumping. At that time in order to let black people know that they could go so far and no farther, if a black man was seen out there talking to a white girl, the police would rough up the white woman but they would beat the hell out of the black man, say, you leave these white girls alone. Now what made it more aggravating is that over here going on out toward Broadway on 7th Street was the red light district. The white girls wouldn't do service to black men in the district. But they'd gravitate sometimes over here into the Negro district and some gullible Negro said ooh, boy, I've got me a white gal tonight. . . . The police, whenever they'd catch a white girl and a black man walking down together, they'd beat the black fellow up. Wouldn't take him to court. Just beat him up. "Don't even look at them. If you were down south, we'd lynch you. We're not going to lynch you, we're just going to beat the hell out of you." Then they'd rough up the girl.

Lyman Johnson, Louisville

When I grew up in [Fayette] County, I grew up in a place called Cadentown . . . out there at Todds and Liberty Roads. If you could look on certain Fayette County maps, you'd see a lot of those little towns. These were black towns. I can mention Uttingertown, Fort Springs, so forth and so on. Associated with the city of Lexington, there are a lot of little pockets or towns . . . I mentioned Speigle Heights, you can mention Smithtown or Taylortown or Pralltown. . . . People in those neighborhoods probably felt just as much or maybe more pride sometimes in the communities in which they lived as anybody else in Lexington felt at that time. . . . I think while we are very much aware that we were segregated, we weren't sitting there quietly. We were doing the things that most people did in their communities, the church groups, the playground groups, just the neighborhood clubs. People had good times together, people would fight each other and when I say fight, I'm not talking about the literal, I'm not talking about the physical fighting, I'm talking about, you had your differences and that kind of thing. But I think those communities were ones where people felt very strongly about themselves and their kinship, not necessarily blood kin, but their kinship to those people in those communities.

You could always say, hey, look over there at what's happening in the other communities—I'm referring to the white communities—from time to time, we might go into some of those other communities. When I [worked in recreation programs at] the old Douglass School playground, we from time to time went down to Athens community, [state representative] Scotty Baesler's community, and played against the kids down there . . . baseball. It was a baseball game, they beat us, we beat them. Of course, while you were in that community, you were going to see some things there that you wish you had. . . . So I don't know to what extent the kids dwelled on, hey, they're different or their park's different, or they have more than we had. I think they loved to go play somewhere else from the competitive point of view. They, of course, would see differences, but I don't think anybody at that time had such a negative feeling that they were going to go back and do nothing, or even do something because of that. You go back into your vital neighborhoods, and you [feel] just as good about that as anything.

Wilfred Taylor Seals, Lexington

I was born in Henderson, Kentucky, February 18, 1939. I went to high school at Henderson Douglas [and] I graduated in 1957. Of course, the schools were segregated then. My memory of that time was receiving hand-me-downs, so to speak, from the other school, the white school that was in Henderson at the time. We were in the band. We had no uniforms, and we received uniforms from Henderson High School, and we were glad to get them. They were used uniforms, you know. They were passed down from the main high school. We were very privileged to get them. Also, this was the way we received our textbooks.

Well, [once I was grown] I was young and energetic and I saw some things that needed to be done. There were other young, energetic people around and we were just not satisfied, sitting back, letting things go the way they were. We wanted to get involved. We wanted to make sure that the youth had something to look forward to. We weren't as concerned about ourselves, as we were about the youth, the children coming up. I guess that is how I got involved. I was asked to coach one of the little league baseball teams. Well, this was the Jackie

Robinson league. Our kids have so much talent, but we were not allowed to play any other teams in the community. We had to play the teams in our league. I didn't think that was fair. They were all black teams of the Jackie Robinson league, where you had other leagues in the city that we weren't allowed to play. We would have allowed them to play us, but they didn't want to play us. But we weren't allowed to play them, so we had our own league. I knew in order for our kids to get their talents recognized, there had to be some exposure.

Ricardo Sisney, Henderson and Bowling Green

Kentucky Village [where I taught for seven years and was principal for eight years] was a reformatory for delinquent boys and girls from all over the state. . . . Everything was segregated during that time [when I started working there in 1957 or '8]. Even the eating facilities, even the boys and girls did not eat together. And I thought nothing. I knew they were separate but I did not realize that the dining room for the white workers was different because we were eating over there with our children. It was neat as could be and the food was just fabulous. It was all the same food. But just, you know, served separately. Then I did discover that they had this fantastic dining room where all the other [white] workers were. I guess I had been there maybe six months, and then I decided, well, we couldn't have this, so I integrated the dining room. I walked in and took a seat and destroyed the lunchtime for everybody, even those who supposedly were friendly, you know, and glad that you are here and all that. All right, glad you are here as long as you stay in your place. I decided that my place was going to be in th[at] dining room. There was a male teacher from Paris, Charles Buckner, who I told that I was going to do this. And he said, well, I'm not going to let you do it by yourself. So he went in with me. A whole lot of people threw their food in the trash can and on the floor and everything else and marched on out, but I was there to stay. They reported it, naturally, to the superintendent. At the time I had become president of the local NAACP.

[So I was called in to see my supervisor, a white man.] I had to share with him some things of how as a race of people we had more accidents on the road because we couldn't stop at the motels. We had to keep on driving. He was shocked. He says, "What do you mean?" I had to go ahead and tell him. I said, "Yes, some places in some of the communities coming across the country, they would open their homes up to people for overnight. For us to be able to stop at a motel and just rest, no. . . . Sometimes we could stop at a filling station and sleep in the car. But this is the reason that we did not travel."

Audrey Grevious, Lexington

No, we swam in the little river. We didn't go into the park. Now if you went to a ballpark, they had a place in the bleachers just for us . . . just like they did at the show. You could go sit up in the balconies.

See, there's another thing where you couldn't get insurance with say Metropolitan or Lincoln Income or National. That's why you had, what we call now, the black company, because we couldn't get insurance with the white ones. We'd walk all through the country, everywhere, selling five- and ten-cents policies. We'd go weekly. See, most of our premiums were weekly. Now there may be some people who were able to pay by the month. But that's the only way. You pay five cents and get a dollar for sick and accident. You pay ten cents, maybe you can get a policy for paying you a hundred, two hundred dollars a death, something like that, if you get it every week. That's when we used to sell what they called the little endowments for ten cents. We'd sell them on the idea that you pay this ten cents a week and the child finishes high school and you've got a thousand dollars to send him off to school somewhere. We called them educational policies.

[In World War II] the Signal Corps was looking for technicians. They had a Signal Corps School in Lexington, and it was established at Transylvania, what we called Johnson School. So I applied for that and I got in. I'm trying to escape getting in combat, you know. [*Laughs.*] So we studied radio, telegraph and telephone, all of this communication. So I said, we may have to get in the front line doing the technical work. It was integrated. We took that course. We were up there almost a year. Then I got called. I'm a World War II veteran. Everywhere I went, nobody wanted to use us. They just didn't want a Negro, didn't want to do it. Well, I didn't like it, but there was nothing I could do, because it was a hopeless situation. We were down at Maxwell Field here. A man laughed and put us in Valdosta, Georgia. I told the major that I was a technician in radio, telephone and telegraph. He laughed and said, well, by God, the closest you'll get to that is riding a bicycle over to the message center. And he was right. That was the Air Force. That was just the way it was.

F. E. Whitney, Hopkinsville

In growing up in Paducah as a young boy, segregation was not as rigid as in the Deep South, but it existed. We had a swimming hole down at the river. We went there to swim and we kind of thought that was our own private swimming hole. Whites had a nice swimming pool out at the Noble Park, the municipal park. There was a kind of a mixed pattern of segregation. For example, we could sit anywhere on the bus in the bus system. We didn't have to move back and give our seats to whites as they did in places like Birmingham, where the civil rights movement really got kicked off. We couldn't ride in white taxicabs, but at that time there were four black taxicabs in Paducah. Down at Kresge's, I remember that we could stand up at a counter. It was a five-and-ten store. 'Course they don't have it any more now. It's a dollar-and-up store. [*Laughs.*] Well, at the five-and-dime store, there were a lot of black people worked downtown and you could stand up, but you couldn't sit down at the lunch counter. The schools were segregated. It was kind of a caste system in a way because some people of affluence, some African Americans of affluence, they could go downtown and be treated quite courteously. In fact, they might allow them to try on some clothes. But as a general rule, you just had to guess your size and buy.

The churches were completely segregated. All of the eating establishments were segregated, restaurants and dairyettes. Of course, with dairyettes you could go to the window and carry out. There were a lot of places where you could carry out stuff, but you couldn't sit down. I remember a place down on Second Street where people, including myself, went. I worked downtown at the time I was a young boy and going to school. You could go back in the kitchen and eat but you couldn't sit out front. It was Lambert's Restaurant. They had plate lunches back then for thirty-five cents. [The food was] quite good. They had black cooks in the kitchen.

Gladman Humbles, Paducah

I worked in a white church forty years and the restaurant was right across there. Well, sometime, like if they had something on Sunday, I had to keep [the church] clean all day. You'd have to go get your food out the window. I remember that.

When we'd go on a train, we got on a train in Fulton. It was all "colored" here and "white" over here. Then one time [*laughs*] I come home, and I went back with somebody kin to me, [a light-skinned relative who looked Caucasian], and they said, move, you have to go to the front. She says, "I'm happy here, I've been right in here all the time." She said, "I know, but you have to go." But there was a time we had to ride in the back of a train.

Jennie Wilson, Mayfield

The library here was the result of a will or an endowment from Mrs. Ella Goodnight and of course, at that time, she had requested that it was for white only. We knew it was for white only. But now there was a [black] family of guys that didn't pay that any attention. Whenever they wanted to read, they went to the library and they read. No one asked them out. But I don't think everybody wanted to trust being humiliated.

The hospital has moved and the type of hospital they had in the '40s, '50s, and '60s was completely segregated. They had only certain rooms that blacks could be admitted. They had separate waiting rooms.

Lucille Brooks, Franklin

The blacks lived on a few streets and most of the white people lived on what was called Main Street. But [segregation] wasn't visibly noticeable, [because] the town was small and even though we didn't attend the same schools, all the kids played together. What might have separated us may have been an alley. [*Laughs.*] So we grew up playing basketball in the back alley together, or playing football together all the time. Another thing you have to remember in a coal-mining town, all of those men went into the same mine to work. You knew everybody. Ninety-nine percent of the men in the town had the same jobs. For the women there was very little out-of-home work. The women were housewives. All these men knew each other.

One of the things that I was very close with my father [about] was fishing. Most of the men in that town, that's what they did on weekends, fished and hunted. And you know, black and white men fished together. There was still a lot of close-knitness in this small town. They depended on one another when they went into that dark hole to make a living.

Porter G. Peeples, Lynch

After I finished grade school in Millersburg, we had to go from Bourbon to Paris to take the examination and believe it or not, it was a two-day exam. We talk about segregation, but the black and the white children took the exam together in the courthouse. Now it's true that schools were segregated, but we took the exam in the courthouse together. I think there were over a hundred kids who took the exam and I made the highest mark in that grade school exam. Then after that, Mr. Whitney Young Sr. was recruiting kids . . . and came to my home and prayed my parents to send me to Lincoln Institute. Lincoln Institute was an exceptional school for black children and children came from all over the state. Whatever [the tuition] was, there were a lot of people that didn't make much and most people out in the state made their living either farming or working. They were very beautiful days. I enjoyed the time at Lincoln. I don't sing now but I sang with a quartet. This [quartet] was to project and advertise the school. We did have integrated teachers. The woman who was head of the music department was white and her assistant was black and the woman heading the math department was white and she was from the state of New York. There were other white people who taught there. They taught carpentry and such courses. The people around there [in the community] hadn't become accustomed to this day. Lincoln Institute wouldn't be closed if it hadn't been for the people there in Simpsonville. It was closed in 1970 by the legislators from Shelbyville, all because it was all integrated.

Mae Street Kidd, Millersburg and Simpsonville

Whites' Memories of Racial Segregation

Coming out of western Kentucky and Madisonville, then a town, I would judge, of twelve to fifteen thousand people when I was a youngster, and a county seat town in a county of probably forty thousand people, 30 percent of all the citizens were black. There was little mechanization in the mines and a good-sized coal mine would employ three hundred men per shift underground every day. Most of those men, except those in a supervisory or foreman capacity, were black. There were so-called colored towns built up on the perimeter of Madisonville on the east and the west and the south, particularly, because there were three large coal mines on the edge of town in those directions. I grew up associating with blacks. We had black servants in the home. I played marbles against black boys. I played baseball against them. But there was always sort of an unwritten, unspoken, recognized situation that the blacks were the blacks and the whites were the whites.

The blacks tried to beat us in marbles and did, in baseball and did. But still, there was no socializing beyond the game. There wasn't any rapport between black children and white children. Sometimes the servants would bring their children to the house around Christmas or on some special function when they were six and seven years old. We played with them with our toys but after you got up to eight or nine, you didn't associate with the black children anymore until you got to be thirteen and fourteen and fifteen when you played marbles and baseball against them. I knew a lot of black people. I expected them, when I got to be a boy thirteen or fourteen, to call me Mr. James. They did, those that worked on the farm and things of that type. Even the older blacks who ran the threshing machines would address me as Mr. James. I never really gave it any thought because things were just that way. Everybody accepted it.

The blacks seemed to look up to my father and believed that he was their friend, I guess. I can remember at his funeral a great crowd of them came. The funeral service was in the home in those days. We didn't have fancy funeral homes in the country. I can remember just a very long line of blacks, a great crowd of them in the back yard. My mother let them in the back door and they walked through the kitchen and through the dining room and into the living room where the casket was, turned to the right and went down the hall, back through the kitchen and back out into the back yard. They came to pay their respects. My father had been a very active foe of the Ku Klux Klan and the Night Riders and Possum Hunters when he was on the bench. The Possum Hunters were dedicated to driving black labor out of the coal mines. They wanted to drive them out so that only white men would work in the coal mines. They were very active in western Kentucky. The Night Riders were riding down the tobacco crops of people who sold their tobacco to the trust. They burned tobacco warehouses in Princeton when my father was judge; that was in his circuit. One of the early things I can remember as a child of three or four years of age was a cross being burned in our front yard during a resurgence of the Ku Klux Klan in the early '20s.

Judge James F. Gordon, Madisonville

There was a shocking thing that happened here in '36, I guess it was.[9] They hanged a black man, just down where the Executive Inn is now. And . . . no one did anything, really. [There was a] perfunctory cross-examination of witnesses. So these lawyers from up in Louisville came down and filed a petition in the Federal Court to set aside this whole proceeding, and that was not successful. But the tragedy of the thing, was that people, thousands of people, gathered to watch this. I have to admit that I was guilty as one of them. I was a sophomore at Harvard Law School then. He [had been convicted of raping and murdering] an elderly white woman who lived here in the town. He was feared, really, in the black community. . . . But nonetheless, I think that public spectacle, of thousands of people gathering to see a black man die, cast a sort of pall over the black community. Rainey Bethea was his name.

My father was rather furious at me, for coming in to watch that. I told him, of course, I would get a thousand questions at Harvard Law School about this event and I wanted to see what went on. Oh, I remember it vividly. The elected sheriff had died, Everett Thompson, I believe was his name, and his wife had succeeded to the office. When the verdict was sustained through all the procedures, it was widely speculated that she would hang Bethea. Instead she employed a professional hangman.

The jailer brought the prisoner out, just a short distance from the jail. . . . Then he was led up to the platform where the hangman and the deputy jailer, deputy sheriff were standing, waiting for him. They put a drape over his head, sort of a sack-like thing, it came down to just below his shoulders, as I remember. And the hangman put the noose around his neck. I can't remember now whether there was a minister there or not. . . . There was a deathly silence over the whole crowd. They were gathered around about as far as you could see around there. The hangman then tripped the trapdoor and he fell to a point where his head was maybe three or four feet below the platform. As he hit, dropped to the end of the rope, the rope snapped his head around like this to the side and his feet convulsed a few times, then quit. Anyway, they pronounced him dead.

They had the so-called hangman parties the night before, some of the places around town. Every bar, you know, they take advantage of every opportunity to sell drinks. So it was jammed up close to the gallows. I was standing back maybe fifty, sixty feet [back]. . . . I don't recall seeing any women there. Then they took his body down and I don't know where they took it. I guess they buried him out in the Potter's Field for black folks here.

It got this town an awful lot of bad publicity. Every newspaper in the country carried the story, and it was carried in Europe. . . . Everybody wanted to know what kind of justice we had down here. It was the last, I'm sure the last public hanging in the United States.[10]

Morton Holbrook, Owensboro

Our first public swimming pool here opened in 1922. Ware's Crystal Swimming Pool, and it was definitely segregated. It would become Carter Swimming Pool later, and I would say it was not integrated until the late '60s. There was Ware's swimming pool for white children. There was Moore's natatorium for the African American children. Along about 1948, the Hopkinsville Kiwanis Club undertook a fund-raising effort to build a municipal swimming pool out on Richards Street. From 1948 through about 1956 or '7, they held an annual fund-raising event in the auditorium at Hopkinsville High to raise money to build a segregated municipal swimming pool, which they did and which opened and operated for a number of years and finally closed when integration was upon us.

Now the annual fund-raising event [was] a blackface minstrel. This is what I mean about the paradox of this whole thing. We had a group of very prominent [white] businessmen here in town, who blacked their faces and put on an absolutely fantastic minstrel. I've got programs for it. I attended nearly every one of them. It was a big event. Remember that I was a little [white] boy growing up before TV. So the Kiwanis Minstrel along in November before Thanksgiving in the auditorium of the old Hopkinsville High School would run for three or four nights to a packed house, and 800–900 [people] can be packed in that auditorium. It was big. They sold tickets and raised money to build a segregated municipal swimming pool by blacking their faces.

William Turner, Hopkinsville

Sometime around age five maybe, when we lived in Campbellsville, I remember trying to sort out this black/white thing and asking my mother were all black people Republicans and all white people Democrats, because we were Democrats. I must have been trying to make sense of this on some level. My contact with African American people had been people working in homes, someone who helped Mother with laundry. When I went to visit some of my relatives they had what they called their "colored help."

Betty Gabehart, Campbellsville

I grew up in a small town, Hopkinsville, Kentucky, which at that time had about a ten thousand population. It is much larger now. It had about a 40 percent African American population. The southern half of the county was very rich agriculturally, and there [had been] many slaves in that county. In fact, Christian County still has the highest percentage of the population of African Americans of any county in Kentucky. I knew those people. I did not have any great sense of the problems of segregation as I was growing up because I grew up in a segregated culture, but there was a general feeling of live and let live and get along in the community. There was no active Ku Klux Klan group or ultra-rightist group, but the [white] people felt that African Americans had their place and they ought to stay in their place. It was typical.

We had people that worked in our home. My mother was a gardener and we had a person who worked for her who was African American. I got to know them pretty well. I played with a little black boy who was one of my best friends growing up, but I never thought about it really . . . [until] I was in the Air Force. Then I was with a diverse group of people in World War II. There were no African Americans in my cadet unit. I was training for flight training and I went to Vanderbilt for a year to train as a meteorologist before I went into flight training. There were no African Americans in our class. My roommate had gone to Purdue as an engineering student and he couldn't understand it, either, because the Big Ten had been integrated . . . He was from Evansville, Indiana, right across the river from Henderson, Kentucky. I thought just that river and just that mile between those communities made such a difference. We had many discussions about it. Philosophically I began to see, and I could not understand why we in Kentucky couldn't see that.

Governor Edward Breathitt, Hopkinsville

I can't tell you that any one incident triggered in me a real deep passion to try to set the equation right. Maybe it was my junior year [of high school], I guess, I decided I wanted to do a study of the American Negro, which is what we called black people back then. I went down to the Louisville Urban League in Louisville to get some data and some reports . . . and got sort of fascinated by the situation. I don't know what turned me on to that. . . . It certainly wasn't anything that was in the air in 1951 in Louisville. I mean, it was like nobody talked about race. I know I joined the student NAACP because of this paper that I'd done in high school and my realization that there was gross inequity. But it wasn't something I confronted on a daily basis.

One of the friends I made when I went up to Indiana [University] was a graduate English student from New York City. I invited her home with me one weekend, and she readily accepted. We got home on the train, pulled in to Union Station, we're walking down the platform to go into the station, and I turn around and Sandy is white as a ghost. I mean, she's stopped in her tracks and she's white as a ghost. I said, "What's the matter?" And I followed her eyes, where she was looking, and what she saw was white/colored: white drinking fountain, colored drinking fountain, white waiting room, colored waiting room. She was horrified. She would never come back to Louisville after that. That had been a situation I had been exposed to many, many, many times and not seen. It took this experience with a stranger for me to see it. That had a profound impact on me—not only that I saw it, but that I hadn't seen it [before].

Suzy Post, Louisville

Jesse Crenshaw

AT the dawn of the twenty-first century, Jesse Crenshaw was one of only five African Americans in the Kentucky General Assembly. His district—the 77th, which he has served since 1993—includes parts of Lexington and Fayette County, and he was the first African American ever elected to represent that area. Crenshaw also teaches law and politics at Kentucky State University.

Born in 1946, Crenshaw came to Lexington as a young adult, part of the first generation of African Americans to attend the University of Kentucky Law School, from which he graduated in 1973. Crenshaw's childhood, however, was spent on his parents' and grandparents' farm, which straddled Barren and Metcalfe counties near the tiny hamlet of Knob Lick in southern Kentucky. Generations of his family had farmed in that area, and Crenshaw and his three brothers continued that tradition as youths. Because Crenshaw's grandfather and namesake, Jesse Filmore Crenshaw, was a landowner who at times rented out portions of his tobacco land to whites, he commanded some respect. But that status could not fully protect his grandson from the racial discrimination endemic to their rural community, which he experienced in schools and other organizational settings.

Although the elder Crenshaw had only a second-grade education, he and Jesse's mother, Magdalene Brewer Crenshaw, who had been a teacher, emphasized to young Jesse the importance of education, self-determination, and political involvement in overcoming the obstacles he would face because of racism. Although he never took part in any protest march or even saw one, Jesse Crenshaw was vaguely aware as a teenager that segregation was being widely challenged elsewhere by others not much older than himself. Because of the models of self-reliance and achievement in his midst, he shaped a strong sense of self and of possibility that led him to respond calmly to the blatant racial discrimination he recalls here from an adolescent summer job. The clash described in this narrative revealed to Crenshaw that racism was about power, not skin color, and strengthened his resolve to acquire the skills and position to make change. The interview begins with his reflections on growing up in a segregated community.

* * *

When I was growing up, the nearest elementary school was one mile from where I lived. [It] was segregated and all white. The elementary school that I attended was . . . three miles away, thus three times [farther] from where I lived than where the nearest school was, and it was segregated and all black. The nearest high school was three miles away and was segregated and all white, and the high school that I attended was in Glasgow, Kentucky, and twenty miles away, one way, and segregated. And we were bused . . . for forty miles round trip, five days a week, to go to school when the nearest high school was three miles away.

We raised tobacco, corn, we had cows that were milked. We had all kinds of things that my grandfather sold to various stores and markets. He sold Kentucky Wonder Beans, Silver Queen corn, tomatoes, lettuce, butterbeans. . . . One hundred and sixty-eight acres. He had a four-acre and thirty-nine hundredths tobacco base at the time, it was acreage then rather than poundage. And that was considered a very large tobacco base for that small amount of land. My mother and my father lived on the part of the land that was in Barren County and my grandparents lived on the part of the land that was in Metcalfe County. My father decided to sell or to allow my grandfather to buy the portion that was in Barren County. My father had previously, many years before, to my understanding, worked in Detroit, Michigan, in the automobile industry. At some point in time, he decided that he no longer wanted to farm and he decided that he was going back to Michigan to work for the automobile industry. My mother and my brothers, for a very short period of time, lived in Michigan and I suppose I was there for a year. And then I went back and lived in Kentucky with my grandparents. At some later point in time, my mother and my brothers moved to Glasgow and my father remained in Michigan.

My grandfather worked in many, many [Democratic] political

campaigns. My mother worked in every campaign that I can think of in Glasgow, my grandfather in Metcalfe County. So in terms of being exposed to the importance of matters that affected electing candidates and government and the impact of that, then both of them were very active in conveying information to us. In terms of teaching you to be proud of the fact that you were black and proud of the things that you could accomplish, my mother, my grandfather, my grandmother, all were active in . . . instilling in you that . . . whatever you want to become, you can accomplish that if you are willing to work hard. . . . We were never taught that because you were black, that you couldn't go on to be whatever you wanted to be.

I decided when I was fifteen that I wanted to be a lawyer. You have to understand [that] when I was thirteen years of age, my grandfather was leasing part of the tobacco base to a white farmer. And . . . my grandfather was saying to me, "Here's what I want you to have Mr. So and So do today." So I was, as a thirteen-year-old who was black, saying to a fifty-some-year-old white man, "This is what my grandfather wants you to do today." And that white man was saying all right and was going on and doing it. And at thirteen, my grandfather would send me from Knob Lick to Glasgow to buy fertilizer, grains, all kinds of things that he needed for planting and things that he needed for the farm. And I was going from the farm, with my uncle driving the vehicle, and going into the Southern States Cooperative store and saying, "These are the things my grandfather sent me to get." And they were saying, "Where do you want us to load them up?" And they were put in the vehicle and I signed for the thing and went on home. So at the same time that you had segregation, I never had the feeling that I couldn't do what I was supposed to do in life.

Prior to going off to college, I worked at a hospital there, the T. J. Sampson Community Hospital, and it was an interesting experience there in which even though you had no legal segregation per se, they had a wing of the hospital that was where all black people were put. Black people and poor whites were put on that wing of the hospital. And when I was working there, I was working as a janitor and again, this is segregation and discrimination in its most blatant form. And what happened, there was a man there, Mr. Henderson I believe was his name, and he was a janitor and he always kept his floors just spotless. And so I worked just as hard at sixteen years of age as he did and kept the area that I was assigned [to] just as well.

Well, in the hallway in the basement, there were four different locker rooms. The first one on the farthest end said "women"—no, I take that back—the farthest one said "ladies"; the next one said "women"; the next one said "men"; and the one that was the farthest up said "gentlemen." And the one that said "men" by and large was black males who had their lockers in there, there might have been one or two whites but almost all black. And blacks and whites would congregate in there at different times and play cards and gamble. Well, I being the sixteen-year-old who had no interest in gambling . . . would go sometimes when the entire locker room was overflowing with blacks and whites and so . . . would take my break in the one that said "gentlemen." Well, anyway, there was a time when the supervisor of the janitors came to me and said, "There's been some complaints about you using the white men's restroom." And I as a sixteen-year-old had no idea where the white men's restroom was, because of the fact that on the wing that I did my work, which was this one that was predominantly black and a few poor whites, you had both whites and blacks using the restrooms that were available . . . on this end of the hallway. And so as I cleaned up those, I had never known that there was a difference. And then when you cleaned in the front of the hospital, there was a restroom out there that was used by both white and black visitors. So, when she told me that there had been a complaint about me using the white men's restroom, it befuddled me for quite a spell there, thirty or forty minutes, the morning that she told me that. And so I went back to her later and asked her, "Mrs. Parrish, where is the white men's restroom?" And she then explained that it was the locker room where Mr. Henderson went.

So I explained to her that if I was not good enough to use the white men's restroom then I was certainly not good enough to clean it up. And her explanation to me—this was in 1963—[was] that there was nothing racial intended. And so she said to me that I should go home and talk with my parents, think about this, and then . . . come back and let her know what I'd decided. So I went home and told my mother. I was [then] living in Glasgow, I was not living on the farm anymore. So I suppose now—this is my speculation—that Mrs. Parrish had felt that if I had talked with my parents, that I'd be told, "You must accept this.". . .Well, I explained it to my mother and my mother hit the ceiling. And rather than say, "You should accept this," it was the same thing I had said: "You should quit, you should not even think that you're going to work there."

Well, I went back and the next day was . . . it was amusing as it could be because we started work at seven o'clock in the morning and usually by eight-thirty at the latest, Mrs. Parrish would make rounds to observe and make known that she was in the area. She was the supervisor of both the janitors and the maids. And so anyway, [on] that particular day after I'd gone back to work . . . rather than be assigned to where I had been working, I was assigned up on the third floor, way over in another area that I normally didn't work. And so instead of her coming by at the usual interval that she would come by to make sure that everybody was working hard, it was like—I'm guessing, this is a guess—eleven, eleven-fifteen, or something before she ever came up on the third floor. And so she came over and asked me if I had talked to my parents and I told her I had. She asked me what I had decided. And I said, "Well, Mrs. Parrish, I'm going to quit." And she said, "Well, if you're going to have to quit, then before you do that, Mr. Kimball (who was the administrator of the hospital) wants to talk with you." So anyway, it was kind of just totally amusing to me because there was a portion of the hospital that they called the chapel that was utilized for funerals or [maybe] just religious services for patients. And so the chapel doubled as a conference room. But anyway, this was such a significant area that Mrs. Parrish always cleaned the chapel herself. She never allowed the maids or any of the janitors to clean it.

She explained to me that I had to meet with Mr. Kimball [there], so we go down to the conference room and we were at this beautiful conference table. Mr. Kimball sits at the head of the table, I sat to his right, he had me sit to his right . . . I had been working there for a long time and I had never been allowed in the conference room until we were talking about whether the hospital was—and nobody ever said this—but the real conversation was whether the hospital was about to get sued for racial discrimination. It wasn't about anything else because if you are receiving federal funds, the last thing you want is some sixteen-year-old black kid to file suit against you for racial discrimination. So anyway, we were sitting down there and Mr. Parrish goes through thirty minutes, at least, of conversation. I will always remember this [because] when you're cleaning the hallways and you're mopping and you're waxing . . . here's a man who at his best would barely grunt to you as an acknowledgment or as a greeting, and now here we are down in the conference room with him . . . explaining to me what life was. We went through all of this about his children and his wife and his family and the various—to use his words—"colored" people that they knew and had interacted with and all. And the phrase that he used, after he got through summarizing all these racial differences and distinctions, was what he was really trying to explain. The phrase that he used near the end was, "Now there are some things in life that you just can't change."

At sixteen I knew that was not true. I knew there were many things that you could change. And the reason that that didn't bother me at all when he was saying it was because all of my childhood had been one in which my grandfather and all of my family had taught me to do what I wanted to do, become what I wanted to become. And I'm trying to think: by that time I had already graduated from high school and graduated valedictorian of my class and so it wasn't like I was intimidated by the room, by him, or any of that. And one of the things that really, really was noteworthy: he was going through all the various comparisons between black people and white people and he was pointing out that his wife did not work and that she stayed home . . . and made sure that their children were well cared for. And as he was explaining that, it was something I thought about, how stupid it was for him to be using all the explanations . . . because as he was comparing the fact that his wife had gotten to stay home and have the ideal set of circumstances in terms of raising their children, my mother was working at a chicken factory, picking hen feathers, and had to be at work at four-thirty in the morning. And so as he was trying to explain all of the wonderful things that went on in his and his family's life, it was stupid as you sat there knowing that [it was] a result of the difference in economic standing and the difference of what was allowed economically for black people versus white people.

Here is my mother—who was an educator and had been an elementary school teacher prior to her going back to Michigan—back here in Glasgow working in a chicken factory because the chicken factory paid more than being a teacher. And yet, at the same time, he's telling me that there's some things in life that you just can't change. So now here he is under the threat or the possibility of some federal intervention adversely affecting their funds, he's now got plenty of time and he's got all of these personal things to tell [me] about life. I will never forget it, we get to the end and he looks over to me and he says, "Well, now what have you decided?" And I said, "Well, Mr. Kimball, I'm going to quit." He says, "Well, if you just quit then I can't give you a recommendation in the future. If you work two weeks and give the proper two week notice, then I will be able to give you a recommendation." And I thought to myself as he was saying it, how could he be so stupid, how could he think that I would be such a fool to believe that he will ever give me a favorable recommendation?

So anyway, I worked two more weeks [anyhow] to pay off another payment on my car, and I quit, and I left there to go off to work in construction. I went to work for the Ernest Simpson Construction Company and I worked there until I left and went to college. And I told the other orderlies and janitors who worked there at the hospital that I was going to work in construction and I would not be back. This one particular person told me, "You'll be back, construction work is extremely hard, and you will be back."

And I have been back to the T. J. Sampson Community Hospital—visiting patients, but I've never been back there to work. . . . And I never envisioned that I would need a job there in the future, so when you ask me about discrimination, yes, I understand it, yes, I was exposed to it. . . . So in terms of the way I have approached life as best I could, . . . when I enter a center of power, I am impressed with its beauty but I'm not awed. I'm neither awed nor overwhelmed with it, and so as the years have progressed, when I try to do things to help improve the lives of people, I see it as something that anyone can do who's willing to work hard and put their mind to doing it. And so, you know, it was like when I went to law school. I mean, I didn't have any feeling that this is something that I won't be able to accomplish or achieve.

My grandfather always taught us that we should be our own boss, as he put it, and it revolves around being self-employed. So every morning I'd go out there to drive the cattle in for us to milk the cows. One morning there was a beautiful view and mist on the ground and a beautiful sunshine reflecting off of that and it really was beautiful. And the cows were out there grazing and they didn't want to be bothered or pestered at all and it finally dawned on me, these cows don't want to have to be brought in here to milk and there's got to be more for me in life than bringing these cows in every morning, [*laughs*] milking these cows everyday. So . . . at that point I then decided, if I'm going to be my own boss, then what should I become. . . . The only careers that I knew of then were either being a lawyer, a doctor, or a teacher. . . . I didn't feel I could stomach the blood and all that went with being a doctor. . . . I didn't at that age think that teaching was the wisest thing because you always had to go to summer school to keep working on all of your certification. . . . So anyway, my choice was to become a lawyer and I went from there working toward becoming a lawyer.

Now in terms of working [for] civil rights and that kind of thing, . . . my view of things is that you're better able to make changes . . . going back to my grandfather's philosophy . . . if you are in positions that you make decisions. You are able to make a lot better improvement than if you are always on the outside. One of my law professors, Professor Eugene Mooney, once taught us in constitutional law that the most important part of a decision is deciding who gets to decide. And so, my way of viewing life is that I like helping decide who gets to decide.

* * *

After studying history and political science at Kentucky State University, Crenshaw completed law school at the University of Kentucky. Practicing law soon led him into a career in politics, part of the first generation of African Americans in Kentucky to experience even a veneer of equal opportunity in public life. Such opportunity, he found, had to be seized rather than simply assumed.

When I was in law school, [in 1973] I was a third year student and Harold Green was a second year and he was president of the Black American Law Students Association and I was vice president of the organization. We decided that we were going to desegregate the law school faculty because the law school had never had any blacks on it. We felt—or I felt especially—that black law students and white law students needed to see a black teacher. Black law students needed it because of the fact that we needed to see a positive reflection of our own self-image, and white law students needed to see it to see that, in fact, black law professors are able and capable. So anyway, we went to the [then-] dean of the law school, a man by the name of George Hardy, and asked Dean Hardy had he ever considered hiring a black law professor, and he said, "Oh, yes, we tried." He pulled open the bottom of the drawer—and this was in good faith, I mean, he was not trying to stifle us in any way, form, or fashion—he pulled open his desk drawer and he had all this list of files of people they had tried to hire.

So again, the most important part of the decision is deciding who gets to decide, so rather than going in saying, "Oh, please, please," we went in with a name of a specific person, name was Kleckly.[1] Ultimately, a man by the name of William James was hired. So he became the law librarian and became the first black law professor at the University of Kentucky College of Law, in the fall of 1974.

Well anyway, four years later, I was [by now] the first black Assistant U.S. Attorney for the Eastern Judicial District here in Lexington. So I go in, and this is with no authorization from the U.S. Department of Justice whatsoever, I ask Dean Lewis—different dean—"Have you all"—same phrase I used in '73—"have you all ever considered hiring a second black law professor?" And Dean Lewis reached down at the same drawer, pulled out the same things and said, we worked and we've tried and tried. Well, anyway, after we posed the request—the demand, as Frederick Douglass would have called it—Dean Lewis went forward and worked very diligently with me in trying to find a second black law professor.[2]

Now I'm jumping back to my efforts at the U.S. Attorney's Office. Patrick Malloy, who was the United States Attorney at the time, came to me and asked me if I would consider coming to work for the U.S. Attorney's Office, and I said yes. And Jimmy Carter was president of the United States at the time. And it's my understanding, now I never saw this in writing, but when President Carter became president, it is my understanding that Carter made it known throughout government, "I want to see more black people hired." And it's my guesstimate that that filtered down to U.S. Attorneys as well as everything else. So when I went there in April of 1978, the office had been operating since 1901 and there had never been a black Assistant or a full-fledged U.S. Attorney, in the history of that office. In terms of the state, I would have been the second in the state, but in terms of this local Lexington office, I was the first.

So later when I became the first black state representative from Fayette County, it's not like I saw [either of these jobs] as something that I could never do. It's back to when Mr. Kimball was telling me that there were some things in life that you can't change. Well, that's not true, and it wasn't true then, I knew it wasn't true. When you look at the Civil Rights Act of 1964, that legislation that Martin Luther King was able to get enacted, you may not be able to change the hearts and minds of people, but you can change their conduct. Through the utilization of the law, you can change their conduct. Now you asked me earlier a question that I have to restate. Yes, it became clear to me at a young age that through the use of the law and a law degree and its impact, you can improve society, you can change society.

I always felt that you should—this may have been one of my grandfather's phrases because he had many of them—practice what you preach. It's fine to be eloquent in recounting all the historical . . . and the political activities, but you ought to be able to have some involvement and practical experience in it. So as I teach students, I think I'm a much better teacher because I've left the courtroom two days before having to encounter just what I'm telling them about. In terms of political activities, in 1973 there was a mayoral race here in Lexington in which Foster Pettit was running for mayor and he asked this friend of mine, Harold Green, and me to help in his campaign. Well, we started by trying to help register sanitation workers to vote.

My finally running for political office—it was almost a common, natural thing to do. As I had sat there as a twelve-year-old watching [my grandfather] at fish fries and this, that, and the other, where he was working in whatever candidate's campaign, it became very, very natural [for me to see later] as a young adult, that working in someone's campaign or being involved in the decision-making process made sense. I worked in every mayoral race in Fayette County from 1973 to the present. I've worked in every presidential race, I worked in many congressional races, I worked in city council races, I worked in judicial races, so it wasn't like . . . there was some big thing that said, "I think I will do this today." No, it was sort of a natural progression.

This particular district was a combination of a part of what used to be the old seventy-fifth, a part of what used to be the old seventy-sixth, and I believe, I want to say like the seventy-eighth, that became the newly created seventy-seventh [because of] the Voting Rights Act of 1965, where there were federal efforts to try to see that we had more blacks voting and that you had more black elected officials. So as a part of the federal efforts to see that across the United States there were districts that were designed in such a way that blacks were more able to be elected, this district was designed in such a way that it had a larger number of black voters.

* * *

Crenshaw's reflections conclude with situating his own experiences of racism in what he has observed as a troubling and persistent national trend.

I don't think our country ever has addressed the problems of race in a way that makes sense. I mean, we address it, kind of like Mr. Kimball did, "My God, we've got to do something, he's about to sue." When we went to the dean of the law school and said, you never had a black professor, it was like, "Oh, my God, we've got to do something." I go back in four years and I say, "You've had one and you haven't gone out on your own and gotten a second." And they say, "Oh, my God, now that you've brought it up, let's do something." Well, we do the same thing in almost every [area].

Chapter 2

Desegregation in Education

EXCEPT for a handful of tiny private schools operated by free people of color, very few opportunities existed for African Americans to obtain an education in antebellum Kentucky. Although literacy was not criminalized for slaves in Kentucky as it was in some southern states, many owners punished slaves who sought education, while free people of color were exempted from paying school taxes in 1837 because of an assumption that no schools would serve them.[1] Racially segregated schools then became the norm in every former slave state once a system of public schools began to be instituted across the South after the Civil War. African American leaders in the commonwealth began almost immediately to demand equal funding for all-black schools—a measure achieved in principle through an 1883 U.S. circuit court ruling in *Edward Claybrook v. Owensboro*, but the ruling often went unenforced. Their efforts also led to the establishment in Frankfort in 1886 of one institution for teacher training: the State Normal School for Colored Persons, which eventually became Kentucky State University.

Despite these nominal gains, in 1904 segregated schooling in Kentucky was reinforced by the Day Law, which required that all schools in the state, both public and private, be racially segregated at all levels. The measure was aimed at the only college in the state to admit blacks prior to 1900: Berea, whose mission of educating disadvantaged Appalachian Kentuckians put black and white youth in classrooms together on an equal basis and defied the increasing trend toward segregation. When the U.S. Supreme Court affirmed the legality of the Day Law in 1908 (with Kentucky's Justice Harlan again dissenting, as he had in *Plessy* twelve years before), Berea was forced to comply, and it did so by becoming all white. Andrew

49

Carnegie and other philanthropists who had supported African American education at Berea then endowed the Lincoln Institute in Shelbyville. The Lincoln Institute, as Mae Street Kidd mentioned in Chapter 1, was a private "normal school" that drew black students from around the state to its teacher training programs.

Although the Lincoln Institute operated effectively for decades and investors such as the Slater and Rosenwald Funds established other schools for blacks around the state, the segregation of Berea in response to the Day Law effectively ended interracial education in Kentucky and the South for nearly half a century. Despite persistent African American demands for better treatment in all Kentucky schools, several generations of youth grew up in separate and unequal institutions at every level, and schools generally in the commonwealth struggled for success in light of the state's economic tribulations. Although black students were sometimes taught by highly educated African Americans confined to teaching by employment discrimination, most of the "colored" schools (so called by whites) had poorer funding, leading to inferior facilities and textbooks.

In the 1930s the NAACP began its fight nationally against Jim Crow in education by challenging segregation on the grounds that separate facilities were not equal. The organization's strategy was to start at the highest level of education, the graduate and professional schools, and work its way down. One of the first targets in Kentucky, in the wake of World War II, was medical education. Black leaders at that time secured an amendment to the Day Law to enable black doctors to take residencies at all-white hospitals and also to allow integration in nursing programs, in part because their adult, all-female student body aroused less opposition among whites. This was the first of several measures through which civil rights activists were able to chip away at segregated education in the commonwealth.

Within a couple of years, African Americans began successfully opening doors to graduate education at the University of Kentucky and other state institutions. White officials tried to forestall that outcome first by offering supposedly equivalent graduate classes for African American students on the campus of Kentucky State. These proved cumbersome, as illustrated in the case of John Hatch—the first narrator in this chapter—who attended the Kentucky State law program administered by UK in 1948. Off-campus graduate UK classes did not last long. The same year Hatch started law school in Frankfort, Lyman Johnson, a Louisville high school teacher and leader of the local NAACP branch, became the plaintiff in a federal antidiscrimination suit demanding the right to enroll in UK's graduate history program on the same terms as white students. With NAACP lead counsel Thurgood Marshall as one of his attorneys, Johnson won his case. Partly because similar cases from other southern states pending in the U.S. Supreme Court seemed likely to end segregation in higher education—which they did in 1950 (*Sweatt v. Painter* and *McLaurin v. Oklahoma*)—the university decided to comply rather than appeal. In mid-1949 Lyman Johnson became one of about thirty African Americans to desegregate UK.

In the wake of the Johnson suit, and fearing other NAACP challenges, several other Kentucky public and private colleges followed suit in desegregating both their graduate and undergraduate programs. Berea became biracial again in 1951, and Jessie Zander's narrative reflects on the experience of African Americans' return to that campus in the early 1950s. In that same year the University of Louisville became the first of the state's previously white universities to hire an African American professor—sociologist Charles Parrish. His hire was part of the absorption of the Louisville Municipal College for Negroes. The first generation of desegregating African American students continued to experience imposed segregation and discrimination on college campuses, however, as some of the narratives that follow attest.

Despite amendments that whittled away at it, the Day Law remained in place for precollegiate education until the U.S. Supreme Court unequivocally condemned segregated schools in its *Brown v. Board of Education, Topeka, Kansas* ruling on May 17, 1954. While the immediate reaction to the court order in much of the South was surprisingly muted, over the next two years opposition to school desegregation built, enlisting leaders not only among local businessmen, professionals, and politicians, but even from governors and U.S. senators. This rising tide of resistance was enabled in part by the Court's delay in specifying how integration was to be accomplished, and by its decision in May 1955—commonly referred to as *Brown II*—that merely counseled officials to proceed with "all deliberate speed" and left the authority for determining both pace and process in the hands of local officials. By 1956 the region was swamped by a wave of what historians have called massive resistance, which included legal and extralegal means to keep black youth from attending school with whites. This hostile climate was bolstered by rampant anticommunism, fueled by the Cold War, which allowed white southerners to associate white supremacy with American tradition and to defend segregation as a fight against internal subversion.[2]

The response to *Brown* in Kentucky was relatively more positive. State leaders, like those in neighboring West Virginia and Missouri, immediately pronounced a willingness to abide by the new law of the land, as when state Attorney General J. D. Buckman Jr. announced that the ruling nullified the Day Law and Governor Lawrence Wetherby proclaimed his support for integration. The lack of direction from the Supreme Court temporarily put a brake on the momentum for desegregation when the state school board declared there would be no changes until the Court acted further. Meanwhile, a tour of the state by NAACP officials found that not only did school boards in smaller communities have no plans for integration by summer 1955, they had not even discussed it. Nevertheless, although officials adopted a "go slow" approach and many whites showed no enthusiasm for change, several communities around the state did put desegregation in motion, following the lead of nearby border states and contrasting dramatically with those in the Deep South.[3]

Kentucky's first public school desegregation occurred in the summer session of 1955, shortly after the second Brown ruling, when one African American Fayette County schoolgirl unexpectedly applied to attend all-white Lafayette High School in Lexington and did so with no sustained opposition. Communities with small African American populations, which had been financially burdened during the separate but equal era by sending their black students to other districts, also took steps toward integrating their own schools. In the fall of 1956, with the urging of the state NAACP, desegregation began in earnest when more than half of Kentucky's 160 biracial school districts admitted students on a desegregated basis.[4] In places like Louisville, the change was received without much protest: superintendent Omer Carmichael—who received accolades from the national press for the calm transition—called it "the quiet heard 'round the world," by comparison to the white uproar in communities farther south. Acceptance by white Louisvillians took place at least in part because the actual numbers desegregated were hardly more than a token, and Carmichael offered reassignment to any parents displeased with the racial content of their home school—an offer many white parents took advantage of to return to all-white environments while African American youths suffered persistent small indignities in the schools they desegregated.

In parts of western Kentucky, the remnants of a Confederate political identity—as one of the region's historians has argued—yielded more aggressive white pro-segregationism through the formation of White Citizens' Council groups that joined the massive resistance to school desegregation sweeping the South.[5] Among the most extreme reactions were those in the districts of Henderson, Clay (Webster County), and Sturgis (Union County, which had supplied the Civil War with seven Confederate soldiers for every one who stayed with the Union).[6] In all three communities, whites, inflamed by regional media outlets such as the pro-segregationist *Madisonville Messenger*, boycotted the schools and led mass rallies protesting integration. In Clay, every black family was intimidated into backing down except one, the Gordons, whose two children were admitted only with help from the National Guard. The family then endured the dynamiting of their neighborhood, termination of the father's employment, and economic harassment so fierce they could not shop at some stores, only to find that officials withdrew the two children from the formerly white school anyway, prompting the anguished family to flee Kentucky.[7] None of the Gordons could be located later for KCROHP interviews, but narratives of participants from the Sturgis and Henderson conflicts are among those included in this chapter.

While token integration was achieved in many Kentucky communities by the late 1950s, widespread desegregation of schools in parts of rural Kentucky and across the South required multiple lawsuits, especially in areas where there was organized white resistance. Nearly twenty such lawsuits were filed here in the late 1950s by the Kentucky NAACP's crusading lead attorney, James Crumlin, a Louisvillian who reportedly caused white "panic" when he arrived in Kentucky country towns. Many districts adopted "freedom of choice" plans that supposedly allowed students to attend their desired school without regard to race. In truth, however, the resulting "choices" put blacks who made them at risk for white retaliation, while whites exercising "choice" sustained many all-white schools.[8] Still, such inhibitors to desegregation were less successful in Kentucky than they were in the Deep South because state institutions and the board of education were for the most part committed to abiding by the law, whereas many policymakers in former Confederate states were themselves massive resisters. By 1964 about 92 percent of Kentucky's school districts had achieved some desegregation, compared to less than 20 percent in the South.[9]

In light of such marked lack of southern progress, the U.S. Supreme Court ruled in the late 1960s that "freedom of choice" would not lead to true integration and in fact undermined it by placing undue burden on African Americans. A 1971 decision went further, empowering federal judges to intervene more actively in search of a racial mix in schools. These legal changes were not aimed at Kentucky, but they heralded the second, more sweeping wave of K–12 school desegregation here in the 1970s, involving measures such as busing, school closures, teacher desegregation initiatives, and—later—the creation of magnet programs. In Lexington, court actions in the early 1970s brought about dramatic policy shifts, including the closing of many inner-city, historically black schools, but desegregation continued to stall. In Louisville, in response to a 1972 federal suit, Judge James Gordon instituted a county-wide busing plan in 1975 that mobilized massive white protests that rivaled similar upsurges that took place the previous fall in Boston.[10] The new policy proceeded, however, and after several rounds of amendments over the years it eventually gained community acceptance, though not without considerable citizen organizing both for and against busing.[11]

As with many aspects of the civil rights movement, school desegregation is not simply a chapter in history, but a vexing social issue that remains unresolved in the twenty-first century. Conservative policies of the Reagan-Bush era in the 1980s saw a nationwide decline in the push toward multiracial education. Supreme Court decisions of the 1990s then made it easier for school districts to be released from longstanding desegregation orders. In Kentucky, educational reform after 1990 also ushered in new concerns that emphasized racial parity only as one of several ambitious goals for schools across the commonwealth. Although the Jefferson County desegregation order expired in 2000 after twenty-five years, a 2004 court decision affirmed the district's decision to continue voluntarily taking steps to promote racial integration in its school placements. While a report by the Harvard Civil Rights Project in 2003 pronounced Jefferson County the most racially mixed school district in the United States, a close look at its schools reveals persistent racial achievement gaps, and local protest campaigns and interviews with African American residents of Louisville suggest mixed experiences even today.[12] In 2007 the U.S. Supreme Court ruled in *Meredith v. Jefferson County Board of Education* against even voluntary measures that involve racial balancing to keep schools integrated, throwing into doubt the future and legacy of *Brown* in the commonwealth and in the nation.

The oral histories in this chapter are grouped into three chronological sections representing the desegregation first in higher education, then the two distinct waves of K–12 desegregation described above. The first set of narratives describes the process of integrating Kentucky's colleges and universities, and the experiences of African Americans who were pioneers at previously all-white institutions.

College and University Desegregation

John Wesley Hatch, a native Louisvillian, matriculated at age nineteen as a law student at a University of Kentucky program held at Kentucky State in 1948.

* * *

I always saw law as a possibility. I think it had to do with the expectation that if you could change the law, that life could become a lot better. At that point, you could go to law school after your second year of college. . . . I was in the process of applying for that [for Howard Law School] and was informed, hey, that's over. . . . They said, well, now you can do this right here in Kentucky. I certainly understood that UK should have been open, but it wasn't. Actually my application was to Kentucky State and I was a student at Kentucky State Law School because they had said that we'll have law school at Kentucky State. But they didn't have any students until I went forward and said, okay, you've got a student, and they had one.

It was not a good way to get a legal education, to say the very least. I would have a reading assignment and would be asked to react to it. You know, I don't know as anybody'd ever [studied] law that way. [Before law schools were established] there was an apprenticeship system, which would be quite different, where you'd just begin to go in and do things. But to try to learn without the dynamic of an interactive process with other students? Oh, I would on occasion [ask questions]. But I didn't quite know what the law was and so much of the culture of any learning process is from other students, not from the professors. I was missing that.

I was a powerful curiosity on campus as well as down at the capitol. I remember a man, I think he was assistant attorney general. I can remember he was a very decent old man, but he was saying, well, "John, why would you want to be a lawyer? Blacks don't have any business. You know, it looks like you would make a fine teacher or preacher and it seems to me that your people need that a lot more than they need law." 'Course I didn't agree with him, but I realized his sincerity, and in retrospect he was really quite close to target because black lawyers had a hard time eating in a good many places. I hadn't quite seen the law that way, but of course he was saying to me that most lawyers earn their keep through business transactions, and indeed blacks didn't have any businesses.

It was explained to me that I would have access to a law library. Everybody knew it was impossible to teach law without a library. I realized [though] that the likelihood of getting a legal education in that way was not good. After I'd done it, we began to get input from friends of my father, in particular, about the futility of it. And we continued to think, well, if this doesn't work out, then I'll go to Howard. Somewhere, I don't know exactly at what point . . . probably the second semester, I met with Thurgood Marshall and Robert Carter, the dean of the Howard University Law School, and another guy, who had been the NAACP Legal Defense Fund person before Marshall. Anyway I met them and they said, "Look, this is not the way you learn law, and we would recommend that you bail out of this and go on to Howard if you're serious about a legal education." Howard was where I wanted to go in the first place, but money was a big barrier. The African Methodist Church didn't pay a lot, and my father [a minister] always had to work on the side to pay the rent. So that seemed out of reach.

* * *

In 1949, with revision of the Day Law, Hatch was allowed to attend classes on the UK campus.

There were no other black students in law. [Treatment was] not a lot better. It was so uneven really. In some classes, it was mandated [university policy] there should be a chair between me and white students, and then there were some professors that said this is bullshit, I'm not going to have that [chair]. Then, even in the library, I didn't sit at tables with other students. I sat at a table in the corner, and I never really went to a moot court or anything like that. So it was not open. That's a rather profound message when you're sitting at a table in the back of the library and you can't sit down with other people. Or indeed just the physical separation, the symbolism of that empty chair.

[Some white students] would speak or maybe shake hands or share something occasionally. But I really never had a study relationship with anybody. I think the most grievous thing from my perspective was I never got into the system as a serious student, attending moot court. How can you do it without that? I never went to a single session. After

I'd been here and got a dose of this, I knew that was it. . . . It was just a matter of being twenty and not having sufficient resources, even if I could handle the psychological piece of it. But I was pretty sure that it was nobody's real agenda to see that I got much of an education anyhow. I couldn't imagine really that once the court decision had gone down that these insults would have continued. But you can't be a part of a class, you know, sitting in a box.

John Wesley Hatch, Lexington

* * *

The next two narratives also center on UK and the experience of African American graduate students, who, still rarities on campus, were the subjects of hostility, controversy, and scathing insults.

In September 1951, I was admitted to the University of Kentucky as a graduate student. My experience the first day was quite humiliating. I was assigned to Dr. [Thomas] Clark's Kentucky history class for the first hour. I went in. There were seats for forty people. I always pride myself [for] being on time, so I was about five minutes early. I sit down. Everybody else came in and I noticed they would take a look at me and stare and then stand up against the wall. Nobody else would take a seat. Finally, a young man from Bardstown named Jess Gardner came in and he introduced himself. Said he was a veteran, and asked me did I mind if he sat down beside me. I said no and we continued to talk. But nobody else came to sit down. They just stood against the wall. Finally there were thirty-eight people standing and two sitting, me and Jess. When the bell rang, Dr. Clark came in and I guess he was just astounded, because his face turned red as a tomato. He turned and wheeled and went outside. He went to his office and stayed about three minutes. I guess he was getting his thoughts together. He came back and he said, "There are forty seats in here and there's only two people sitting down. You either take a seat or get out." That was reassuring to me at that particular time.

But the next morning, everybody came to class early. They took a little rope and put around the seat I had sat in and put a sign on it, "For Colored Only." Everybody was sitting, and when I came in that was the only seat available. So this day I stood up, because I refused to sit in that seat. Poor Dr. Clark came in that morning, and oh, that shocked him. So he came back in the room, and he asked me, "Mr. Logan, would you go over to the student center, have a cup of coffee or something? You will not be marked absent. I need to talk to these students. Don't worry about it, but tomorrow, you will be treated as a human being." So I said, "No, I don't mind." I went over to the student center and got some coffee, but it was humiliating because every time I would sit down, I don't care how long the table was or how wide the table was, if I sat down [or] sit a cup of coffee down, everybody at the table would get up and leave. But I had been schooled on that and I had expected some of those things. It was quite humiliating for a human being to put up with. But at that moment, I made up my mind that as long as I went to UK, I knew that I was going to excel in my classwork.

George Logan, Lexington

Having grown up around where [black and white people] don't interact, you're in your world and I'm in my mine, I still have that trait. I can walk into a crowded room anywhere, size it up, and say okay, you're over there, and I'm over here, and get along just fine. Talk with anybody who needs, or wants, doesn't mind my talking to them, and the rest of them, I don't even know they exist. It was sort of like that [at the University of Kentucky]. Nobody said anything, or as I recall, did anything [hostile]. Nobody spoke to you, nobody engaged you and stuff like that. But after I was around there a while, a few people did. One of the things that I do remember is that they discouraged my ever participating in class. If I raised my hand to get involved in a discussion, they just ignored the fact that I had asked permission to comment. In retrospect, I have thought that they possibly thought they were sparing me being noticed by other people. That if you say something and get something going here, you are going to instigate something that maybe wouldn't happen if you just keep your mouth shut and sit over there quietly. Maybe that's what they were doing. I don't know.

Iola Harding, Yosemite

* * *

Racial conflicts at UK were certainly the most publicized and perhaps the most pronounced in Kentucky higher education in this period. That was so in part because UK was the centerpiece of the state's post-secondary system and thus possessed more symbolic power for those wishing to maintain white supremacy. Yet the commonwealth's other post-secondary institutions—public and private—experienced similar turmoil in the 1950s and 1960s. In 1951, Jessie Zander was recruited to join the first generation of African American students since the passage of the Day Law to attend Berea College, where she found it challenging to be both black and female.

When the opportunity [came] to go to Berea, there was no question whether I would go or not go. It was the only opening I saw. [My grandmother] could pay whatever she was able to pay and I could work, and so it could happen that way. When I got to Berea I learned that Dean Allen, who was Dean of Women at the time, and a very beloved lady, had selected a roommate for me in anticipation of my coming. I think they were concerned about how I would be treated. So they had found someone who did not mind rooming with a black student.

I must have been real protective of myself. Probably I wasn't my true self maybe the whole two and a half years because it was a strange situation. I cannot say I was not treated well. But I could, looking back on it, gauge that I chose things to be part of that were safe and regretted not being a member of the singing group, for instance. Probably what kept me from doing that was I knew I didn't read music. Even though I know now that wasn't important, to be able to read music, to be part of the musical group. Being told all your life you have to be three times as good in order to make it meant I wasn't going to chance being embarrassed. I did not join the players, the acting group, because I observed that if a black person became a part of the acting group they were doing servant roles. But there was one young woman who had a lot more nerve than I did and she protested that those weren't the only roles. There were other roles to be played and she became a vital part of the acting group. But she had a little more guts than I did in challenging that.

When I went to Berea I was straightening my hair because, well, the real standard of beauty was as straight as you could make your hair. And you were concerned about whether your "kitchen" was going back—we called it the kitchen at the back of your hair. We didn't go swimming. That's another thing. A lot of black young women never took swimming because it meant your hair would go back. So at Berea there wasn't and I understand there is no provision still for black students who are interested in hair care, that there is anything in the college life that provides for hair care. Anyway I would wash my hair in the dorm and go out, there was a family who was the custodian at the school and named after John G. Fee [the founder of Berea], which was interesting. They lived right down under the college. His name was Fee Moran, and they befriended many, many students—there weren't that many, but all black students ended up at that house. So it was through them I learned of where I could go to get my hair done. So I would wash my hair in the dorm and then get out before my roommate would come in because I was embarrassed of my own hair. I didn't want her to see it washed. Then I would walk to the home where someone would do my hair in their kitchen, you know, with the hot combs on the stove or [with the] paraphernalia they used to do hair. Then I'd come back all beautiful. I had an aunt who used to say, if she didn't believe you, she'd call you, "lying haint," you know. In my mind I was repeating "lying haint." I don't know how to tell you better but it was a word we used in the community if we didn't believe you. So in my mind, I was saying that because there was no idea that my hair could be beautiful. Even though I have very soft hair and I ruined it all those years straightening it when it shouldn't have been. I'm glad to have gotten to the point where I wear it natural.

Dating at Berea, you see, was problematic for me. I did not have dates at Berea. I think once I went to a movie. A young man had enough nerve to ask me to go to the movie, a white student, but we both were so nervous. We went to that movie, [*laughs*] and we never invited each other to do anything again. I don't even remember that guy's name. Then there was a young man in the community, he was a relative of [another African American female student] . . . and I remember dating him once, but that didn't pan. So my social life was really curtailed at Berea.

Jesse Zander, Berea

* * *

The same year that Zander entered Berea, undergraduate desegregation also began at the University of Louisville. With its urban location and a higher percentage of local blacks than elsewhere in the state, U of L none-

theless proved less than fully hospitable to its early African American students, in part because of the segregation that surrounded it in the city, as
the next narrative illustrates. Mattie Jones enrolled in the early 1950s after
first attending Indiana University.

I needed a course in P.E., so I signed up for bowling, not knowing that
Louisville at that time did not have a public accommodation law on
the books. Then when I signed up for my bowling course, I carried my
little card over to my instructor, and the instructor said to me, "Where
will you bowl? You cannot go over there to Parkview Bowling Alley
and bowl." And my reply was, "Why?" He said, "Colored people can't
go over there." That was just like someone had cut my leg off, I tell
you. There's no words to explain how I felt. . . . I left that campus and
I was crying; I was completely upset. When I got home my mother
wasn't there, and I guess I drowned myself in my own tears. That night
when she came in, I was pretty angry.

So I told her what had happened to me. She says, "Well, you can't
do anything alone all by yourself." She says, "There is a difference
here with how they treat"—at that time we were using the word "colored"—"colored people and how white people are treated." She says,
"But you can't run from everything." She says, "Now, what you need to
do is get yourself in an organization." Said, "The NAACP has always
helped colored people."

Mattie Jones, Louisville

* * *

Although not among the original pioneers of desegregation at what is
today Western Kentucky University, Howard Bailey's generation of black
college students was the first to attend Western en masse (he enrolled in
1966). Their numbers gave them a greater measure of assurance, yet they
encountered lingering discrimination.

I remember going to the guidance counselor's office [in high school]
asking for an admissions application for Western State, and she looked
at me and said, "I don't know." This was some of that subtle racism
you saw. She said, "I don't know whether you're really the type material that you need to try to go to a school like that. You might want
to consider Kentucky State." "No, that's where I want to go. If you

can't get me one, I'll have to write out for it." She eventually gave it to me, but she also said, "If you're wanting to go to that part of the state, you might ought to look at Western Kentucky Technical School in Paducah." It was a black technical school. She was still trying to tell me I didn't belong at a white school. I was hell-bent that I was going then, even though I'd never laid eyes on it, didn't know where it was even, but I was going then. But when I got to Western, we saw discrimination here on campus, saw it in the community—because I came ironically in the first critical mass of black kids that hit Western's campus. Before then there had been just the athletes and a few kids that lived in boardinghouses along State Street . . . that commuted in here for graduate classes and left. But other than a few of the athletes that lived on campus, there hadn't been any real mass of kids. We showed up—there were probably seventy-five, eighty freshmen. We outnumbered all the other black students twofold or more when we showed up that year.

This was thought to be the Promised Land 'cause there were no other black athletes being recruited on scholarship in the state of Kentucky. . . . I was first turned down [for housing]. They sent me a listing of Negro boardinghouses in Bowling Green, that I might want to contact . . . and get a room. [After a family friend intervened on my behalf] not long after that I got a notice that there was a room. When I got here, I found out that Western only assigned black kids rooms if they had a pair because they want to make sure that they put you in a room together. They roomed us in certain sections of the halls, and they scattered us so that there wouldn't be too many of us in any one building. It took us a while to figure that out. But as you got to know other black kids, you would notice that [in one dormitory], all the black kids were in the "fifteen" room: 215, 315, 415, 515. That meant that the staff knew where the black kids were all the time, and there were never too many of us together. I was in West Hall, and in West Hall everyone was in 101 and 103, all the way up. I had [some] instructors that were racially negative toward me. I can remember being a moment or two [late]. The bell was ringing as I was stepping into the classroom one day, and the instructor said, "Well, class, I guess we can start now that our black member is here"—to emphasize that I was late. There were people that were very nice to us, but there were other people that made it clear that they tolerated us.

Howard Bailey, Bowling Green

The First Wave: *Brown* Era Public School Desegregation, 1954–1969

Between 1954 and 1969, Kentucky schools went through the first wave of desegregation in response to the *Brown* decision. The story for which the state won national publicity took place in Louisville, where the opening of integrated schools occurred on September 4, 1956, with no violence and a minimum of vocal opposition. Here Evelyn Jackson, African American principal of Douglass Elementary School, and Ruth Higgins, white principal of Morris Elementary School, share their memories of the preparation for integration led by school superintendent Omer Carmichael, and the impact of the transfer option—two elements widely credited with securing Louisville's relatively peaceful transition to nominally mixed schools.

* * *

Mr. Carmichael was a person who always discussed the moves he was going to make, or anything he was thinking, with the principals. At first he talked with us and then we met. . . . The whites met in the morning and the Negroes met in the afternoon for the first meeting. He stopped that and we all met at the same time. So we had become quite accustomed to meeting, and he would discuss the issues with us. Then he would proceed to go out into the community. He contacted the city fathers. . . . He'd discuss it in political groups, he'd discuss it in Lions and Rotary clubs and all. He had quite a few meetings at the library there at Fourth and York and he began to talk about it. He began to feel out the people to see how they felt about it. He kept saying it was going to be the law of the land. . . . His premise was this, he was going to obey the law of the land. So then the time finally came when he said he was going to do it. He called us together again and discussed it and then he just went on and told us that if we had any trouble to call. He said we'll just go into it naturally and this is the thing to do.

We had many meetings to get us ready to prepare our faculties. He talked with us on such things as name-calling. Parents in public were probably saying that one group of teachers were better prepared or better teachers than another group. He talked about such things as that and he showed us that there were fallacies in these things, and that we would go into it naturally. . . . We had to meet with our parents, because a lot of the parents—I don't know what the white ones said about coming to me, but a lot of the black ones said they didn't want to send their children to Morris School. They were afraid they'd be mistreated and be outnumbered. I had to convince them that they were going to be in the majority there. I told them what we were trying to do and I hoped that they would go along. . . . I can honestly say . . . I never had one minute's trouble, never had any trouble and Mrs. Higgins [at Morris School] didn't have any trouble either.

Evelyn Jackson, Louisville

[The board of education] decided to integrate and they decided to avoid making it a forced thing by saying that a child could choose to go to a school if he wished. If he didn't want to go to the school to which he was assigned, he had the privilege of choosing to go to the other schools. This was recognized as a very liberal sort of thing throughout the city. It was Mr. Carmichael's idea. He was our superintendent. It was also written up in *U.S. News and World Report*, of course, and it impressed the president, who invited him to come to Washington. . . . I think that it gave [parents] more the feeling of integrating because we wanted to rather than integrating because we had to. Morris School became 25 percent black after integration. I don't know what the other schools did. . . . I think probably a great many of [the white students assigned to Douglass] did avail themselves [of the transfer option to return to Morris]. . . . I don't know that it was necessarily the idea that they didn't want to go to a black school; it might have been because they loved Morris so much because the teachers had been there for a long time and they had a sort of motherly attitude toward some of the children and the children seemed to be proud of the school and liked it.

* * *

In reflecting on the major factor contributing to the relative success of Louisville's school integration, Higgins pointed to the transfer option.

I think [it was] the chance to choose to stay in the school you wanted to or to transfer to a school—I think it would go both ways. I think the transfer was that you could transfer to your own school. . . . Some people were trying to get to a school where there were no Negroes. I

know some whites [did]. I have an idea it was the other way too. . . .
But anyhow, it got so there weren't any schools that didn't have some
Negroes or some whites. Not very many anyhow.

Ruth Higgins, Louisville

* * *

The transition was not so smooth in other parts of the state, where boycotts
and mobs, in scenes foreshadowing the more well-known Little Rock crisis
of 1957, greeted young would-be students. James Howard was born and
grew up in Sturgis, which became the site of one of the state's greatest
conflicts surrounding early school desegregation. Instead of taking a bus
to Morganfield, as generations of blacks had from Sturgis, in 1956 the
young Howard and nine other African American teens enrolled in Sturgis
High School, only six blocks from his home. He and his peers endured har-
rowing opposition in order to remain at the school, but within weeks they
were forced to return to the all-black school after the school board mandated it. Howard's closing comments here reveal the roots of his resolve
to return the following fall. In spite of persistent opposition of the sort he
describes initially, Howard graduated from Sturgis High School and went
on to a career in education.

The first day in 1956 it was really uneventful. I saw some [white] kids
that I had played with growing up. And quite honestly they welcomed
me to the school when I first went in. . . . It was a decent response
from the children. I can't say that was the general attitude of some
of the teachers, but as far as the children, it really wasn't a problem
on that first day. . . . On the second day when I [arrived], there was a
crowd of people there that had shovels, pitchforks, that were outside
of the school, name-calling. The state police and National Guard were
called in, I believe it was on the third day. During the weekend people
had come from all around. Not only from Sturgis, but people from all
around the county that had come in to voice their disagreement about
our attending school there at Sturgis. So it was after that that [the
Guard] were called in. . . . And quite frankly, it was somewhat com-
forting to see them present. Because given the attitude of the people
who were here, it was close to a riot. . . . There were threats about
"you niggers won't live to see another day if you come back to school
here."

There's a park that was right across the street from where my grandparents lived. The park had a large barbecue pit and it had a couple of old basketball goals, where black children went to play. On one night the park was completely filled with cars and trucks, and there were people in that park, whites, some of whom had on sheets with the Klan insignias. Sheets with the cone heads, with the holes in the eyes of the sheets. They burned a cross out in the middle of the park and they rode around bumper to bumper with guns and rifles and were speaking to the fact of what they were going to do if we continued to attend Sturgis High School. We're one block away from the park, and I recall the trucks, the tooting of the horns and the screaming, the epithets. My father had to go to work, and he had told my mother she needed to be on the lookout. We had one shotgun and one .22 rifle that had been given to us. That was going to be our protection against the mob that was riding up and down the street. So we laid on the floor [so] if they began to shoot, hopefully the bullets might miss us. . . . We laid on the floor all night, and it wasn't a matter of us sleeping. There wasn't going to be much sleeping going on that night.

I was thirteen at the time, and [what I felt] was fear and anger, probably as much anger as fear. Because some of the people, I had known for a long time, some of [them] I had worked for. At that point in time I really had no idea that they felt so strongly about my attending school. For no other reason [than] we were going to [that] school, there would be a mob of people that would ride around with the thought, and some screaming, about burning down this entire community.

* * *

Howard recalled that there were a few white youths, however, who expressed acceptance and even support for the African American students, both that first year and when they returned in 1957.

They were called "nigger lovers" and of course because they lived in the white community day in and day out, they were treated with disdain. In fact, some were beaten up . . . for no other reason than they didn't participate in name-calling or cursing or any agitation towards us. So in many ways they paid as big a price as many of the black students that they befriended.

* * *

Despite ongoing protests, Howard and eight others desegregated Sturgis High School for a few more days that first fall. To do so, they had to be escorted by the highway patrol past crowds of jeering whites. At times, both in and out of the school, they were spat upon, showered with rocks, kicked, and shoved.

Had the [highway patrol] not been there, there is little question in my mind that more would have happened other than having rocks or eggs or tomatoes thrown at us. . . . [But I couldn't fight back because] clearly there were two sets of rules from the outset [one for blacks, one for whites]. Any black child who put up any resistance at any time was expelled. . . . That's why I did not.

One day, we were read a letter by the principal of the school, Earl Evans. Fortunately for me, I knew the principal; in fact, I worked for him. He was a good man. He read a letter to us that had been provided to him by the school board that said we would not be permitted back in the school, and that we would have to attend Dunbar [the all-black high school in Morganfield]. For many people that was a relief. It really wasn't for me. I was disappointed that we would have to go back to Dunbar after all that we had gone through at that point in time.

James Howard, Sturgis

* * *

Despite the turmoil he encountered, Howard was determined to return the following year, and did so. Only thirty-five miles north of Sturgis, Henderson schools saw similar outpourings of white resistance, but with a different outcome—due in part to the efforts of two pro-integration white ministers who worked through their local ministerial association to oppose the boycott. Its collapse a week later allowed school desegregation in Henderson to proceed, whereas the Clay and Sturgis schools required a federal lawsuit to do so. Below is the narrative of Ted Braun, the United Church of Christ minister who, along with Sumpter Logan, a Presbyterian, helped pave the way for desegregation by calling on whites to accept it.

Integration began in Weaverton School, which is on the southern edge of Henderson. I think they integrated the first three grades down there.

And the White Citizens' Council called a meeting on a Saturday evening in the main courtroom, on the second floor of the courthouse, to organize . . . to oppose the integration of the Weaverton School. It was at that point that the ministers' group started, got it together and got into action. Sumpter called a meeting of the Ministerial Association. The outcome of that meeting was to attend as a ministers' group at that White Citizens' Council meeting, and to have Sumpter present a statement in favor of continuing desegregation, of supporting this development at the Weaverton School, that he was going to write. We all agreed, there must have been a dozen people there, representing most of the denominations in Henderson. So I forget what time the meeting started, maybe 7 o'clock, and we all went upstairs, had a huge American flag in front. And the meeting started, we got there quite early, because we wanted to get seats, we knew it was going to be crowded. We got the first two rows of seats, we were up there. It was an organizational meeting, kind of a pep talk, all this stuff about how desegregation was wrong, against the Bible, against human nature, against everything. At the end Sumpter got up and asked to read a statement, from us, the group. At first they were a bit leery, but they decided, well, to do it. He got most of the way through his statement when they had enough. They started booing, and the meeting broke up at that point.

Then, the next day, the White Citizens' Council sent a sound truck through town, urging the parents to keep their kids from going. Attendance [at school] was down quite a bit. . . . Then we started putting ads in the paper, and also spot announcements on the radio. The head of the radio [station] was a member of Sumpter's church, as was the newspaper editor. That was interesting, it was the upper class church, except for the Episcopalians there. But the White Citizens' Council called another meeting, a second meeting, to help this process along, at the courthouse again, but outside, where the meeting couldn't be interrupted. We decided to have a parents meeting at the same time. We got the names from the school of all the parents who had their kids coming, to invite them to this meeting in our church, which is two or three blocks from the courthouse. A lot of parents couldn't come on such short notice, but they were all encouraged by the fact that we were having a meeting. We had it in our sanctuary, and had the chief of police there, and the superintendent of schools. Our process was to just ask parents to share why they were having their kids come to school. . . . These were white parents. I'm not clear whether we had the black parents—I think we had some black parents there, too. They got up to share why their kids were going and people could ask them, well, why are you sending your kids to school, so that they could share and have this time. You could feel this be resolved. After the meeting, we went up into the fellowship hall for coffee and cookies and fellowship. And, there—we had feedback from parents who were so grateful for meeting like this. The next day the attendance started going up.

Theodore Braun, Henderson

* * *

Although pitched battles in places like Clay, Sturgis, and Henderson made national headlines, other parts of western Kentucky that fall found African American students facing less dramatic hostility that nonetheless took its toll. In Mayfield, for instance, in the far west corner of the state (Graves County), Alice Wilson, an incoming black freshman, and a group of friends desegregated the formerly all-white high school in 1956.

Absolutely the biggest difference was in material—textbooks, workbooks, library materials. . . . When I changed schools, I saw books that I had never seen before, and certainly a lot within those books that I did not know, so it was extremely hard to catch up. Because I was way behind . . . I had to work twice as hard to keep up, especially changing into a new situation.

All of us had read information about what was going on in other parts of the country with the integrated schools. The ten of us were friends, and I can remember we sat one night and we said, "Ah, I bet that would really shake up everybody if we decided to go to Mayfield High School." We laughed about it. Oh sure, sure, we're going to do this, and nothing was said. As time went on, we kept talking about it to each other, and we decided, the ten of us, that we were going to try it—and we did it. We had adult support, once we made a decision, but adults didn't help us make that decision. I think we just registered the first day. Instead of going to Dunbar High, we went to Mayfield High, walked into the office, and said, "We're here to register." . . . They were shocked, I do remember that. They were absolutely shocked that we had walked in, and we did register. . . . I'm sure it threw everybody into turmoil, but it wasn't blocked by those who were making decisions at the time.

We were all at the same level; we were all ninth graders. Most teachers were good. A few didn't like the idea at all, and never did the entire time we were there, and those differences were definitely felt in their classes, by what they did. By not calling on you if you held up your hand, not giving you the extra time, if you requested. By generally ignoring you within the class. Because they really didn't agree with it. Some others who were just students, they didn't like us very much. They opposed the idea totally. For the first two years, it stayed that way. Our schedules [were prepared so] that there were never two of us in the same class, in the same time period within a class.

The only sit-ins were the demonstrations that had to do with us attending Mayfield High School. There were days when the white students decided that they weren't going to classes with us, and all the students would come out on the campus and just stand there. I remember one morning. The other person that graduated with me (her name was Dorothy), we were walking to school and we saw quite a few state trooper cars along the way. We said, "This is very unusual, for Mayfield," and we saw more and more and more, and we realized, "Ooh, there must be something going on today," and sure enough when we got closer to the high school we could see all the students standing on the outside. They weren't going to class with us, and we walked through the door anyway. They just taunted us as we walked toward the school. The teachers were inside. The principal was standing at the door. We went in and we started classes. The principal's way of handling that was to just go in, and let them know that nothing was going to stop because of what they were saying, and they had a choice to stand out there all day or come to class. He probably felt that was the best way to handle it, to not have a huge fight, or a real riot during that period of time. I think he was trying to keep it as quiet as possible without anybody getting hurt. Local police would come regularly, too. At the beginning of the day they would ride around the school, around the block. We had family friends who came, too. Sometimes they would drive us there, because we didn't have a car at the time, and if they heard anything on the radio, or they suspected anything was going on, they would come and pick us up. It was hard, but we thought it was the right decision, because we all wanted to go to college.

The advantage of going to Mayfield High School? There were many disadvantages, and I guess the disadvantages were about joining extracurricular organizations, and we really didn't do that at the time. Later on I wished that I had tried for some of them, but I think it was so hard to get through the classes, that I didn't want to fight through that for an extracurricular activity as well. . . . It was a very interesting time because everything was changing. The climate was changing. African Americans were changing their attitude about themselves. It was changing toward being very proud of who you were.

Alice Wilson, Mayfield

* * *

Local school systems experimented with a variety of models for school desegregation. In Owensboro, as the first narrator below explains, it began a grade at a time from twelfth down, with black high school students selected individually—and based on merit—to begin by attending just one class at the formerly white Owensboro High. In Horse Cave, however, as the second narrator—Newton Thomas—explains, a biracial committee prompted the simultaneous integration of K–12. Thomas went from being principal of the high school that had served African Americans to becoming one of the state's first black teachers in an integrated classroom.

I have three boys. The oldest one, Reginald Johnson, was one from Western School that was chosen or selected or asked to go out to Owensboro Senior High School because of his being a decent, upright person, clean-cut, not a trouble-maker. There were others besides him that were chosen to go out there during this integration period. He wore out a lot of shoe leather because he walked from Western School out to Owensboro Senior High and from Senior High back to Western School for class. He went for a history class. One class. He wasn't stubborn; he was scared stiff. You throw a youngster into an environment like that that he hadn't been in before, that's what he said. We learned that had been said. But he wasn't stubborn; he was scared. Others were, too. They didn't know what was going to happen or how they were going to be treated or accepted or—they just didn't know. They had to find out for themselves. That was how integration got started here and it did real well. It was a smooth change. . . . We needed some of the things that they had out there that other students were getting that black students weren't. I thought we had a right to it. One of the reasons we learned about this was the [African American janitorial staff] that they had cleaning schools. They would tell us, "Well, they got so-and-so and the kids do this and the kids do that." . . . They had equipment that we didn't have, didn't know about.

Gustava Hayden, Owensboro

[In 1955] we organized a committee from all segments of our community—the black and white—to make a study. So we would meet, and we would discuss, how we felt about integrating the schools. They didn't even have any idea how it would work. I had to convince them that it would work. We'd meet with the Women's Club, the Rotary, the Kiwanis Club, the PTAs, and all of them. We'd meet with those people to try to convince them that it would work and we wouldn't have any problems. I would have to make the speech to convince them that it will work. So then they finally said, "Well, what about just integrating the high school? We'd be willing to do that, if you would stay and be principal of the elementary school." I said, "Well you can just forget it, 'cause I wouldn't stand and be principal of the elementary school if just the high school was integrated." They said, "Well what would you do?" I said, "I'd find me a job someplace else." So then this one woman said, "I think Mr. Thomas is right. If we're going do it, you start down here with the elementary students." I told them, "Let the kids get used to each other before they get to high school. They'll grow up more knowing with each other. Then we won't have problems when they get into high school." So the board finally decided that this would be what they'd do. So they built that new school down there on the highway [which became Caverna, an integrated high school serving both Horse Cave and Cave City].

Then, the question came up, what they going do with me? They said, "If he doesn't stay it won't work. He's the one that convinced those people it would work." So the fellow at the bank, Mr. Alston, I can remember him, he called me and said, "Mr. Thomas, the board is kinda concerned about what to do about you? They don't think this'll work unless you stay here." He said, "They'd put you up in any kind of business you want to go in, just so you stayed in the community." And I said, "No, I figured on going in the school." So now, they said, "Well, now then, would you take a teaching job?" I said, "I'll take a teaching job, but you pay me a principal's salary." So they agreed to that so I would stay. That was in 1957.

Newton Thomas, Horse Cave

* * *

The remaining narratives in this section suggest how desegregation experiences varied among Kentucky school districts in the 1950s–1960s. Two themes emerge: the role of athletics in enacting and responding to integration, and the sense of regret over the closing of black schools and loss of black teachers and staff.

Home ec. teachers work ten months. I always had to work this extra month after the rest of the teachers were through. They came over during the time I was working in this tenth month. I said "they," I mean the superintendent and some of the white principals came over one day, and they were looking around to see what was there. They said that we were going to integrate the next year. That was like in June. I think they just took it in their stride, you know. I mean I don't remember any particular talk about it. I didn't like it at all. . . . My concerns were that we had been like a little family over here. [We had] small classes. The children were just like our children. I was having a fear of this larger student [body]. We were going to Cumberland. To me that was a large school at that time. I really just dreaded the large atmosphere, you know, that was going to take away our little closeness. But when I got there it wasn't like that. I tell you the first day the children there wiped that out. They were just like my children here and I felt just as close to them and I loved them and they loved me. I had a beautiful time at Cumberland.

Every black teacher was given a job. My principal was the highest educated principal around here. Mr. Cawood had told him a few years before integration that he would not be a principal, you know. They were going to hire him but he was going to be a teacher. He wasn't going to come down like that so he and his wife went to Tennessee where it was still segregated. They weren't going to have a black principal. A lot of [the black teachers] left anyway. I think they thought it was going to be a struggle, you know. I really don't know that they had job offers but they were from other places and I guess they thought they could go there and get a job. They mainly left here to go to work in the cities. Eventually I got left as the only black teacher there. . . . Well, it was just understood when the kids got out of school, they were going to leave here [too] because there was nothing to do unless they wanted to mine coal.

Constance Ellison, Benham

Most [black teachers] left the county and got jobs elsewhere. Some of our teachers, before they would be subjected to [demotion], left. This area was really raped of the black leadership when they integrated the city schools here. It was kind of piecemeal the first year. They had one black teacher there. Our black students got lost in the crowd. They didn't have the role models, and they didn't have the teachers that took the time with them as individuals. We lost a lot. . . . Black people . . . lost just about everything. The only thing that I see that we gained here in Harlan was that they recognized that we were human beings, and we had access to science labs, and we got new school books. Because at Rosenwald, we didn't have a science lab. We got the used books from the white schools. They got the new ones and we got the used ones. But we lost our teachers. We lost that personal touch. Our kids are outnumbered, and so they've been kind of lost. We lost our cheerleaders. For years we didn't have any and then I said, "It's a shame. Our black boys get out there and help win the games, and then there's nobody to go running out there to hug them."

Nancy Johnson, Harlan

We had a very successful basketball team here—The Bunche High School. At the time, the white high school's team wasn't as strong as ours, and we had gone to the state, and we had a lot of support. We['d] win a lot of favors, as you know. So this sort of made us prominent in the community and in the area. And we were then frequented, our ballgames and whatever, by the whites in large numbers. But anyway, we finally got a gymnasium, and we got a lot of association from the other groups due to the athletic program and that sort of smoothed out things. And then when integration came it wasn't too difficult to just make the transition. But I would say that the single, largest thing was our athletic program.

It was the racial relations that had developed through our athletic program and through my constant effort in this community to upgrade the blacks and to make the whites conscious that we were of the same as they. We were more alike than we were different, except for opportunities and color of skin. And this sort of thing prevailed.

Luska J. Twyman, Glasgow

[In Middlesboro] we integrated in 1964, which is a clear decade after the *Brown vs. Board of Education* Supreme Court decision. So there was obviously some foot-dragging going on, some people that avoided it. The excuse that we were given was that the white school was over-crowded, and it was. . . . So by 1964 the actual integration of kids in the same classroom took place. Two years prior to that, in '62—and this is, has some racial greed, I guess I would call it—in 1962, Middlesboro integrated its athletic program. Well, not just athletic but school ex-tracurricular activities were integrated. Our school, [its] numbers had gotten so small that we couldn't man a football team anymore. So that had stopped, I think, in about '59. But we had an outstanding basket-ball, baseball, track, state choir . . . so in '62 the decision was made to integrate the extracurricular activities. So we were for the first time bused, as student athletes, over to the white school to be on the then-Middlesboro High athletic teams. And needless to say, Middlesboro High, which had been a very mediocre athletic program, flourished and boomed immediately. So that's how it actually started, was in '62, the integrated extracurricular. So the bus then would show up at our school in the afternoons—you didn't get a ride home, but if you were going to the white school to take part in some extracurricular activity, you got a bus ride over to the white school . . . still had to get home the best way you could.

Howard Bailey, Middlesboro

* * *

The final story in this section gives some hint of the continuing discrimina-tion and poor treatment that faced black students and staff in the newly integrated schools.

[In Bowling Green] there was still a resistance. We went into school integration with the same stereotypes that blacks were inferior, that blacks stole, that blacks were ignorant, that blacks couldn't learn. Even when Western integrated, the average college professor said that he couldn't teach blacks. So we went into an integrated situation in which you still had these racist and prejudicial thoughts. A lot of our kids were expelled, suspended. They were excluded. They had been used to having teachers personalize with them, help them. But it was a turmoil. Black kids hated the high school. There were constant race, I wouldn't say race riots, but race confrontations, on up until the early '70s.

George Esters, Bowling Green

The Second Wave of School Desegregation, Post-1969

The second generation of school desegregation followed the U.S. Supreme Court's condemnation of "freedom of choice" plans in Green v. New Kent County (1968) and extended into the 1970s. The few narratives included in this final section center only on Louisville and Lexington, sites of the largest movements and the largest racial upheaval in schools as a result of more aggressive court enforcement of school desegregation in this period.

* * *

I think back some years ago, when this district [Fayette County] was ordered to integrate under court order. The city board made what I consider to be a very sinister decision to avoid having cross-busing. Cross-busing meaning bringing white kids downtown and black kids out. They made a sinister decision to close down several of the downtown elementary schools, which robbed the downtown neighborhoods of elementary schools, which if we fast forward to today, there is a lot of discussion about the merits of having neighborhood schools. That's fine for the suburbs who have neighborhood schools, but that's not fine for the neighborhoods downtown, who no longer have those neighborhood schools. But during that time, there was a lot of controversy around here about that decision. I can remember being part of marches on the school board members about that decision. I can remember when we started to hire the first school superintendent not too long ago, and under KERA [Kentucky Educational Reform Act] there were rules about who was supposed to be a part of this school board selection process. It was very controversial. We insisted that there was going to be some way, somehow, some avenue for [African American] participation. It ended up even having to have the governor come down and do some intervention. We're still fighting this district through my Equity Council role, about closing the achievement gap between black kids and white kids. There is still an abundance of issues in education tied to equity.

Porter G. Peeples, Lexington

In 1969 I became the president of what was then KCLU [Kentucky Civil Liberties Union]. In 1970 we were approached by some black people, most notably Lyman Johnson, who had desegregated the University of Kentucky graduate school. We were approached by Lyman and some other people about suing the Board of Education of Louisville. We studied it and we debated it and we had endless meetings as to whether or not we wanted to undertake that. It was a big, ambitious proposal. We even had hearings in the black community to find out what black people wanted. It went on and on. Finally, in 1972, Bob Sedler, who was our volunteer general counsel and a tenured law professor at U. of Kentucky, filed suit. In the course of putting that suit together, he thought he would like to have a white plaintiff who had white children in the public schools, so I said, "Sure." . . . They [my children] were all in public schools so it gave me some legitimacy to go out there and try and promote peaceful school desegregation. I got real immersed in it. The thing dragged on from '72 to '75 when it was finally implemented.

There was enormous opposition in the county. Just enormous opposition. I mean, it was an organizing vehicle for the Klan and for every little [white] Save Our Community school group. The county was just ringed with opponents and organizing against school desegregation because it meant busing their kids. It was very tempestuous. It was the most tempestuous period I've lived through in this town.

Suzy Post, Louisville

* * *

The court-ordered busing to integrate the Jefferson County schools inspired a wave of violent opposition unseen before in Louisville during the civil rights era. As local whites organized mass demonstrations and boycotts especially in the South End of the city, extremist organizations took advantage of the turmoil to try to make inroads in the community. The result was a year of conflict and confrontation as opponents of busing marched and rioted. Civil rights advocates and those in the black and white community who abhorred the rise in racial tension counter-organized. As this narrative from Howard Owens makes clear, school integration continued to be contested and to inspire civil rights activity more than twenty years after *Brown*.

It was a time of national fervor, especially during the busing. We went to a Klan rally out at McNeely Lake. I swear to you, it looked like it was a couple of hundred people in hoods and another three or four hundred out of hoods who were attending the Klan rally there. But at McNeely Lake, what had happened was it appeared that a [black] guy's family, that their house had been dynamited. Someone had put dynamite in their driveway. This is what we understood to have happened. So some of the people went out there and stood vigil as they did in a situation like that. Some even spent the night. As we were leaving there was word that there was a Klan rally at McNeely Lake Park. So we did not go out there intentionally to go to the Klan rally. We weren't looking for trouble. It was just coincidentally that as we were leaving it would have been in our path anyway. So we went there to the McNeely Lake Park and like I said, there were uniformed Klansmen. Many, at least a hundred. Very well armed. We went by them once and they were facing the speaker and we came back the second time and they were facing us. That's when you saw the arms. There was a jeep with an M-16 machine gun mounted on. Hard to miss by the police, who were, no doubt, carefully monitoring the situation. Like I said, the second time they were highly armed and we just went past them. There wasn't any stopping and there wasn't any confrontation. But they were upset that their rally was being that closely observed by [what they called] "leftist liberals, niggers and communists."

What happened in the schools was not put in the newspapers. The people in the community knew that. So therefore, that's why you got a lot of blacks who were either neutral on the point of busing or, [as] I stood, in favor of busing more or less as a reaction also to the violence that the whites had put during the busing thing. Serious violence, like they tore up downtown, they were breaking out windows. They put a policeman's eye out. Afterwards, [when] the whites saw that their violent protests were not going to get them what they wanted, then they take to the political ends. Standard mode of operation, when you see that your street protests and stuff don't work, then you go to the political arena. Black Protective Parents began to react to the violence and the difficulties that was placed on the youth during the integration process. If a child had been attacked, academically or et cetera—there were a number of problems on entry to the school. It was oftentimes difficult to gain entry into the school because it appeared, although it may not have been true, that whatever the instructor or the counselor did that was detrimental to the youth, the principal would stand by them.

Howard Owens, Louisville

Chapter 3

Opening Public Accommodations

COURAGEOUS high school and college students facing arrest or verbal and physical abuse to get a simple hamburger at a lunch counter form some of the most poignant images of the civil rights movement. In many people's minds, those images are the movement. Such sit-ins—captured on camera and replayed on the evening news in an era when television itself was an innovation—helped expose the moral bankruptcy of segregation to the American public in the early 1960s. Yet they were only the most public and mass-movement phase of a collective struggle that had been building for quite some time. As narrators in this volume have suggested, African American demands for access to public accommodations began long before 1960, and spontaneous confrontations over unjust treatment have taken place throughout U.S. history. The sit-in itself was not new to the 1960s either. It was the same basic form of protest that Louisville African Americans, for example, had used as early as 1870 to obtain the right to ride public streetcars seated inside the coaches. Such mass protests make a dramatic statement, but they have also nearly always preceded or precipitated negotiations with political authorities to seek policy changes.[1]

The public accommodations battle was much wider than access to service in privately owned businesses, which became its focus only in the late 1950s. Although African American residents paid taxes like other Kentuckians, they were prohibited by a combination of law and custom from many public libraries, pools, hospitals, and parks, including twenty-four of the twenty-five state parks.[2] But segregation had been written into law in early twentieth-century Kentucky in a patchwork fashion—there were laws segregating mental hospitals, for example, but not hospitals, while some towns with very small black populations had no local statutes mandating segregation at all. These variations reflected the commonwealth's mixed embrace of a southern identity and its relative disregard of race as a major policy concern because African Americans formed such a small proportion of the state's citizens.

With one or two exceptions, campaigns against segregation as it hardened in early twentieth-century Kentucky were rarely successful. The first Kentucky chapter of the NAACP formed in 1914 Louisville as a result of a group of local African Americans petitioning the national association for help. Soon after it began, the chapter got a boost through its victory against segregated housing in a case that had national import because it reached the U.S. Supreme Court (*Buchanan v. Warley*, 1917, discussed in chapter 5). Yet for the next two decades, even in Louisville, where the black community was large, activist, and prosperous enough to wield a limited amount of economic and political clout, African American leaders were unable to break down any aspect of Jim Crow, settling for negotiating relative improvements in conditions within the system of "separate but equal." Thus, while Louisville cultivated an image of itself as a progressive, moderate city with good race relations, in truth blacks there were excluded from or severely restricted in their use of most public and private facilities—libraries, parks, restaurants, hotels, and theaters—just as they were elsewhere. Even the retail shops that welcomed their purchases nevertheless prohibited their trying on clothes or eating at the lunch counters.[3]

Only in the 1940s did race relations begin a profound shift across Kentucky, the South, and the nation. Widespread suffering and unemployment engendered by the Great Depression invigorated protest movements that at times united blacks and whites nationwide, including the Black-Belt South. Then World War II raised public awareness of the importance of democracy even as discriminatory treatment of black soldiers and defense workers exposed uncomfortable parallels between American racism and Nazi fascism. Although President Franklin Roosevelt responded to African American labor demands by signing an executive order in 1941 banning discrimination in defense industry jobs, the military itself remained segregated. Across the South, black soldiers confronted discrimination most frequently on public transportation and at lunch counters, so it was no surprise later that these two sites became focal points for postwar civil rights activism.[4]

Once the war ended, the more than twenty thousand African American Kentuckians in uniform returned home with raised expectations for equality. In keeping with an upswing of African American protest nationally, they increasingly challenged discriminatory practices. Whereas previous protests had mostly centered on Louisville, the number of NAACP branches across Kentucky more than doubled in the ten years after the war (1945–1955), with most of that growth occurring in the immediate postwar years (1945–1947).[5] The NAACP had become the primary organizational vehicle for the achievement of equal rights, nationally as well as in Kentucky, but its tactics tended more toward litigation and incremental change than they did direct actions to confront the morality of segregation. Local ad hoc initiatives arose to augment NAACP efforts. In 1950, for example, the Louisville-based Interracial Hospital Movement spread to sixty Kentucky communities and generated more than ten thousand signatures that resulted in a gubernatorial investigation and a statewide order requiring nondiscriminatory treatment in all hospitals receiving public funds.[6] Such battles picked up steam in the state after the desegregation of higher education and once the Brown decision of 1954 declared racial segregation to be contrary to the Constitution.

The use of direct action against segregation emerged on a large scale—as did the movement's most renowned leader, the Reverend Martin Luther King Jr.—in 1955 in Montgomery, Alabama, where blacks sustained a thirteen-month boycott of city buses to end discriminatory treatment. The boycott came in the midst of the reaction to Brown, which, while it brought the hostility and repression of massive resistance, also fostered optimism among African American communities that change was on the way. Throughout the remaining years of the decade, smaller local protests against Jim Crow broke out, including in Kentucky's largest city, Louisville. There, the NAACP Youth Council—led by the same Lyman Johnson who had desegregated the University of Kentucky in 1949—instigated after-hours and weekend sit-ins that in 1957 desegregated downtown dime stores that depended heavily on black clientele.[7] The youth met more resistance from drug and department stores, and the decade ended in December 1959 with pickets—as described by Raoul Cunningham in this chapter—in front of the Brown Theater protesting the exclusion of local blacks from Porgy and Bess, a musical with an all-black cast.[8] In Lexington, student protesters also picketed lunch counters near the UK campus without much success, and were turning their sights to downtown Lexington businesses as 1960 dawned.[9]

Other than sheer numbers, what was newest about the Montgomery movement and the campaigns that followed it as the 1960s arrived was the inspiration they took from Mohandas Gandhi's nonviolent civil disobedience campaign that had ended British rule in India less than two decades earlier. On February 1, one month into the 1960s, students in Greensboro, North Carolina, instigated nonviolent sit-ins at their local Woolworth's. A mass sit-in movement focusing on downtown lunch counters spread like wildfire through more than eighty communities in twelve southern and border states over eight weeks' time, including first Frankfort and, shortly after, Lexington, beginning in late February.[10] The sit-ins were not strictly an urban phenomenon, but they proved most successful in cities or in college towns, where they were more likely to find a substantial base of youth support and to generate sympathetic or widespread publicity. Those who sat in were predominantly African American, but another distinctive feature of the new wave of movement was that it drew more white participants.

The NAACP had groomed the new generation of dissenters, but it was not always equipped to contain or support their commitment to direct action. New civil rights groups emerged to challenge the association's longstanding leadership, and those who appealed most to the young included the Congress of Racial Equality (CORE), formed in 1942 Chicago by an interracial group of Christian pacifists, and the Student Nonviolent Coordinating Committee (SNCC), formed in North Carolina in 1960 as the student sit-ins became a mass phenomenon. Kentucky college students attended SNCC's regional meetings and applauded the energy of the young militants who became the "shock troops" of this new generation of movement. But the organization never really took hold in Kentucky except as a source of inspiration emanating from the Deep South.

CORE, on the other hand, which had been active in nearby Cincinnati since 1946, sent regional organizers to hold workshops on nonviolence with student groups around the Bluegrass. In response, a CORE chapter arose in Lexington in the late 1950s that worked closely with the NAACP branch throughout the 1960s. In Frankfort, a Students for Civil Rights group came together and affiliated with CORE in the spring of 1960, while a small CORE chapter also formed in Louisville that spring through the course of nonviolence trainings. Held prior to any sit-in, the trainings prepared young people to accept the abusive language that might be hurled at them and offered tactics for shielding themselves from physical blows without retaliating.[11] The development of direct-action and student groups in many communities also served to galvanize preexisting NAACP chapters into more direct action, and that proved to be the case in both Louisville and Lexington. Black churches served as nurturing forces for civil rights activism in many Kentucky communities, but the extent of religious leadership varied widely across denominations and localities.

Kentucky's most dramatic and highly publicized student movement in the spring of 1960 took shape in its small capital city of Frankfort, home to the state's one historically black college. Such campuses were most often the germinating points for the youthful civil rights activism that took the South by storm that year. The civil rights drive that grew out of Kentucky State College involved downtown sit-ins but also a demand for on-campus reforms (predating by several years the nationwide campus-centered movements later in the 1960s). Rufus Atwood, an African American educator who had held the KSC presidency since 1929, counseled the students to exercise caution and extreme propriety in dealing with local authorities on whose support he relied, yet he was initially sympathetic to their plans to protest racial discrimination in stores and restaurants. But Atwood and the college executive council reacted harshly when the focus of student discontent turned to conditions on the campus itself. After a student boycott of the school cafeteria due to its poor quality, he publicly repudiated the student movement, and the executive council undermined their plans for downtown desegregation when it expelled twelve student leaders and fired two faculty members. That action deepened student unrest, resulting in the torching of the school gymnasium and the early departure of nearly the entire student body. The furor set back the Kentucky State movement—as KSC professor Gertrude Ridgel describes later in this chapter—but did not dispel it, and direct actions resumed that fall.[12]

Although the situation at Kentucky State was not entirely typical of student movements in 1960 because it involved campus as well as community, Atwood's crackdown does illustrate the harsh punitive measures that could result against young people who undertook radical protests involving direct action. Yet their dramatic acts also received national television coverage and increased public awareness of discrimination, in some cases opening a new path for reforms initiated by their elders through more traditional political channels. In this regard, Kentucky lawmakers proved more receptive to change than was the case in former Confederate states. The movement here achieved an early victory when African American leaders negotiated with soon-to-be Governor Bert Combs's administration for the creation in 1960 of a state agency established to monitor and publicize racial injustices, the Kentucky Commission on Human Rights (KCHR). The

KCHR was the brainchild of African American Frank Stanley Sr. (publisher of Louisville's weekly *Defender*), but it evolved under intentionally biracial leadership. Robert Estill, a white Episcopal clergyman and native Lexingtonian, became the first chairman. Within a few years, local commissions had been established in Lexington, Louisville, Frankfort, and Henderson, and more than twenty formed over the next decade.[13]

As the KCHR began documenting racial discrimination (having, initially, no enforcement authority), the battle for public accommodations moved into other communities in the commonwealth. Despite its history of African American activism and the moderate leadership that Louisville image-makers treasured, full desegregation of public accommodations in Kentucky's largest city proved difficult to achieve, with the result that public facilities and a few privately owned stores and restaurants ended discriminatory practices, while many other businesses and especially entertainment facilities stubbornly resisted. Throughout 1960–1961, African Americans and their white allies sought passage of a local public accommodation law to eliminate those inconsistencies, but both the mayor and the board of aldermen opposed it, claiming that all desegregation should be voluntary. By early 1961 local high school students—members of both the NAACP Youth Council and CORE—initiated a new wave of sit-ins and demonstrations in front of the most outrageously discriminatory businesses. They did so without sanction from the local adult NAACP or any other group, although leaders of civil rights organizations soon joined the students to form a steering committee to coordinate the protests. The steering committee also inaugurated a "Nothing New for Easter" drive that boycotted downtown department stores, costing merchants thousands of dollars in sales and culminating with a march of more than three thousand, known as the Easter Prayer Pilgrimage. That spring, amid dozens of arrests that were controversial since many of those arrested were juveniles with no criminal record, more than 80 percent of downtown businesses acquiesced. In the fall civil rights leaders switched tactics from demonstrations to politics and launched a concerted voter registration and election campaign that contributed to the ouster of the Democratic board of aldermen and mayor. Despite this victory, it would take two more years of negotiation and threatened demonstrations until Louisville passed a city ordinance banning discrimination in public accommodations, the first such law in the South.[14]

Lexington, seventy miles to the east, yielded more easily, possibly because it was a college town and had already faced, with some difficulty, campus desegregation. It did so in spite of a nearly absolute ban on local protest coverage by the city's daily newspapers, the *Herald* and the *Leader,* denying the movement there the media spotlight that became so crucial to its success nationally. Fred Wachs Sr., publisher of the two papers, directed his reporters away from covering Lexington protesters, whom he allegedly considered "rabble rousers."[15]

CORE and the NAACP led six months of ongoing sit-ins and pickets in downtown Lexington that by October of 1960 had achieved desegregation in downtown drugstores, dime stores, and lunch counters. Then activists turned their attention to movie theaters, which after another half a year of "stand-ins" desegregated by May 1961. The civil rights movement for public accommodations also reached new heights nationally that spring as the news media followed the risk-taking Freedom Riders, black and white youth who tested the limits of segregation by riding desegregated Greyhound buses through former Confederate states. Although the Freedom Riders did not reach Kentucky, their presence was felt here, and the threat of similar confrontations propelled some communities toward greater reform.[16]

In spite of disclaimers that "we don't have any trouble here," pockets of resistance remained in Louisville, Lexington, and around the state, convincing civil rights leaders and their allies in elective office—including Governors Combs and, later, Breathitt—of the need for public accommodation laws.[17] Combs made moves in that direction in 1962 by advancing legislation clarifying localities' right to pass antidiscrimination ordinances. A year later he went further, issuing a controversial "Fair Service" executive order directing state agencies that licensed businesses to work toward the provision of fair, racially neutral treatment to all patrons.[18] Meanwhile, the state Commission on Human Rights drafted a public accommodations bill, and a group called Kentuckians for Public Accommodations Legislation, headed by Lexington businessman Joe Graves—a narrator in this chapter—began the uphill climb of building public support.

The drive for a statewide law became the high-water mark of the open accommodations movement in Kentucky. As the bill was introduced to the legislature by a biracial group of three state representatives in January 1964, a coalition of civil rights groups planned a massive March on Frankfort for that spring. On March 5, 1964, buses and carpools from around the state delivered ten thousand Kentuckians to the steps of the state capitol to join the Reverend Martin Luther King Jr. and baseball's Jackie Robinson in calling on lawmakers to act. When they refused to do so, a group of twenty-five demonstrators staged a hunger strike in the capitol gallery for a week. Still the bill did not succeed. But as the movement reached fever pitch regionally and three highly publicized murders of activists in Mississippi rocked the nation that summer, a federal Civil Rights Act that had been similarly stalled became law on July 2, 1964. When the Kentucky legislature reconvened next in 1966, it relented, approving one of the nation's strongest public accommodation laws—and the first in a state south of the Mason-Dixon Line.[19]

Narratives that follow highlight some key moments and experiences from this series of events. More than in previous chapters, the voices here speak predominantly of Louisville and Lexington because the largest, most embattled public accommodations campaigns were centered there.

Open Accommodations Protests in the Post–World War II Era

In this first section narrators discuss public accommodations activism that arose in the 1940s–1950s after World War II. Many of these fairly short excerpts concern Louisville, which at that time was still home to the state's most visible activism.

* * *

After [World War II], civil rights activity really stepped up in Louisville.... There was a little activity, I understand from the history books . . . in the '20s with the Lincoln Party and politics and that kind of stuff, but not much during the Depression. People were poor and they were trying to make a living. But during the war and particularly after the war—one of my friends came back after the war and he decided he wanted to play tennis. So right over here at Triangle Park, University of Louisville owns it, he came over to play tennis and they arrested him. His name was John Stubbs. Nobody would ever have that in any documents anywhere, but if you check the *Leader* or the *Defender*, they were operating at the time, there's a story about one of my best friends, John Stubbs.... They arrested him and of course the NAACP came to his defense and there was a big case that was involved.

Joseph McMillan, Louisville

About that time [1950], which was before my oldest child was born, we got active in a thing here [in Louisville] called the Interracial Hospital Movement. What happened was there were three black men hurt in an automobile accident down near Hardinsburg, Kentucky. They were taken to this hospital that didn't admit blacks and they wouldn't let them in. They let them lie there on the waiting room floor and one of them died. There were a lot of incidents like that. It wasn't that unusual. But . . . there was a woman who was a good friend of mine, Mary Agnes Barnett, a black woman. She decided (we had worked on other things together) this was one time something was going to be done about this. She came and talked to me about it and we started a petition to try to get a law passed, just get something done about this. I think this was the general idea in the beginning, to get hospitals open to everybody. Eventually we kind of focused on getting a law passed that said hospitals couldn't be licensed in Kentucky—they were just passing the hospital license law, they didn't have one before—they couldn't be licensed if they refused treatment to anybody. We finally got that passed. . . . It was modified. The best they could do was get it [so] they couldn't be licensed if they refused emergency treatment, not any kind. Anyhow, we were working on that so we got a petition and were going around to different groups and churches, black and white, to try to get them working on this thing. We finally formed a coalition organization called Interracial Hospital Movement. The hospital movement was not only working to get that law passed, which we finally did, but just trying to get the hospitals around here to voluntarily begin to admit blacks. Except for General Hospital . . . none of them did at that point. Gradually over the next few years most of them did. The one hold-out for so long was Norton Infirmary, which was the Episcopal Hospital.

Anne Braden, Louisville

* * *

In this story Clarence Matthews, a reporter for the *Louisville Defender*, describes his role in testing lunch counters in the era before the mass sit-ins.

Some people forget this, but black reporters used to go out and test lunch counters, even before the students did in North Carolina. . . . I remember going in the old hotel, I think it was Fourth and Chestnut, and sitting down. And of course they refuse you, you go back and write a story about the refusal. . . . Black reporters used to do that all over.

I remember in St. Louis, they were doing it. They may have done it
in Nashville, I'm not sure, and Birmingham. I know they did it in St.
Louis and I did it here. You just go in with a photographer, maybe
lingering around somewhere and take your picture while you're sitting
at the counter or something. But it wasn't a bad incident. They just
didn't serve me, that's all. They said, "We don't serve Negroes here." It
wasn't any confrontation 'cause I wasn't being paid enough for that, to
go to jail. . . . I don't know whether Frank [Stanley, the publisher of the
Defender] was involved with it or not; I'm kind of hazy, but I know the
guy that was managing editor at the time, by the name of Nathaniel
Tillman, we talked about it and we decided to do it.

Clarence Matthews, Louisville

What really got me involved in the movement, after I had been elected
president of the NAACP I had an opportunity to go to [the NAACP
national] convention in New York one year. And I met these two
young men and we started talking about their section of the country
and mine. . . . Both of them were from Ohio. So one of the leaders
of the thing was having lunch with us one time, and we were talking,
he said, "You know, we have always wanted to do an experiment and
we've never had anybody to really, really do it. How about you three
doing it?" Well, first I wanted to know what kind of experiment, you
know, being the only woman sitting right there at the table. And he
said, "We'd just like to have somebody to just go across country down
south and stop at all the places, and see if they'd be served to eat." We
looked at one another and decided that would be a good thing to do.
We had a car, a fairly good little old car, not fancy or anything, just
a good, old, running car. We just dressed and we stopped and documented every place we stopped from New York all the way down to
Lexington through the southern states you know, including Washington, D.C. We came through that area. And we weren't served any
place. Now a couple of places said they would fix us some food in a
box, in a sack if we came around to the back door to get. Of course,
naturally you were not going to do this.

Then the plan was to get back to Lexington, the NAACP rented
a limousine for us, furs for me, jewelry, kind of a, not African dress like
they do now so much, but different. I was to sit in the back, one young
man was to be dressed up in a suit all the time, and the other was to be
the chauffeur. We were to head back and stop at the very same places

all the way back to New York. We were served at every place that we stopped except one. The conclusion that we came to was that they weren't quite sure who I was. Same people, we were still clean when we went before only this time I had some furs in the hot summertime wrapped around me and jewelry, and all this fancy other stuff, fancy car, chauffeur and everything, so they weren't quite sure whether this was a foreigner coming through and they served. Well, this is what made me decide, this is ridiculous. Nobody needs to go [through] this. The same people—we were no different. . . . Now keep in mind this is around the '50s, late '50s, [they didn't know] whether this was a diplomatic something, an African queen. Something has to be wrong. That's what really got me into the movement one hundred and ten percent. . . . When I came back they thought the enthusiasm was from the convention. No. It was not. It was from those two trips.

Audrey Grevious, Lexington

* * *

Louisville and Lexington were not the only communities to see stirrings of activism in the postwar era. Here Helen Fisher Frye, longtime leader of the Danville NAACP, describes an early effort to bring some integration to the campus of Centre College.

I worked in church all my life from the time I was—I guess I [was] around ten or eleven years old [when I] was made secretary of my children's department; and I served in some office all the rest of my life, all the way to church treasurer and superintendent, you name it. I was president of an organization called men and women's auxiliary, and we brought Todd Duncan—I don't think you've ever heard the name Todd Duncan. Todd Duncan was a native Danvillian. He was the first African American on Broadway in New York. He played in the stage play *Lost in the Stars*. This play centered in Africa, this African minister and his son. . . . My mother said he was born here over on [Danville's] Walnut Street. He had attended Simmons University, which was an African American college in Louisville. Of course, he knew a lot of Danville people. . . . But for us, as a small group, to bring a Broadway star to Danville was something to be proud of.

Up to that time, African Americans had not been able to go to Centre College concerts. Of course, they bring in outstanding artists.

The only way an African American could get into a Centre College concert was that he worked for some [white] person who wasn't going and said, "You use my ticket." So if I use Miss So-and-So's ticket, I could go. So, when we got ready to have Todd Duncan, the only place we knew of that would accommodate our anticipated audience was to use Centre College facilities. The president, the secretary of this organization, and our minister went to see the president of Centre College to see if we could use their facilities for Todd Duncan. Well . . . he was very open and receptive to the idea. He said, "Well, when you have it, will you have seats for white people?" I said, "No." My members and my minister still tease me about it. I told him, "No, we will just have seats." And that's what we did.

People from all around central Kentucky, even from Cincinnati, came down because a lot of former Danvillians were all around. A lot of them knew Todd Duncan . . . he was a world-famous tenor. . . . Then the fact that he was starring on Broadway, and a Kentuckian—we filled the house. The concert was a great success. It was on, I think, a Saturday night, Friday night or Saturday night, and on Monday morning the chairman of Centre College—I'm going to say they called it their Lyceum Committee, their artists program—called me at school to come by his office that afternoon. I went by, and he said, "We had a called meeting of our committee this morning, and we were so impressed with how you presented your concert that we have decided that we will open our concerts to African Americans." And [he] said, "I'd like for you to head up the campaign to try to get African Americans." We succeeded and we've been going ever since. I've had a season's ticket ever since, and that was back, back in the '50s, the early '50s.

Helen Fisher Frye, Danville

The New Mass Movement: Early 1960s Protests

As the previous section reveals, the mass civil rights movement that swept the 1960s began brewing much earlier. Indeed, as is clear in Raoul Cunningham's opening narrative in this section—which describes events of the Christmas season, 1959, among Louisville youth—no magic bell tolled to differentiate a new generation as the 1960s opened. Yet a substantive change in the level of activism unfolded along with the new decade, and students led the way. This section includes stories that reflect on that new wave of student-initiated activism—bringing perspectives from Louisville, Lexington, Frankfort, and half a dozen other smaller communities that were touched by the upsurge in varying degrees. Also included in this section are the voices of several reformers who were not of the student generation but who, inspired by it, also found new openings for civil rights reforms—for example, the formation and public accommodations efforts of the Kentucky Commission on Human Rights, which was established in 1960 soon after the sit-in movement erupted. Although some of the Lexington and Frankfort protests described later in this section actually predate much of Cunningham's story, it appears here first because it demonstrates the emergence of students at the forefront of protest and illustrates continuity between the new mass movement and the civil rights crusades that had gone before it.

* * *

Porgy and Bess was opening in the city of Louisville, on Christmas Day [1959]. All black cast and we could not be admitted to go see the production. But the Brown Theater had—they later learned they made a tactical error—ticket sales in advance, through mail order, so that those of us in the youth chapter purchased our tickets through mail. On Christmas Day [we] presented ourselves, knowing that we would be turned away. We already had our picket signs made. Once they turned the first group of us away, we immediately started picketing. Not only because it was an all-black cast, but I think the younger generation of African Americans were beginning to reach the point, of [being] willing to tackle the barriers of segregation.

It was shortly after that, in '60, when you had the sit-in demonstration at Woolworth's in Greensboro. Through SNCC, NAACP, CORE, the movement began to spread. The next major city that encountered civil rights demonstrations was Nashville. The Nashville story was broadcast across the country. After Nashville you had Atlanta and Houston. These were all college students. In Louisville we did not have a black university. By this time I was a senior. CORE was picketing the Walgreens at 4th and Chestnut. The president of CORE and I were classmates in school. We decided, hey, we can combine the NAACP youth chapter, CORE, double our numbers, and make a concerted effort. For fear that if *we* didn't do it, it would not get done in Louisville, for as I said, we didn't have a college chapter, a black university in the city.

Segregation was on the forefront. Nashville, Atlanta, Houston, Greensboro. It caused you to think about your situation, your life, your city. We weren't thinking about history. We weren't thinking about making a difference. We were thinking about breaking the barriers of segregation. Because we wanted to go to these restaurants and eat, we wanted to go to the movie theaters. So although there was a great deal of commitment, there was some selfishness involved in what we wanted to do. . . . Segregation made me angry. Simply because I was denied what I considered to be a right. They didn't lower the prices for the garments to blacks. We were charged the same price that everyone else was. It . . . made you feel less than a human being. It was a custom that you, we, became used to, in order to survive. At least our parents became used to it. I think that's one of the things that we rejected. . . . You've always had that generation gap.

We started [the mass demonstrations] in February of '61. At that point I was seventeen years of age, and a senior in high school. I felt scared, the first time I was arrested. . . . I understood civil disobedience, and had made a conscientious decision that I would break the law, at that time. Because I thought it was an unjust law. But I was still scared about it, and nervous about it. That first time, there were eighteen of us . . . who attempted to sit in at Stewart's. They gave us ample time to leave, should we decide to. When they said they would arrest us, we had a quick group meeting, and decided, fine. With none of us having gone through that process before, we were all nervous. When they took me down, oh, about ten minutes later, fifteen minutes, when they had me in a holding room, two more came down. One was a first cousin, I was never so glad to see him. Then two white girls came down, who had been demonstrating, the only two white folks who were demonstrating with us. They didn't put them in the same holding room with us, they took them to the "white" section. So we immediately began to sit-in there. How did I feel? Scared, nervous. Second time, all that had been removed. And by the fourth or fifth time, it didn't make any difference if they arrested us or not.

The first day that we were arrested, the adult chapter had asked us not to sit-in that day. They didn't think that they were prepared to cope with it. But . . . [five of us] were arrested, [and] the adults were a little bit miffed at us. But we were in high school, all under the age of eighteen, so therefore there was no bond to be paid. . . . It was really funny, that morning my mother [had] told me, "You've got to make some decisions." Because we had been down there the week before, and we had closed Stewart's every day. And she advised, "Stewart's is not going to let you continue to close them. There's going to come a time when they're going to arrest you. Are you prepared for that? Do you think you can continue to take the nonviolent pledge?"

It was a pledge that had originated with SNCC—Student Nonviolent Coordinating Committee—and Dr. King. Everyday before we would demonstrate, we would raise our hand and take a pledge that we would be nonviolent as we were demonstrating. No matter if rocks were thrown, eggs, if we were spat upon, or arrested. We would remain committed to the philosophy that we would not physically retaliate. That was true of every sit-in movement across the country. In addition to being arrested, passer-bys [*sic*] would throw eggs, rocks . . . call you "nigger." . . . If they got close enough to you, spit at you. . . . I remember one afternoon, a guy spat on me and I wanted to grab him so bad. . . . But I'd taken the pledge and I couldn't. I would like to have seen him after I got off the march, but we didn't see him.

[That next day] we went down, we were arrested. There were some who couldn't [take the pledge] and therefore they did not participate with us. . . . The next day, there were about forty-five of us. The next day, seventy-five. And we built up to as many as three hundred and fifty people demonstrating. . . . As we began to grow, we then could take on the movie theaters, and Blue Boar [Cafeteria]. By the third week of demonstration, we could take on the entire downtown area, where we could close it. That was our after-school activity, from February, through March, into April. Easter was coming up. CORE, the NAACP adult chapters got together, with the youth, and we decided we would try an economic boycott. Our slogan became "Nothing New for Easter." And it was successful. We did decide not to demonstrate during Derby. It was then that we began to get some pledges, from local politicians, that they would support a Public Accommodations Ordinance in Louisville.

Raoul Cunningham, Louisville

* * *

The next narrators continue the story of Louisville sit-ins with observations about how the public and store employees reacted to the demonstrations.

It was mixed. Well, the deal with black passer-bys [*sic*] [was they] would either immediately applaud or go to the other side of the street and walk down the other side. No black person was going to cross that picket line. I don't think in all the number of times I went downtown, I [ever] saw a black person go by us and go into a store. The white reaction was mixed. I don't think you had very many, as I remember, you didn't have very many [who] exhibited a real cohesion. There was not a cohesion feeling with regard to white patrons that refused to go into a place. I mean, nobody was going to say, "Honey, you're doing a good job. I agree with you," or whatever. You didn't get a lot of that. But you did get the feeling at times when you had people that started towards the door of a place and stopped and turned around. They understood why you were doing it even though you were inconveniencing them. So I guess from that standpoint there was some compassion there for what you were doing. They were being inconvenienced but they'd just turn and walk away. Then you had the person that was just going to go in, come hell or high water. They were going to go by you. I don't know that there weren't patrons in town that would see a picket line in front of one of those stores and go there even though they didn't intend to go in the first place. There was some "anti" attitude down there.

Louis Mudd, Louisville

I remember the one time—and I was more upset about this one time that we went because my mom had made me a blouse and skirt outfit. I had gotten these straw shoes because it was in the summertime. We were sitting right there at 5th and Chestnut, there was a restaurant there. And a guy came out and dumped this nasty water with whatever I don't know was in it, all on us. I was so angry because these were my new shoes. My mom had told me, she said, "I don't think you ought to wear that up there." I said, "Oh, yes. If I'm going to jail I'm going to go looking nice." And it was summertime, you know. It was icky, I don't know what was in that water. Old dishwater. I can't even remember the restaurant, sit right there on that corner. That was one time. And then where the Palace is now, I don't remember what the name of the theater was. We marched down there. Like I said, we were assigned to go different places. We were going to try and buy a ticket to get into the movie. They already had the police there when we got there. I don't know if he was a rent-a-cop or whatever. But they had this little wood-like peg that they would shove in the windows when we would try to stick our hands in there with our money. I remember the little rent-a-cop or whatever, he kind of tapped me on the arm with the—it bruised, but it didn't break my arm—when I put my arm up there to try to get my hand in the window to get a ticket. They never would let us stay at any one place too long because the paddy wagons would just back up and load us all in there and we would be gone. And we would be resistant by locking our arms. We'd just sit down and they would have to pick us up.

Runette Robinson, Louisville

* * *

After the Kentucky Derby, when civil rights leaders decided not to resume demonstrations, attention turned toward political organizing and the fall campaign, as Mervin Aubespin describes here.

Then you begin to look at the political ramifications. Let's see what will happen if we can get another person on the board of aldermen. A great example was Mayor Hoblitzell, the mayor during the time when we were doing Public Accommodation. Black folks were so angry at him because he took the obvious worst scenario and was not going to do anything until I saw the strangest thing happen: we got involved in politics. That's why we were doing voter registration and every-body decided we were going to vote Republican. Historically, and through the line, blacks have always voted Democrat. But this time I saw people come to the poll and they had their—there were poll workers—and they had their Democratic buttons on and they'd tell you, "You know what we're going to do." And they got in Cowger. Cowger didn't say he wouldn't sign an ordinance, he said if it passed he would sign it. So they cleaned house and it's the first time it's hap-pened. And it shows the power that the black community coming together could in fact be a swing vote. It actually happened and that was a great day; I saw this and I'll never forget it—when we went to the polls we rode around and we went to the polls and the word was, "You know what we're supposed to do." It went out to the churches, it went out the network, the clubs, the network was, "We're going to clean house." And they did. They even brought in two black Republicans, and Louise Reynolds was one of them.

Mervin Aubespin, Louisville

* * *

The next narratives switch to Lexington, where the adult leaders of the NAACP and CORE cooperated to instigate and conduct the demonstrations. The first narrator is Abby Marlatt, a white University of Kentucky professor who describes the beginning of the demonstrations downtown.

People were concerned about the fact that there was no place in downtown Lexington outside of the cafeteria at the YWCA where any person of color could sit down to eat food. At that time Main Street was the major shopping center, the major source of activity in Lexington. The big department stores, primarily Stewart's but also Grant's, and some of the specialty shops were there. Of course Woolworth's and McCrory's and a couple of the other variety stores had lunch counters. At least one or two of them would prepare food in a bag to take out if you stood at the end of the counter and asked for it. Some African Americans did that, but they would have liked to sit at the lunch counter and eat like everybody else. It was at that time that some of the students at UK, particularly through the YW and YMCAs, decided that they would like to do something about changing this. I had had previous experience in California working with the American Friends Service Committee and the Fellowship of Reconciliation. Some of us had had training in nonviolent direct action in the early efforts of CORE by Bayard Rustin, who was out [in Lexington] to do some training.

[The] first efforts had to do with lunch counters in the variety stores, and the idea was first of all to discover what the situation really was. We heard rumors and people had reported that they weren't served. It was, let's find out. So we would send in a team of at least three, and preferably four to six, people—mixed black and white—who would attempt to sit at the lunch counter and attempt to order. . . . There probably were more women than men, but there was always a good smattering of fellows. Caucasians were agreed that they would defer to the blacks, and unless the blacks were served they wouldn't be served either, or in some cases they attempted to share their food with their partners. If they weren't served they would sit there for a designated length of time waiting to be served. . . . That was, of course, the heavy time for the lunch counters downtown. So you really occupied several of their spaces, and people were waiting to be served, and here they weren't serving you and you were occupying a seat. When you discovered that [on] the first attempt when obviously you weren't being served then, we tried to contact the manager and set up a time when a team might go see the manager, talk about the policy and the fact that it would be to his advantage to serve everyone. Then if you got a negative, then you planned to have sit-ins in which over a number of days throughout the week you would try to get in with several people who would occupy seats at a lunch counter. . . . I don't believe there ever were [any arrests] at lunch counters. We had the foresight to talk with the chief of police ahead of time about what we had in mind, and what we were trying to do, and that it was nonviolent.

Of course, [then] we worked on the theaters, and the final result of these activities was passing the ordinances by both the city and the county for nondiscrimination in public accommodations. And after that then young people began to work on employment opportunities.

Abby Marlatt, Lexington

* * *

The next narrator, Audrey Grevious, discusses her relationship with Julia Lewis, revealing the close cooperation the two forged between the NAACP and CORE, two groups that in other places could become rivals, and the significance of that united front, including in their negotiations with the local police.

We were fortunate here in Lexington. Chief Hale was the police chief at the time. We met with him and talked to him about what we were going to do, and that we were going to try to remain as peaceful as possible. That we were not going into it to start any riots or anything, and that we wanted to see how we could work together. After we had talked for a long, long time . . . he agreed with us that they would not arrest anyone unless the owner of the building took out a warrant for our arrest. That it would not be an automatic thing that the police would come and see us and pick us all up and go. This was fantastic, unique, unheard of and everything else, but he wanted to keep Lexington as calm as possible. He was aware talking to the two of us [he could count on cooperation from NAACP and CORE] because at this time CORE also had organized and Julia [Lewis] was [head] of that.

I was a member of CORE and she was a member of the NAACP, so we kind of bonded together for this. The only difference between the two organizations [was] the CORE had more white members than the NAACP had.... So we did get something done here in Lexington because of the two of us were not in competition with one another. As a matter of fact, she was with the NAACP before CORE even came into existence here. When [James] Farmer came here to organize he stayed here at my home. So it was just a twosome that worked is really what it amounted to.

* * *

Despite this negotiation with the chief of police, there were arrests in Lexington, as Grevious describes here.

The theater was the one time that we were arrested.... That was [the only time] we got publicity the next day.... We were standing in front of the Strand Theater in front of the window so that other customers could not buy a ticket ... and they came down and arrested us, took us all in the wagon downtown. That was the most horrifying experience that you can imagine, being put in the back of that big wagon going to jail for really not doing anything.

* * *

What follows of Grevious's story illustrates her commitment to nonviolence, despite the costs it could exact. She sustained lifelong damage to her leg as a result of the confrontation she describes. Following her account is a brief recollection of the same series of events by her brother, Robert Jefferson. Taken together, these two narratives reveal the differences in the extent to which local activists, even those in the same family, supported nonviolence as a strategy.

The only time that we may have had a confrontation was at H. L. Green [lunch counter] when we were standing in. The week before that, we got in before they knew we were coming, and so we all took up all the seats at the counter. And the young lady there turned over a thing of tea [deliberately] all over my suit. As a matter of fact I still have the suit up as a souvenir in the attic. But anyway, so the next week we came back. But this time [there was] a chain all around the entrance to the lunch counter and the manager is sitting on this stool and when one of his white customers would come he would open the chain and let them in. Unfortunately I was at the front of the line and I guess it must have been about twenty other people, men and women, behind. And he had this chain and he kept swinging it. The chain kept hitting me right across the leg like this and I would move a little bit and he would scoot up and move some more.

So then I started to sing, no—the men, the men decided, we're not going to let him do this to you. I said, "No, go off the picket line. Go home, please go home." Reluctantly they did. I said, "It's okay. It's not hurting." It was but I didn't let them know. And he kept on and I stood there and I'm looking him right on the eyeball and he's looking me right on the eyeball. And he's still swinging and it's still hitting—and I started singing, "Yield Not to Temptation." Now how all the words to that song came, I will never know. I think I sang all of them right, and then I started making up my own for that time. I'm the only person that I know that received any injury . . . because I had to wear Ace bandages for months after that. It did do some damage to the nerve [in my leg]. . . . But we stayed the whole time, and then finally when my time was up then I think Julia stood at the line and she was taller than I and bigger than I. I think he must have just gotten tired because the other young man who came and sat on the stool didn't do the chain. But the actual manager did do the chain.

Now, you're talking about having some control. . . . It took an awful lot for me not to take that chain away from him and wrap it around his neck. Because that's really what I felt like doing to that man. Then I thought, that's what he would like for me to do. And I am looking back at all the ladies because by this time nothing is left but ladies and they kept saying, "Audrey, let me be up there." I said, "No, I don't want. . . ." See, everybody else just about except Julia and I had children. They were either mothers or grandmothers. . . . We [had made the men] leave because, see, they were going to wring his neck. We had to literally make them leave, even leave the whole place. By that time Reverend Jones had also come, like I told you he came to everything that we did. When he came to find out what was going on and they stood outside and he told them, "Please, go."

Audrey Grevious, Lexington

I didn't necessarily advocate violence, but I could not accept the non-violent movement. And specifically my sister was one of the major leaders in the movement in that period. . . . I did [participate] on one occasion, but due to the harassment and the intimidation that my sister was receiving at the head of the line, I attempt[ed] to retaliate on the individual who was, in my concern, abusing her and I was informed by her that that was what she believed in and it was best that if I could not accept the conditions that they were functioning under, it was best not to participate at all. So rather than hamper what they were doing, I discontinued my association.

Robert Jefferson, Lexington

* * *

The following two observations describing the participants in the Lexington demonstrations highlight the involvement of one church but—in the view of one of these narrators—not many.

This is the thing that bothered us with the churches and the ministers here in Lexington. Because with the exception of Reverend Jones at Pleasant Green, no other minister was directly involved with the movement, period. It's a prestige now to say that you were involved with the civil rights movement. I hear [church people say they were there] all the time and I don't remember any of these people. Because the ones who were involved that made the Lexington thing work was not your [professionals]—the teachers were not involved. The ministers were not involved. Most of our people were people who were maids, mothers and things—people who worked for other people, and our thing was that you don't lose your job to do this. We can find something else for you to do. Some of the maids were threatened . . . but the grassroots people are the ones who really worked here in the movement in Lexington, not your professionals.

Audrey Grevious, Lexington

[My husband, Reverend William Jones, minister of Pleasant Green Baptist Church,] never held an office in CORE, but his church was . . . always open to anything that CORE wanted to have or any meetings. Even for training: you know, teaching them what to do and how to react to certain circumstances. There [was a time] when Mr. Farmer, who was the national head, James Farmer, was due in here to make a speech, and the word was that the church was going to be bombed. And before the meeting was held that night the police came in and did a thorough check of the building. It kept quite a few people away for fear that something would happen. But there was never any violence done to our church during all of that period. There were times that things were very serious in this town. I mean, conditions got very bad several times, especially downtown there, at the various sit-ins. But I think it was his stature. I'll tell you this. Reverend Jones . . . had that kind of compelling attraction . . . and I think that was the one thing that helped. Most of the people in CORE were youngsters. My husband used to say, "These kids here are standing on these lines who will never be able to go in these places to see a picture or eat a meal, and a world of folk who aren't doing anything to help the cause will have the money to go in and enjoy it. . . ." And it was true, too.

A lot of people just don't want to get involved, but my husband was a fighter. I was a fighter for rights, and you know, children are like their parents. It just follows . . . but had it not been for the children, young people in this town, CORE could not have survived. I was never arrested or anything like that, but wherever they were, if any were marching off or [having a] sit-in, if I wasn't in the line, I was very close to it, and trying to watch, fearful that something could happen, and I always felt like an adult ought to be around [to be] more sensible.

Mary Jones, Lexington

* * *

The final narrative on Lexington's public accommodations struggle illustrates the role of whites connected to the local power structure, and particularly the Lexington Human Rights Commission, in resolving the crisis.

The other thing about demonstrations I remember, [Lexington] had a police judge named Richard Moloney, who was about my age and he was very strong for civil rights. His father was in the legislature, Irish-Catholic, great sense of humor. We used to talk about the power structure, how they were against change and so forth. So he called me one day and said, "Joe, we are really concerned about the demonstrations in front of these theaters downtown." The Congress of Racial Equality was demonstrating before these theaters. He wasn't really so concerned about that, but what was happening is that people were driving by and yelling obscenities and throwing things at them. He just thought it might really start riots so he asked me to serve on what became known as the Lexington Human Rights [Commission]. That was created in 1960 and the other cochair of that group—I became a cochair—was Homer Nutter, who was a [black] Baptist minister. His church is right up here on Short Street. . . . Another cochair was Dr. J. Farah VanMeter. He was a prominent doctor; he later served on the city commission. . . . And then a third man was James Angel, who was head of the First Presbyterian Church up the street. . . . We met up at Christ Church; Robert Estill was then rector of Christ Church, and he made it possible for us to meet up there in the parish house.

We'd get these members from CORE and the theater managers to come to the meeting. We took turns being chair and I can remember it was a very high-pressure situation. Feelings were very strong and we were trying to keep the feelings down or at least cool so we could talk about this thing. . . . Well, there'd probably be fifteen people there. It was informal in the sense that if several people from CORE wanted to come that was fine. If they wanted to bring three others, why we always welcomed whoever was there. Local [theater] managers came. . . . What became apparent to me was that the local managers really were open to integrating, but with them, it was an economic issue. They were concerned if they let black people in, they'd lose white people; and it would be kind of a net loss, and they would be in jeopardy with their superiors. All the theaters were owned by out-of-town chains. . . . We worked and worked—we even agreed to have integration every other day to see how that would work. They said, "Okay, we'll integrate on Monday, Wednesday, and Fridays and not on Tuesday, Thursdays, and Saturdays. We'll see how that works." Well, you know, we thought it was kind of ridiculous to try it, but that was their first step. . . . I don't think it lasted very long . . . I mean, it was just not [practical], but it was a genuine attempt on their part to move forward, to try things. I think they tried it and I think they [quickly] reached the conclusion, "Hell, this is silly." So they just opened it up and that was the end of it.

Joe Graves, Lexington

* * *

The following narrative shifts us to Frankfort at a particularly contentious moment in that local movement's development—mid-1960, in the aftermath of its first student demonstrations, arson, and the early departure of KSC students that spring.

At the time that [my husband and I came to teach at Kentucky State]—shortly after that, we had not completely unpacked our bags—we met Mrs. Helen Holmes. Helen had been trying to recruit faculty and students for the civil rights movement through the NAACP. Well, she didn't have too many problems recruiting us. At the time they were training and I've forgotten what the group was, whether it was SNCC or CORE or what. . . . Whatever it was, they were training students and faculty and community to sit in at these restaurants and to march in public places, only in public places. We were not supposed to invade any private organizations. So then this group could tell you whether you were capable of participating or not. My husband failed the test.[20] [*Laughs.*] They were just carrying you through a simulated sit-in.

Putz was a little restaurant down at the end of . . . High Street, and it was a popular restaurant, but blacks couldn't eat in it. So we sat in there. There was Mucci's on East Main. It seems to me that it was Mucci that we sat in. There was [also] a drugstore on Main right across from where Penney's used to be, and we sat there or stood there. They had eating counters. There was a five and ten [cents store] where the mall is now. We sat in there. We walked around Frisch's when it was up here and . . . some of them tried to go in. Some did go in but we also did our marches.

We had students from Kentucky State who marched with us around. There wasn't a whole lot, a few, you didn't want too, too, too many. . . . I do know that Atwood had had a lot of pressure from downtown to keep the students and the faculty quiet. When we prepared to have a march on the city of Frankfort [in December 1961], he almost like ignored it. . . . In fact, Mrs. Holmes was around then and she went to him and told him that they were going to have this march and she wanted the students and the faculty to participate. . . . He told her at that time, well, you do what you have to do. So they had a nice march on Frankfort. Some of the citizens of Frankfort didn't participate, a few of them because they were afraid to participate. They worked for some people and they were afraid that if they were seen marching their jobs might be taken from them.

[Helen Holmes] was a professor in English at Kentucky State and her husband was a physician. Of course she was really independent. If they had fired her at Kentucky State, she would have hurt, but she wouldn't have gone into poverty. But I had a lot of admiration for her. She really was interested in the welfare of human beings. She worked very hard, I understand—that was before I came here—to open the pools. Not that she wanted to swim in any of them. She didn't. It was the same way with the integration of the restaurants. She knew all of the people in town. They had a lot of respect for Helen Holmes. In fact, they asked her, "Mrs. Holmes, why in the world are you marching and sitting in these restaurants?" Then after they opened them up, one of them asked her, "I don't ever see you down here eating. Why don't you come to eat?" And she told him, "It wasn't that I wanted to eat in your restaurant. Your restaurant was a public restaurant and I'm a member of the public and I had the right to sit in, a right to come in and eat in your restaurant if I wanted to. It just so happens I didn't want to." She was that kind of a person.

She was able to get a group of students together and a few faculty—I was one of those faculty—and we did this sitting in and walking in during that period. She had a time recruiting people because, see, the students could not forget what happened following the burning of the building. I think there were about a dozen students who were expelled. I didn't know anything about the faculty [who were fired or disciplined]. But you could understand why they were cautious. She could not always understand why these people would not stand behind her. They did jail some of the students, and she would have to go around trying to find people who owned property so that they would be able to sign a bond so that these kids wouldn't have to stay in jail, and she managed to do that.

Gertrude Ridgel, Frankfort

* * *

The six brief narratives that follow offer glimpses of other student campaigns that erupted across the commonwealth in the smaller cities and towns of Danville, Hopkinsville, Franklin, Owensboro, and Bowling Green.

One of the biggest supporters I had throughout my public life was the local paper. They had a city editor named Miss Tipton, and [she] supported me in anything I did. At one time, when they were taking the freedom ride buses to the South, she called me and said that it was rumored around town that I was organizing a busload of freedom riders and was that a fact. I said, "No, I'm not." And she said, "Well, if you are, just let us know, we want to give you some good positive publicity on it." And I said, "Well, I certainly would." Shoot, in her eyes I could do no wrong. That was a big plus on my side to have the newspaper. . . . Now, there were some college professors from Centre College who went down for the freedom rides and the registrations. I knew three of them, and they worked with the NAACP here. Everything was open. I mean, we weren't undercover. What we did—if the NAACP was going to meet, I told Miss Tipton and she put it in the paper. We did everything aboveboard and wide open. We weren't hiding anything.

I was teaching sixth grade, but in church I worked with all ages. I think it was through the church that I got these young high school students, maybe from nine through twelfth grade, and discussed the situation. To make it convenient, we said, "Well, we'll get together after school, at school." And that's what we did. We decided that we would go to one of the drugstores to try to see if—nationwide they were having the sit-ins, so we would go. I talked with a lawyer and so forth, and we got guidance from him. I had these young children to meet in my classroom after school and we worked out our strategy. I don't know how many times they went, but they were never served. They sat and they came out peacefully. No violence, no confrontation or anything. . . . The law was not called in or anything. They just let them sit there and then after so long they left.

Helen Fisher Frye, Danville

Our resistance had begun to occur. We were in about the eleventh grade and a group of us went to the white teen center. We didn't have a teen center. We went to the white teen center and began to dance. We danced with each other and we played the games that they had there. That was a resistance to why don't we have something nice like you have? There was never any trouble, but the next year they built a teen center for the black kids. [Laughs.] I remember, once or twice a group of us would get together and we would go to a restaurant and sit in a seat in the front of the store. When the man would come around from the counter, we would get up and run out. But it seemed like, I believe, that the whole civil rights movement was a spiritual movement, because it happened in places in which people didn't really know the method that was being used, but they felt within their hearts that they had to challenge the system, that they had to say we don't like this, we don't want this, and we're going to do something to make this change. I don't see any type of movement in Kentucky, other than Louisville and Lexington, that challenged the system. The reason why Bowling Green changed was the city fathers heard that Freedom Riders were coming to Bowling Green to sit in. That's when restaurants began to open up and when things began to change a little bit.

George Esters, Bowling Green

I remember one time, I think it was in '61. 'Course, integration had already begun in my hometown, in Henderson, [where] we had the right to go to the front of the restaurants, to order what we wanted to. Well, I remember this incident [in Bowling Green with] two of my girlfriends. Well, we were from the country, we went to school at High Street, but we lived in the country. I didn't know any better, they didn't know any better, because they lived in the country. They didn't know that we couldn't go into the local drugstore downtown and sit down and drink a Coke. It had something to do with—during homecoming, we wanted to get some material to make a float. Well, after we got our material, we decided we'd stop at the drugstore and get us something—a Coke to drink. We went in and had a seat. Well, we had no idea we had to go to the fountain and get our drink and go out. We were sitting at the table—it took forever for them to wait on us, and I just remember at the time the waitress going to the manager asking, "Do you want me to wait on them?" The manager's answer was, "You may as well." We didn't have no idea we were staging a sit-in. So after we sat there and drank half our Coke, we decided we'd been away from school long enough and we needed to get back. So I remember my mother telling me about the slight sit-in that was at one of the local drugstores, which was at the time, I think, was Pearson's drugstore. She had no idea her daughter was involved in that sit-in.

Anna Beason, Bowling Green

The NAACP was going to challenge the Alhambra Theater over here. We had a mayor, Mr. Lackey, who was the owner of the WHOP radio station. This group said to him that we are going to break up this business of segregation here in Hopkinsville. People can't go into a restaurant, can't go into the shows. He made a declaration that he wasn't going to let any riots happen. We were going to stop this thing of segregation. He told all the managers that if any, I think he called them Negroes then, [were] going in there, said, "Don't you call no police, you call me." I said, "We are going to break this stuff up of segregation of theaters and restaurants." He said, "Well, you're in Hopkinsville and I'm the mayor. . . . You [store managers] do what I say or we'll close the place up." That was the turning point there.

F. E. Whitney, Hopkinsville

* * *

Lucille Brooks's narrative suggests how in small Kentucky towns with low African American populations the sit-in movement was less dramatic than elsewhere.[21]

The sit-ins went on in a minor way [here] as it did in the cities. Sometimes they decided they would go to a drugstore counter and sit down to have a sundae, banana split, or whatever. It wasn't that bad. I think it had been done in some larger city to the extent that they felt there wouldn't be too much opposition to that. There may be a situation where [the whites] may have had a small area where they ate, and the proprietors might take the facility out to keep anyone from sitting down, so they wouldn't have to say, we don't serve blacks in here. Just something like that may happen, they may take the facility out, rather than have a situation. . . . I don't remember any particular incident.

Lucille Brooks, Franklin

When I was a youngster in high school, I lived in the community with a man, a strong NAACP man. His name was James Tinsley Sr. He encouraged me to get involved in the civil rights movement. And I did get involved, and I was president of a youth group. And we did some demonstrations. I don't like the word "demonstrations," but we did go out and sit in some of the restaurants to test out their policies and all. One particular restaurant here in town, they served us but we had to make them serve us. But the waitress would just walk by and never stop and we'd have to say, "I want a hamburger." And she'd fix that. "I want a Coke." She wouldn't [ask for our order], she wasn't polite at all.

. . . We just decided, well, they're going to ignore us, so we'll just tell them what we want as they're passing by. And they served us but they weren't courteous with it.

We were just sitting in at the restaurants and . . . the one that I went to was Newberry's. You've heard of the Newberry Five & Ten Cent Store, well, it was Newberry's store. That particular one was. Now, theaters—blacks were not admitted to theaters. I remember [a little later, as a teacher] taking five or six students to see *To Kill a Mockingbird,* and see, they didn't want to let me in. But when I said I was with a school group, well, they let me in.

Wesley Acton, Owensboro

* * *

Not all movement activity in the early 1960s was of the direct-action variety. Both the formation and early emphasis of the Kentucky Commission on Human Rights, established in December 1960, were very much tied to the efforts to desegregate public accommodations. The mere fact that the state sanctioned such an agency set it apart from southern states whose governments stood in firm opposition to civil rights reforms. Here Galen Martin, the executive director of the KCHR for its first twenty-eight years, describes the commission's early work.

[The state Commission on Human Rights] was just this vague thing, you know, to seek fair treatment for all people, as far as the statute was concerned. But we got right into it, in terms of efforts to desegregate everything in sight. We quickly were into the teacher business and I guess [on] a little more gradual basis, we were into the school desegregation effort. But we got into the lunch counter business. That was when the lunch counters were, those demonstrations. That was still going strong in Kentucky when I got up here [in late 1960]. And we were into that. We did things that now would almost seem like Mickey Mouse, but they weren't. They were good things. We would gather information. It's just like we did [earlier] with the Kentucky Council on Human Relations, we would gather information on what had been desegregated and we'd put that out into reports. We would report the progress in terms of desegregation of lunch counters and other things.

We had this discussion with the restaurant owners [in Frankfort], trying to get them to desegregate. This guy at Frisch's, that was a horse's patoot. He told about this Frisch's in Ohio, and he said, well, up there we served them, but we gave them a hamburger that was that big [*gestures a tiny burger*]. And the woman from the Pink Pig [restaurant], she said, "Well, I will never do anything like that." She cut that guy dead. The die was cast when she said that. She's been active in the Democratic Party and now I think works for the Housing Corporation. . . . But it was just so beautiful the way she did that. She just wiped him out. Basically that again is what we had in Kentucky, and this is running through everything we worked on, was a lot of goodwill, not massive resistance. Mostly it was [white] people that sometimes hung back a little bit, hoping for leadership. But anytime we got leadership we moved ahead. It was about like the restaurant situation, throughout a whole lot of things that we were into.

* * *

One controversial aspect in retrospect of the commission's early work was its white leadership, beginning with the first chairman, Bob Estill, as Martin (also white) explains here.

I'm not saying that anybody ever thought that [the leaders should be white]. It's just the way things kind of unfolded, but you know, even reflecting back on it, I think that Combs would have thought that this is a white problem. The problem of discrimination is a problem of whites, and we've got to provide leadership for whites. And as far as the chairmanship is concerned, I could come up with a lot of reasons as to why it was better, what we were into in that time period, to have a white chairman.

Galen Martin, Louisville

March on Frankfort

This chapter's final section concerns the 1964 March on Frankfort, one powerful moment in Kentucky civil rights history that joined thousands in support of a single purpose: passage of a statewide public accommodations law. The first four narrators in this section reflect on the experience of the march itself and how they saw its significance.

* * *

In 1964 in Frankfort there was a rally in support of the public accommodations bill that was in the legislature. It was the only statewide rally that was held. I was there. A busload from Paducah went. I remember so many people. That was one of the biggest rallies I had possibly been to at that time. The March on Frankfort, that's what they called it. I remember it very well. Yeah, I felt like that Kentucky was on the move, making progress. I really do. I think that was one indication, by the reception that that large a group had at that time. I thought it was on the move.

Wardelle G. Harvey, Paducah

I just remember not really knowing what to anticipate, what to expect. I didn't know if we were going to be in the march or if we were just going to come to Frankfort. But I had an aunt and uncle who lived here in Frankfort so I had visited their homes and had a sense of South Frankfort. I remember my mother telling me that I should look out for my Aunt Bea. Aunt Bea was a maid in the governor's mansion, [*laughs*] and for some reason, my mother thought that I would probably see her. I just remember the anticipation of being on the bus. Being teenagers, we were occupied with teenage issues at the time. But there was a certain amount of anxiety because we really didn't know what it was going to be like.

There was a side street and Mr. Welch had parked there. Then we got out and walked over—it was cold that day—all of the people, probably more people than I'd ever seen in one place. State troopers were around, quite visible, and I remember being somewhat afraid and just full of anxiety that day. I didn't have a real sense of what I might be able to contribute to it. I mean, it was just an onlooker kind of thing, and I just remember being afraid. I knew who [Martin Luther King Jr.] was and we were able to get a good view of him coming up towards the capitol. I remember [seeing] Peter, Paul, and Mary playing [music].

Anne Butler, Richmond

It was something to behold. I was in the downtown area and all of a sudden I looked up. Here come bus after bus after bus, people [from] all over the state. When they lined up on Second Street to prepare the march and when you saw the people who were in the line, it was just awesome. Then they marched to the capitol and, of course, by then it had started raining. But in spite of the rain it was beautiful. And as usual, Martin Luther King gave a very stunning address. I think the Kentucky State University choir sang, and some other choirs and bands from other schools. It was just awesome. It was the biggest crowd that I had ever seen in Frankfort. I mean, as far as you could look it was just a sea of people everywhere around that capitol.

Gertrude Ridgel, Frankfort

A couple of things that I remember: Mrs. Breathitt, who's now deceased, and the two Breathitt children—I think there were two at that time. I remember they were watching the demonstration as we marched past. I think that was the first demonstration I was ever in. It was a very interesting experience to be in a demonstration, have other people look at you. You knew conflicting thoughts were going through their minds about what you were doing. But I remember I was marching with Bob Estill, and there were some other members of our church; and I looked ahead in the swarm of people ahead of me, and I saw a head kind of bobbing up and down. It was almost like someone was jumping maybe every other step as they marched. I thought, "That's kind of odd. I wonder why that is?" So I made a point at some point in the march, maybe when we stopped, to look at that person. It was a young black woman, probably college student or high school age. She had a terribly deformed leg so when she was walking, almost every step was just a reminder to me that, boy, black people made a lot of sacrifices and here's one who's has really difficulty walking who's in this march.

Joe Graves, Lexington

* * *

The final set of narratives illuminate the march as part of the larger struggle toward a statewide public accommodations act. They illustrate also the context for the march and the political actions that surrounded it, both by civil rights activists and by elected officials who opted to ally themselves with the movement. The first voice is that of Democrat Edward Breathitt, who was governor at the time of the march and who made history two years later when he signed the first state public accommodation law in the South.

Now during that 1964 session, we had a civil rights march on Frankfort with which I cooperated. In fact, I called Bobby Kennedy and President Johnson's office for advice. The attorney general, Bobby Kennedy, sent Burke Marshall and Senator [Paul H.] Douglas's son, John Douglas, down to help me in the drafting of the legislation and to help me in the ways to handle the civil rights march. I told the organizers of the march to pick their representatives to meet with me after the march and speeches. Among them were Martin Luther King, Jackie Robinson, and Peter, Paul and Mary. And we had a full discussion. Frank Stanley Jr. of the *Louisville Defender* was also part of the group.

[My daughter] helped lead it. [*Laughs.*] She was age 13. She and my minister from Hopkinsville were right up front. When they selected the group to meet with me, they let her come in with them. She came in all excited and emotional about it. She had been active in middle school and she was a freshman at Frankfort High School. . . . Well, most of my cabinet was in that march.

The first time I met [Martin Luther King Jr.] was when he came in the governor's office. I've got a picture in my office with Martin Luther King, Jackie Robinson, and Frank Stanley Jr., who had been an organizer of the march. At that time, Frank thought I would be successful in getting [a civil rights bill] passed. I knew that if I didn't get it passed, my credibility would be destroyed. I saw this as an opportunity to do something with my life that would have real significance in Kentucky and in the South.

I welcomed them when they came to the capitol to see the governor. That was our plan. . . . I later got to know Martin Luther King very, very well when I served with him on that presidential commission.

There was also a sit-in of the legislature in 1964. During the sit-in there was fasting by a number of them during that time. They were up in the galleries and people criticized me, but it is a legislative function that you have to let people come in the gallery. I never did try to kick them out, even though a lot of times they were criticizing me for my failure to get [the bill] passed, which I received from a number of the real activists in the civil rights community and by the *Louisville Defender.*

Governor Edward Breathitt, Frankfort

I had a number of people talk to me [about the statewide public accommodations bill]. I decided to be for it, and every other member of the delegation from Lexington was for it. You had a number from Louisville for it, but everybody else was politically petrified to even vote on it. They were getting a lot of negative comment all over the state. So they just wanted to dodge and duck, not an uncommon activity for the legislature. So when it was sent to committee, the committee would never report it out, just let it lie there. Several of us who were interested in getting a vote on the bill, some kind of a vote, decided to make a motion to take it from committee, which is a rather extraordinary thing to do. Therefore it takes a constitutional majority, which in the House is fifty-one votes. We were certain we didn't have fifty-one votes. At that point, we didn't care. We wanted to know who's going to vote for it and who's going to vote against it and who's going to abstain. So when the vote came up, there were seventeen votes for it. I saved that electronic tally. I remember many of them who were for it. Now at the same time, Martin Luther King came here with his march and that was—a lot of people there. So it was a time of some intensity on both sides. Nothing really happened on public accommodations. Then a few months later the federal [civil rights] act was adopted. In 1966, the very next session, the same bill was introduced. There were sixty-six co-sponsors.

They got brave when the federal act [passed], because, in fact, it probably made no difference. There weren't enough new people elected. It's just that they decided that [supporting civil rights] would not ruin their career. They could go home and say the federal act took care of it. "We just went along with the federal act; you're going to have to live with it anyway." Although I'm not sure [since] the state act covered different things than the federal but they could at least go back and say, "What difference does it make? Might as well be for it."

H. Foster Petit, Lexington

Ten thousand, including me, marched in Frankfort to support a civil rights public accommodation bill in the General Assembly, which refused even to debate the issue, and it died in committee. Then Congress passed [a national civil rights act], of course. I just remember a lot of organizing of getting people there. I had one little aside . . . when actually a parishioner from Louisville had a little camera and was taking pictures of the march. When he came to me—I saw him way down the line—he got ready to take my picture so I made a face at him. [*Laughs.*] Found out he was working for the FBI. I'm in a picture, I guess, somewhere in the FBI files.

Seems to me it was cold, but I can't remember too well. I remember wearing a hat for some reason, which I almost never wore, because I was trying to emulate the Kennedys. But I remember thinking I better have a hat on today. I think we were all fairly naive about big demonstrations like that. We were always fearing that this or that group would descend on us or throw things at us. I didn't go in any great fear, but I went with some apprehension; and it is something to move along with a crowd that big. It showed to me so much build-up of support. We didn't know that we had that kind of support, and I think it made a big impact.

The governor obviously was open to [meeting with us] and it wasn't a forced thing. [And we] needed to be more forceful with the General Assembly. But as I have noted here, they refused even to debate it. By that time, most of us knew practically two-thirds of the General Assembly and had visited them and talked to them. So it wasn't any great surprise. But it seemed to me it marked a time when the average person could say, "Yes, there is a lot of support for this thing. It isn't just some few creatures that are trying to stir things up."

In January of '66, I was busy on TV and radio, traveling the state for the civil rights law that was in the General Assembly, and on January 17, 1966, our bill passed the House . . . we're dealing with Ned Breathitt, and on the 27th of January '66, he signed the state civil rights law on television. That was a great day for Kentucky, I said [on the air], and in many ways, the culmination of my work with the state Human Rights Commission as it turns a corner in the type of work this commission will be doing.[22] I feel my work is done, I said. My last meeting was September 23, 1966, after six years of being there. We have the best civil rights law in the South.

Robert Estill, Lexington

Helen Fisher Frye

WHEN the civil rights movement in Kentucky was at its height, Helen Fisher Frye was both a public school teacher and president of the Danville NAACP. She led that organization in campaigns to end Jim Crow in public housing and accommodations as well as to open city government to African Americans.

Born June 24, 1918, Frye lived her whole life in Danville, moving to a new house only once and leaving her hometown only when traveling or pursuing higher education. Raised in a large family by working-class but economically secure parents, she attended the segregated public Bate School. In 1942 she received a bachelor's degree in elementary education from Kentucky State University, in order to fulfill her dream of becoming a teacher in Danville. She later received master's degrees from Indiana University and the University of Kentucky. She also took courses at both Ohio State University and Danville's Centre College, where she became the first African American to enroll. After World War II, Frye became involved with church-based human relations organizing, and through that and her commitment to community service she got interested in the NAACP. In the 1950s she helped to rejuvenate a defunct branch of the organization and served as its president until 1968.

In this excerpt of her interview, Frye describes race relations in a small southern college town, a setting that has escaped notice in most histories of the civil rights era. Communities like Danville combine the racial and social structure of rural settings with the cosmopolitan influence of an institution of higher learning. Her story provides perspective on the postwar human relations movement, in particular its basis in the cooperation of church women and the influence on it of newly ordained young ministers.

Perhaps most interesting, Frye's description of her motivations and actions roots the civil rights work of the Danville NAACP—a local branch of a national activist organization—in small-town, largely female, church-based and civic institutions and a tradition of community social service. Her story illustrates the kind of leadership that women brought to civil rights activism in similar communities across the South, where community service work sometimes led to bolder civil rights activism that challenged white authority more directly but involved the same sort of patient, day-in, day-out solicitation of the black community's support that had characterized their human relations efforts all along.

* * *

I'm a native of Danville. I was born on Lebanon Road and lived there with my family until I moved to [my current home]. I've moved only one time in my life. My parents were Lydia Moran Fisher and George Fisher. There were nine children. My father was a railroader, which was the best job available for African Americans at that time, and my mother stayed at home with the children and took in home laundry. Danville was a hub for the Southern Railroad and they had what was known then as a roundhouse. It was a hub for repairs on Southern Railway trains. So my father remained in Danville. We didn't live too far from the point of his job.

I attended school at Bate School, which was a twelve-grade, African American school. I lived on Lebanon Road, which is toward the west. Bate School is on the eastern end of Danville. I had to walk about a mile and a half one way each morning and back each afternoon, and I didn't mind the extra three miles if my parents would allow me to go to whatever basketball game. So there have been many times I've walked the six miles per day for school.

I had no way of comparing [our schools with white schools] because we were in our school, they were in their school, and I didn't know what they had. Only the administration knew what we did not have. Everyone was buying his own books at that time. African Americans as well as whites were buying their own books, so our parents bought our books. Whatever other supplies were given to them, we didn't know about them. So we had the same textbooks, we bought ours and they bought theirs. When the state began giving free textbooks, now that's the one point of some discrimination. Some of the used books from the white schools were brought over to us, but not entirely. The teachers' salaries were not equal. I knew very little about that as a student, but as the years went by finally we had a principal who came in and challenged it.

I'm from a Christian home and the philosophy was that you're being mistreated now, but you go to school, get your education, and the day will come that there will be opportunities and you'll be ready for them. You can't change it so try to live harmoniously through it. My mother was a person of great hope that it would not always be like that. Now, in walking the mile and a half from our home to Bate School, we had to pass the white high school. In doing so, there were two or three, maybe half a dozen, white fellows who would make sure we didn't walk on the sidewalk if they were out there. Instead of trying to push back, we just got off and let them have it, because we knew we couldn't come out winners. We were going to be the losers. But I was taught well as I was young and growing up that people who mistreat other people have problems themselves. Contented, happy people don't create problems for other people. Even when I was in school teaching, I'd say, "If someone mistreats you, the person who does the mistreating is the one who has the problem. You don't have the problem. They have a problem and they're taking it out on you." I still feel that way about people.

When I graduated from Bate School I went to Kentucky State College, received a bachelor's degree. I started out for a major in English, which I wanted badly, but I also wanted to remain at home and teach in the local school. My reasoning was that if I were to get in Bate School, there was one English teacher, but there were about eight or ten elementary teachers. So I changed my major over to elementary education. After I graduated, there was not an opening in Bate School. So I taught in three county schools. I started teaching July the 5th, 1942, in Casey County. Rural, rural, rural; I had to walk the creek and everything. But I taught there only one year, and then I came to Boyle County, where there was an opening; taught one year. Each year was a little improvement over the previous year. Then an opening occurred in the Danville system, and I began teaching sixth grade in Danville. I always wanted to come back to Danville. I was in a happy home. I hadn't traveled many places to compare, but since I've been grown I've traveled quite a bit and I haven't found any place that I still would prefer over Danville.

I often compare Danville with Harrodsburg in race relations. Now here in Danville, if a white person is friendly with you that person will come to your house, invite you to his house, her house, and socialize with you. In Harrodsburg, which is ten miles away, my impression is that the whites will give the African Americans and the servants and those who work for them more money than the ones in Danville will give. But to associate with them, cup of tea, sit down, no, no, no, no, no, no. But here in Danville I could name incident after incident where different groups and different individuals have associated very closely race-wise. One of my first friends was a [white] lady by the name of Mrs. Van Winkle, and a Mrs. Oldham, and a Mrs. Erskine. They were three friends—of course, they were church workers. They worked with the United Church Women. I met them through a meeting that was sponsored by the Centenary white Methodist Church.

I'm a Baptist, but the other denominations have done more for race relations than the Baptists in Danville have done. They have an outreach to the minorities more so than the Baptists have. The ministerial association in Danville was made up of ministers of just about all the churches. Evidently these were young ministers who came out with a personal philosophy in the Fatherhood of God and the Brotherhood of Man, and most of the churches had young ministers that worked closely together. They worked for fellowship and human relations. At one point starting from that little nucleus meeting at the Methodist Church, back shortly after I got out of college, that's when human relations in an organized way started and developed, went on from that meeting. I had been to a meeting at Kentucky State College that was sponsored by the Methodist Church, I think it's called central district. I may be wrong on that. One of their main speakers was from United Nations headquarters, and that made an impression on me. When I came back, the Methodist Church had a meeting, and that meeting enlarged and enlarged and continued to grow and did a great deal for brotherhood here in Danville.

From that we formed the human relations council, and that really was a city-wide, county-wide organization with ministers from all churches. We had one friend, Jim Lawless, who was minister of the Presbyterian Christian Church. They said his congregation pressed him until he left Danville because of his human relations efforts. And there were some others, too. The Presbyterian Church had some good, strong human relations ministers. They organized youth groups, and had youth fellowships between the churches and within the churches and so forth. So there have been many outstanding, productive efforts in human relations. It has not been overlooked. Some group or some agency or some individual has always pressed for better human relations.

I attended a national Sunday school convention once out in Denver, and one of the speakers was from Morehouse College. Now, if ever I got an outside influence, I think that was this speaker. He left with me the philosophy that a Christian should be involved in all aspects of human life. You shouldn't just be praying on Sunday and living piously, but a Christian has a place in politics. A Christian has a place in social action. I feel that being in the NAACP was a [fulfillment], an extension of that philosophy and what I learned at home and from my mother. She told all of us, if you think you're right, go ahead. Don't back off. If you think you're right, you take your stand for right and stick with it. So my becoming president of the NAACP was an extension of my home training and my Christian conviction.

In my childhood, whenever there was a drive—of course, then there was a Red Cross, and March of Dimes, and you-name-it drives. When we were ten, twelve, we were selected to canvas our neighborhood and solicit funds for this different drive and so forth. I can think of very few committees in Danville that I have not been on: family, service, Salvation Army. I was chairman of the Public Housing Commission. You name it, I've been on it. That is an extension of my philosophy: service. The bottom line is service. I think maybe that there is a common misunderstanding of the NAACP. The NAACP is not a militant group, never has been. I'm not a militant person. I'm an aggressive person, but I'm not a militant person. I'm ready to run from militancy—I'm chicken. But aggression and taking a positive stand for my convictions, I can confront anyone. I remember at one time it was announced in the paper that there would be a meeting to get involved in this [federal program called First Cities]. I had a young lady say, "Miss Frye, how do you get into everything? Everything that comes along, you're in it. How do you get in it?" I said, "Well, if I read it in the paper—the paper is out there for the public and I'm part of the public. And if it interests me, I go to the meeting and see what it's all about." So they don't select me, I select causes. That's how I got involved in the NAACP during the '50s and '60s.

A minister in the Methodist Church, a Reverend Hodrich, was

As the twentieth century dawned, many African American Kentuckians still worked in agricultural labor, as depicted here on a hemp farm in Mercer County, circa 1900. Courtesy of Ford Photo Album Collection, University of Louisville.

This company store operated by the Consolidated Coal Company in the small town of Jenkins in Letcher County served both black and white coal mining families in the manner described in Julia Cowans's profile. Courtesy of Special Collections, Alice Lloyd College, Pippa Passes, Kentucky.

Winnie Scott (right) in front of the Winnie Scott Memorial Hospital, in 1914, which she operated for African Americans in Frankfort. Contributed by Josephine Calhoun to the Community Memories Project, Kentucky Historical Society.

During the first half of the twentieth century, African American Kentuckians were frequently hired only for the dirtiest, most dangerous forms of labor, as seen with these storm sewer workers in Depression-era Newport. Courtesy of Goodman-Paxton Photographic Collection, 1934–42, University of Kentucky.

Lyman T. Johnson (right) leaves the federal courthouse in Lexington with Rufus Atwood, president of Kentucky State University, after the court rules in favor of his admission to the University of Kentucky in early 1949. Courtesy of the University of Kentucky Libraries.

The earliest African Americans at the University of Kentucky attended graduate and professional classes, as seen here in 1949. Courtesy of the University of Kentucky Libraries.

Governor A. B. Chandler signing the proclamation to open the Kentucky State Police Force to African Americans before a group of NAACP representatives in 1959. Contributed by Archie Surratt to the Community Memories Project, Kentucky Historical Society.

Prayer vigil on the steps of the Fayette County Courthouse in the early 1960s. Courtesy of Calvert McCann and the *Lexington Herald-Leader.*

Rev. Henry Jones and his son at head of a line of marchers in downtown Lexington, circa 1960–1961. Courtesy of Calvert McCann and the *Lexington Herald-Leader.*

Helen Fisher Frye. Courtesy
of Helen Fisher Frye.

Second graders in Valley View School at Elizabethtown pursue their studies
in integrated harmony. The presiding teacher is Mrs. J. V. Robinson. Circa
1963. Courtesy of the Photographic Archives, Special Collections, University
of Louisville.

Vanguard of the civil rights marchers at the March on Frankfort, 1964, included, from left: the Rev. Olof Anderson, Louisville; thirteen-year-old Sherman McAlpin, Louisville; Dr. Martin Luther King Jr.; the Rev. Wyatt Tee Walker, executive secretary of the Southern Christian Leadership Conference; the Rev. Ralph Abernathy; Dr. D. E. King and Frank Stanley Jr. Baseball celebrity Jackie Robinson is behind Abernathy and to the right. Courtesy of the Photographic Archives, Special Collections, University of Louisville.

Long view of March on Frankfort, 1964. Courtesy of the James N. Keen Collection, Special Collections, University of Louisville.

Georgia Davis Powers with dignitaries at the March on Frankfort, all wearing Allied Organizations for Civil Rights (AOCR) ribbons. Courtesy of the James N. Keen Collection, Special Collections, University of Louisville.

This scoreboard illustrates how the Kentucky House of Representatives voted on the civil rights bill in 1966, with lights on left denoting "yes" votes. The bill passed the House 76–12. Courtesy of the *Lexington Herald-Leader* collection, University of Kentucky Libraries.

Open housing rally in Louisville, 1967. Courtesy of the Robert Doherty Photographs, Special Collections, University of Louisville.

In what was covered in the news as a "friendly but inconclusive session," Madisonville mayor David Parish (right) met with representatives of the National Association for the Advancement of Colored People (NAACP): Margaret Williams of Madisonville, Louisville attorney Neville Tucker, and the Rev. W. J. Hodge, president of the state NAACP conference, with Madisonville city councilmen in the rear. Courtesy of the Photographic Archives, Special Collections, University of Louisville.

This array of literature in support of fair housing was part of a campaign undertaken by the Kentucky Commission on Human Rights. Courtesy of the Kentucky Commission on Human Rights.

Movement Is 'Not Anti-White ...It Is Just Pro-Black'

By CHARLES WALDEN
Louisville Times Staff Writer

Blaine Hudson was in the group of black students that set out to disrupt administration of the University of Louisville, hoping it would speed implementation of a broad program of black studies.

Why?

Excerpts from a taped, 90-minute interview with Hudson provide some insights.

Questions are drawn from among those often heard within the white community and sometimes in the black community.

The answers are his.

What is behind the black movement on the U of L campus?

This is a revolutionary struggle, because to fight for black people means automatically to fight against white institutions which are against black people. This is the thing that a lot of people don't understand.

This is not an anti-white movement. It is just pro-black.

Why did you, as an individual, decide you would participate?

I was fighting for something that was a little bit more important than my own education. We did know that we would be expelled and that we would be arrested.

I still think the action we took, the ultimate goal we hope to achieve, justified the risks involved. It was something that had to be done because we had exhausted our means of dramatizing our commitment to the proposal through rhetoric.

There is a general belief that a young, black college graduate can ask premium salaries from business and industry. Do you believe that?

The average black graduate with the same major, the same grade-point average and the same type of job as a white person with the same qualifications still will make $3,000 less on the year. That is, unless he wants to be a token.

There is a great competition for tokens.

Staff Photo
Blaine Hudson led group that set out to disrupt administration of the University of Louisville.

you know. This is essentially what integration is. If you really love the psychological energy or physical stamina it requires to be a token over a period of time, this is all well and good. I think it is rather demeaning.

Why do you think it is such a psychological and physical drain?

Tokenism is integration on the terms of the white society.

To integrate in this manner means to surrender all ties we have to our own cultural history, all our history. It always seemed rather absurd for me, a black

See EXPELLED STUDENT
Back page, col. 3, this section

Hudson Grew Up in Louisville's West End

Blaine Hudson, a sophomore, has been dismissed from the University of Louisville and convicted in Police Court of disorderly conduct for his part in the occupation of an office building on the U of L campus on May 1.

He is one of 17 persons who were later appeal for reinstatement at the U of L. Hudson, an honor graduate of Male High School in 1967 and one of few black students who were National Merit Scholars, had a wide selection of schools.

He chose U of L, he said, because Hudson was born in Louisville's West End 19 years ago. He began school in the segregated, all-black Fond Elementary School and attended Russell Junior High School before going to Male

The *Louisville Times* coverage of the 1969 Black Student Union uprising at the University of Louisville features a photo of and interview with BSU leader and suspended student J. Blaine Hudson. Courtesy of the *Courier-Journal*.

James Cortez and Black Unity League of Kentucky leader Sam Hawkins (right) speaking atop a car at the May 27, 1968, rally at 28th and Greenwood in Louisville, which led to the city's largest civil disorder. Courtesy of the *Courier-Journal.*

As Governor Wendell Ford signs Senate Bill 78 into law, declaring January 15, birthday of the late Martin Luther King Jr., an official holiday, the bill's sponsors look on—Representative Charlotte McGill, Senator Georgia Davis Powers, and Representative Mae Street Kidd (right). Courtesy of the Kentucky Commission on Human Rights.

Associated Student Movement voter participation drive at Western Kentucky University, 1968. Courtesy of the Kentucky Library and Museum, Western Kentucky University, Bowling Green, Kentucky.

Julia Cowans is shown here with her husband, Hugh Cowans. Courtesy of Julia Cowans.

Roy Wilkins (center), executive director of the NAACP, and John Johnson (right), president of the Kentucky State Conference, with an unidentified man. Circa 1970s. Courtesy of the Photographic Archives, Special Collections, University of Louisville.

Jesse Crenshaw, representing Fayette County's 44th legislative House
district, was elected in 1992. He is shown here in 1996, and still served as of
2008. Courtesy of the Kentucky Legislative Research Commission.

the first one to my knowledge to organize an NAACP chapter here in Danville. My twin brother—we were quite similar as a family—we would challenge a cause if we thought it was wrong. We would stand up and speak up. He was secretary of the, to my knowledge, first chapter of the NAACP. After a period of years, it died down. Now this, of course, was before World War II. Then, after the war and the servicemen had come back home, they felt more keenly the discriminations that they had undergone in the war overseas and then to come back home and not have full citizenship and so forth. My Christian conviction told me that was wrong and I should do what I could on the home front to change.

So we were going to re-organize an NAACP chapter. There was a need for it in Danville, and we announced that in all the churches. We set the date, and had the meeting, and there was much support for the idea. We met in the Baptist Church. That's where I belong and that's where the mass, large number of African Americans belong. That was the organizational meeting, but our regular meetings alternated back and forth from the Methodist Church to the Baptist Church. We had quite a few outstanding speakers during that period of time, while I was president. We had Martin Luther King's brother here, we had one of the vice presidents of the national organization. Centre College worked with us, with this individual from the staff of the national NAACP. We made arrangements, and this person spoke to a number of classes on the Centre College campus, and, of course, that, that brought the races together.

We had committees on education, public facilities, other committees. Among the things that I feel that we accomplished while I was president—Danville had back at the turn of the century had African Americans on the city council. Then, I don't know whether it was a matter of no one running for the council or what happened, but from the 1920s until the 1950s or '60s, we had no African American on the city council. So one of the things the NAACP accomplished while I was president, we spearheaded a campaign for an African American, and we got the first African American in forty or fifty years on the city council. His name was George Harlan. He had come to Danville from Detroit, and he sort of impressed everyone so they were willing to vote for him. We put on a well-organized campaign, and got him on the council.

We also, with the Human Rights Commission and Galen Martin,

working through them, we integrated public housing. There was a white project, and there was an African American project, and the NAACP attacked that. We used more than one approach. There were persons who wanted to live in the vicinity of the white project—I don't know that we had any whites who wanted to move into the vicinity of the African American project or not—but those people had made requests that they would like a unit in the white project. Then we did a little testing. We would send an African American to the housing headquarters and ask for a unit and so forth. We just didn't get out there, as my husband said, "get out there with your hair flying back and don't know where you're going." We had a sense of direction and we went about it legally. We did not go about it in a militant manner.

In my time as president I had a few threats. Once I went to a service station to get gasoline in my car, and the attendant was putting gas in my car, and a white lady came up. He left my car with the hose in my car and went to this white lady. And I told him, "I'm ready to go." And he said, "Well, I'll take care of you after while." So with the hose in my car I started moving, pulling off. [*Laughs.*] He told me, I was going to get in trouble or I could cause damage or something. I told him, "Well, you come and finish my car or else I'm going." So he came on and he said, "I'm going to talk to the superintendent of schools about you. You're just too smarty aleck." I don't know what answer I gave him but that didn't stop me. And a church in Louisville, the largest African American church in Louisville, we had their minister to come here to one of our NAACP meetings. I told him I had had several threats about my teaching and possibility of being released from school. He said, "Don't stop. They wouldn't dare, they wouldn't, [*chuckles*] they wouldn't dare release you from school." Of course, that gave me more courage to go on and continue what I was doing. My twin brother would say, "Listen, Helen, now if you want to stay with all of that, you just get on out of here, get on out of the house and get you some place 'cause we don't want to wake up one morning with this house on fire." Now he had been in the NAACP, but they weren't doing the kind of aggressive action that we were doing. I stayed there. I guess my brother said that partly in jest, but he just felt I was going a little too far.

A lot of the members did not want it publicized that they had membership in the NAACP. Now one person that we had, our reorganization treasurer, was working at the state hospital out on Shakertown Road. I noticed that when I would call wanting to ask about money or a check, his wife would never let me speak with him. She would take the message, but I could never speak with him. Finally, he explained that since he was a state worker for the government, he was afraid that he would lose his job so he didn't want it known that he was working with the NAACP. Whenever his supervisor did learn that he was a member, the supervisor encouraged him, said, "Well, that's a respectable organization. You just keep your membership." Of course, you couldn't trust anybody; they might have encouraged him and then used it against him. But anyway, he finally gave up the position but his job had not been threatened at all. But I don't know of anyone who suffered any retaliation at all. There were people who went to my superintendent, and my superintendent didn't look favorably on me at all. The first time the organization wanted me for president, he told me or somebody else that he had something else that he wanted me to do. He didn't want me president at that time. He had something, but that something else never did develop and come through.

I was also watched by the FBI. One day I was at the A & P store, which was across from city hall. I was going out to my car and one of the city councilmen was coming out of the police department. He hollered across the street, over to the parking lot, "Miss Frye, FBI is looking for you." Of course, to have any contact with the FBI back then [meant] you had to be red, and pink, and communistic, and everything else. I said, "Well, you tell him I'm on my way home. If he wants to see me, come on out to my house." [Laughs.] All while I was president of the NAACP they stayed in touch with me. They were really double agents, the news reveals. They gave the African Americans the impression that they were backing them and supporting them and wasn't going to let anything happen. And if it did happen, they'd be on hand; and if it got out of hand, they'd come in and enforce and so forth. But, again, as we have learned, one of the biggest enemies that African Americans and the NAACP had was J. Edgar Hoover. He did more to hurt than to help. I told one of them once on the telephone—he asked me what activities did we have planned and did we have any marches planned and so forth—I told him we did not have any planned. And I said, "You know, if I were planning something that was illegal or unacceptable, I would not talk about it on my telephone, because I know you have my phone tapped. And so if you get me, you'd have to get me some other way."

I was president up until 1968. I do remember that, because people were making progress and interest was dwindling. We were getting what we wanted—some of it—and so interest was dwindling. You had to work hard for memberships, to get them to give you their membership. At that time, my mother had had a stroke and was sick and in the hospital. And in soliciting those memberships, we just didn't get the support. My mother was my idol, so I gave all my time to her, and I told them I could not at that time serve.

Since then, I'm a Democrat and I work for candidates, but I've never run for office. I could not win. Now I have been voted into many, many positions. For instance, the Human Relations Council and when the Danville government first organized the Danville-Boyle County Human Rights Commission, I was president. I've been placed in a lot of positions, but I don't think I could win a public vote. I'm too rigid. I'm not flexible enough. People love me but they don't like me. I know there are a lot of people who don't like me. They'll tell me that. They tell me I'm too hard and firm. I don't yield enough. I stick with my conviction. You just can't change me. I paid a price for it, but I'd rather have lived and believed as I have than to have been blown with the wind.

Chapter 4

Open Housing

ONCE African American Kentuckians had won the right to eat in restaurants and shop in stores, the next great battle in the state's civil rights movement was for equal opportunity in housing. Since emancipation, black and white residences had become increasingly segregated. As freed people and their descendants left rural areas and moved to small towns and cities, they congregated in black-only neighborhoods. In part this practice of seeking comfort and moral support among people who shared family, church, and culture mirrored a tendency that was true among all urban emigrants, including those from abroad who found homes in urban areas across the North and Midwest. But across Kentucky, as in the nation, blacks ended up in segregated communities in large part because of white efforts to restrict their housing choices. Strategies for keeping African Americans out of what whites thought of as their neighborhoods varied from place to place, and included over time community pressure, violence, restrictive covenants (i.e., clauses in deeds prohibiting sale of the property to blacks or other minorities), city ordinances, and a consensus among white realtors, builders, and lenders that blacks should be barred from all-white areas. The result was a varied pattern of housing. In rural areas African American tenants and sharecroppers may have lived near white landowners, though as George Wright points out they were "far from being 'neighbors' in any sense of the word."[1] In some urban areas black families lived on alleys behind white blocks, occupying former slave or servant housing in what one historian has called a "layer cake" pattern.[2] In most Kentucky cities, however, African Americans lived in scattered neighborhoods—Smoketown and the West End in Louisville, the Kingdom in Glasgow, Normal Heights and the Bottom in Frankfort, and Pricetown and

125

Cadentown in Lexington, for example—that although often nearby, were entirely segregated from whites.[3]

The struggle against housing segregation in Kentucky began early and reflected a national strategy of using the courts to prohibit discrimination. In May 1914 the Louisville board of aldermen adopted an ordinance that sought to guarantee housing segregation by mandating that no one could move into a neighborhood in which the majority was of another race. This law was one of about a dozen such measures around the country, including one in Madisonville, Kentucky. Almost immediately black leaders and their white allies in Louisville mounted a challenge to the ordinance. Robert Buchanan, a white businessman, sold property in a majority-white neighborhood to William Warley, an African American newspaperman. When the law barred Warley from occupying a home built on the property, he refused to pay for the land and by prearrangement Buchanan sued him. The case eventually went before the U.S. Supreme Court, which ruled in 1917 in *Buchanan v. Warley* that city laws mandating housing segregation were unconstitutional. The next major national blow to housing discrimination came thirty years later, also from the Supreme Court, which ruled in *Shelley v. Kramer* (1948) that restrictive covenants, which were quasi-legal neighborhood agreements to maintain segregation in home sales, were likewise unconstitutional. Though together these two cases made it clear that governments could not mandate nor enforce residential segregation, neither one had any impact on the private practices of realtors, builders, and lenders, nor on the community harassment and violence that undergirded Jim Crow in housing.[4]

The incident that most dramatized the continuing problem of housing segregation in Kentucky in the post-*Shelley* period was the dynamiting of Andrew and Charlotte Wade's new home in Shively, on the outskirts of Louisville. In the late 1940s and early 1950s cities across the South, including Birmingham, Dallas, Richmond, Chattanooga, and Charlotte—as well as non-southern cities such as Chicago—saw waves of violence, including bombings and mob attacks, in response to African American efforts to move out of older black sections and into newer housing. Meanwhile, in Louisville the housing situation for African Americans was becoming dire. The postwar expansion of home ownership and suburbanization made possible in part by the G.I. Bill was in full flower locally as well as nationally, but developers were determined to keep blacks out. At the same time, the neighborhoods reserved for African Americans were becoming increasingly crowded with only deteriorating housing stock. Ex–World War

II serviceman Andrew Wade and his wife, Charlotte, had one child and another on the way in the spring of 1954 when the couple went looking for a new home with space for their family to grow. After many thwarted efforts, blocked once the sellers learned the Wades were black, Andrew sought help from white allies. He eventually secured the aid of Anne and Carl Braden, white civil rights and labor activists in the city, who bought the home the Wades wanted in a new subdivision and transferred the deed to them. Within days the white neighbors realized their enclave was now home to a black family. Harassment and violence began the night the Wades moved in and climaxed six weeks later on June 27 when the house was partially destroyed by dynamite. The perpetrators were never caught and punished. Instead, the commonwealth attorney prosecuted the Bradens and five white associates on a largely symbolic charge of "sedition," claiming they had bombed the house as part of a communist plot to stir up racial hatred. The hysterical anticommunism that engulfed the nation throughout the 1950s then swept over Louisville. As a result, the plight of Andrew and Charlotte Wade, and the violence that was meant to keep blacks literally "in their place," was all but forgotten, and the Wades were never able to reclaim what had begun as their dream house.[5] Little progress was made in the area of housing in the city or in Kentucky for the next decade.

While there was relatively little action during this period toward opening the private housing market, local forces in Kentucky, in conjunction with a national campaign and eventually backed by federal law, worked to integrate public housing. In the wake of the *Brown v. Board of Education* decision on school desegregation, the Louisville NAACP filed suit against the Municipal Housing Commission, and in May 1957 the Sixth Circuit Court of Appeals used a precedent set in Detroit to order the commission to integrate its units. In response, the city adopted a freedom of choice plan wherein tenants could request housing in any project. Although a few black families did move to formerly white-only buildings, public housing in the city remained overwhelmingly segregated. Meanwhile, John F. Kennedy had promised in his run for the presidency to attack Jim Crow in public housing, implying that a "stroke of a pen" could erase the problem. Once in office, he hesitated, and it took a nearly two-year NAACP-led lobbying campaign to force him in November 1962 to issue an executive order requiring housing agencies to prevent discrimination in any federally built, owned, or supported residences. This inspired some action in Kentucky, as activists in Louisville and Danville began pressuring housing officers.

The issue of public housing integration in the state seems never to have garnered significant official attention, however. Thus, despite those local efforts, the state Commission on Human Rights continued to document segregation in public housing across Kentucky well into the 1980s and 1990s.

The major citizen drive for equal housing opportunity in Kentucky started with the campaign for an open housing ordinance in Louisville.[6] In the wake of the adoption of the city's open accommodations law, civil rights advocates began calling for a similar measure against residential discrimination. When the board of aldermen refused to go beyond an impotent statement of principle, black and white leaders formed the Committee on Open Housing, and in spring 1967 they launched demonstrations, first at the homes of city officials and then into white neighborhoods. They focused on the southern end of town, where affordable housing costs made the neighborhoods the most attractive to blacks, but where opposition was highest from working-class whites who had recently fled the inner city. During three months of almost nightly marches, the level of harassment and violence against demonstrators went beyond anything seen in the early 1960s sit-ins in the city, and it attracted negative national media. After movement leaders turned their attention to voter registration and campaigning to remove the recalcitrant members of the board of aldermen, in November 1967 African Americans and their white allies voted en masse and swung the election. The almost entirely new board they ushered in passed the open housing law within weeks.

As this struggle unfolded, open housing advocates across Kentucky began campaigning for similar measures in other cities and at the state level. The Commission on Human Rights developed a model ordinance and promoted it across the state. Bardstown-Nelson County became the first community to adopt the model when in July 1966 it passed one of the "broadest and strongest local anti-discrimination" laws in Kentucky. This, along with the Louisville law and other small-town measures that followed, meant that by the spring of 1968, seven hundred thousand Kentuckians were living under fair housing ordinances. That strength helped to pave the way for the state legislature to act. When the 1968 session opened, Senator Georgia Davis Powers (the state's first African American woman in its senate) and Representatives Mae Street Kidd and Hughes McGill secured passage of Kentucky's Fair Housing Act, again the first such measure in the South. One provision of the bill facilitated the adoption of local measures, leading to another round of city and county ordinances.[7]

While these fair housing measures were cause for pride and celebration, they did not bring down the walls of segregation in housing. Across the state, enforcement depended on investigation by local and state human relations commissions and on civic leaders voicing support for fair housing. Above all it depended on individuals pushing realtors to show them housing in formerly white areas and then withstanding the resulting resentment and resistance. Most people were unwilling or unable to do so. As a result, even with laws supporting integration, to a great extent Kentucky's African Americans have continued to experience housing discrimination. Research on the 2000 census reveals that in most of the state's major cities blacks and whites continue to live separately. Specifically, while evidence shows that African Americans are spreading out and moving into mixed neighborhoods, white Kentuckians still live in overwhelmingly white areas.[8]

The narrators in this chapter recount how Kentuckians, led by civil rights advocates in the state's largest city, used demonstrations, politics, and legislation to secure the first open housing laws in the South. The narratives open with descriptions of housing patterns around the state and personal confrontations with the residential color bar, including the Wade family's traumatic experience of violence in 1954. Louisvillians then share their memories of the late 1960s open housing movement in their city, focusing in particular on the South End demonstrations. Shifting to the rest of the state, Georgia Davis Powers explains how she got the Fair Housing Act passed in the senate, and Galen Martin introduces how the Commission on Human Rights sought to enforce the measure. The chapter ends with stories from around Kentucky about the passage of local ordinances and continuing efforts to win equal housing opportunities.

Jim Crow in Housing

You were strictly segregated. Now one advantage [for a black real estate agent] is, if a black man wanted to buy a house, he had to come to a black man, because a white one wouldn't fool with him. Because the segregation pattern was then that there weren't any new houses that a black man could build. They didn't have but two groups or two classes of our people—they may be the doctors, undertaker, principal of the school and maybe independent business person—who has had his own funds. They were about the only ones who could buy and build a new house. Of course, we were the secondary market. See that's where the white person, who wanted to move out of a neighborhood, if he couldn't get his neighbors to buy it, he'd sell it to that colored man. And that's the pattern all over, especially all over the South, anywhere you go. Louisville in the West End used to be white years ago, but you know the Negroes would buy those houses.

F. E. Whitney, Hopkinsville

Blacks had lived all over Bowling Green, but in a black section. In other words, there was never any integration. Blacks lived in where Western [Kentucky University] is, blacks lived in the Delefield area, [and in what] was called Shakerag. Then they lived off on the small house roads. So blacks in Bowling Green have never been concentrated in one area. They've lived all over Bowling Green, but always together, never in an integrated type situation.

George Esters, Bowling Green

The powers that be would select certain streets or certain areas where we could live. When we moved to Ohio Street, [it] had just been opened to blacks a very short time. They first opened the 300 block and then the 400 block . . . [The powers that be were] unspoken but understood. . . . I don't really know if there was a law, but we wouldn't have been able to buy if they didn't say it was okay. Even then I know the first [black] man [who] moved on Breckinridge Street moved right on the corner, and he had a rough time. [The neighbors] just made his life a. . . . They would put bombs on cans and throw them on his porch, and put garbage in his yard; they just mistreated him terribly. But he didn't move, and eventually others moved there. But we couldn't move just anywhere.

Amanda Cooper Elliott, Lexington

There were two worlds in Louisville at the time I got here. My mother was living on Thirty-second and Virginia Avenue, she and Ed [Davis, my step-father]. Right across the street was Ed's father and right next door to them was Ed's brother. So he had his whole family kind of in the thing. But there's the most interesting thing had happened before I got here. It appears that my step-dad had seen a house right down the street. Right at the entrance to where Chickasaw Park is, is a stone house, a Bedford stone house facing the parkway. He decided he wanted to buy that house for Mother. So he sent Mother and his sister-in-law, who was also quite fair with straight hair, and so was my mother, and he sent them and they bought the house. The neighbors did not realize that blacks lived next door until one day he was cutting the grass and the neighbor asked him what did he charge to cut the grass. And he says, "I get the opportunity to sleep with the lady of the house." And it was then that they realized that the home had been sold to blacks.

Do you know what happened? The entire neighborhood rallied and put together enough money to buy the house from them at a reasonable profit. He was a businessman enough that he took it and he told them, "It doesn't matter because one day we're going to be here." And he went right up to Thirty-fourth and Virginia Avenue, which was then all white, and bought another house. And that's where they were living when I came out of college.

Mervin Aubespin, Louisville

* * *

In this short narrative, Norbert Logsdon, a white homeowner in Louisville's West End, shares his view of efforts to keep blacks out of the neighborhood.

We hadn't been here two weeks when we got a visit from one of the neighbors up on 47th Street and [they] apprised me of the fact that they had a neighborhood association here. The reason for the association was to keep black people out. They had bought one house over on the parkway and they had been successfully renting it to whites. But there was another house on the parkway going up for sale and they wanted to make sure that black people didn't buy, see, so they wanted my permission for the association to buy that house.[9] I just refused, I said as far as I'm concerned anybody has the right to live wherever they want to live and wherever they can afford to live. Well, it wasn't long after that ["for sale"] signs started going up or people started selling, and after they started selling that's when signs started going up everywhere.

Norbert Logsdon, Louisville

* * *

Devices like the agreements of which Logsdon speaks were not always successful at keeping blacks out, but moving in was only one of many hurdles.

Overt violence was sometimes employed to drive out African American residents from all-white neighborhoods, as Andrew Wade's family discovered in 1954 when white friends Anne and Carl Braden bought a suburban Louisville home on their behalf.

Too many individuals and realtors and legal advisors and what not had advised I should buy where I was designated to buy. After looking around, and I did look around quite extensively, I became very much dissatisfied with what I had seen and I wanted to buy a house that I wanted to buy. I'd see a house that I liked, then it occurred to me that this was in the forbidden area and I said this doesn't make any sense. I served in the [armed] services and felt highly right in trying to buy what I wanted to buy with my own money. I wasn't begging. I was ready to buy, so why not get what I wanted? I said if there's a wall built that I'm not supposed to penetrate . . . then I'm going to penetrate the wall and get what I want. So I really felt that it would be a repercussion. They had to object to me coming in the forbidden area. But I figured right would prevail and I would end up with what I wanted.

It happened that the builder [who] developed that area, he lived right in the same neighborhood. So I talked to the builder's son and I told him he should have no objection to me moving in, that he was a young fellow, he had a future ahead of him, and how could he live in a democratic kind of society and aid and abet such things and spirits to keep me out of the neighborhood. I tried to shame him out of it. But that didn't work.

Andrew Wade, Louisville

I think it was about Thursday of that week that [the builder] came over and asked Andrew if he was doing some work for us or something. Andrew told him no, he was moving into the house, that we had transferred it to him. Either Thursday or Friday night the whole mob came down here [to our house]. I wasn't here. [They] threatened Carl and told him he was wrong. . . . Carl just told them to get out and to quit trampling on the grass, and they did. That's the first inkling we had that there was going to be trouble. We figured that would die down too. Then it was that Saturday night [the Wades] actually moved out there and they were living there. That's when there was a cross burning in a field nearby and there was a rock thrown through the window and somebody shot at the house, which was pretty serious because it could have killed somebody. . . .

It was on Sunday morning [June 27]. There were two people who were the guards who were there. . . . Andrew and Charlotte had been out for the evening. I think it was the first evening they'd really gone out because they felt like things were quiet enough and they could sort of begin to live their life. They came in and Rosemary, the little girl, had come into town to spend the night with Andrew's parents. . . . They usually did that on Saturday night. We never knew if the people who blew up the place knew that habit of theirs or not because the bomb was set right under Rosemary's bedroom. They may have known the child wasn't there on Saturday night because she never was. They had just come in and there was sort of a side porch to that house when you drove up the driveway. . . . They were still standing on the porch. I don't remember if the two guys who were doing guard duty were in the living room or whether they had walked out on the porch. The dynamite went off on the opposite side of the house. It jarred them where they were but they weren't hurt. If it had gone off on the other side of the house they would have been killed. That's what happened.

Anne Braden, Louisville

Louisville's Open Housing Movement

The Wade house incident failed to make a significant break in the barriers African Americans faced in finding housing, or to inspire a movement against residential segregation. That movement began thirteen years later, after the open accommodations sit-ins and as fair housing was becoming an issue in the North. Here, Hal Warheim, a white Presbyterian seminary professor and civil liberties activist, outlines the emergence of the city's open housing demonstrations.

* * *

I guess the next step comes with this Open Housing thing, 1967. As I recall, the civil rights organizations were trying to get an open housing bill, or ordinance, passed by the board of aldermen for about two years. There was a Republican administration, Mayor Schmeid, and Republican board of aldermen, who vacillated and postponed and promised and didn't do anything. Consequently, the black leaders, and the white leaders, but mostly the movement was led by black leaders at this point, got tired of the game, and decided to go to the streets with it. I was on the board of the [Kentucky] Civil Liberties Union at that time, and I was chair of their Minority Relations Committee. I think it was in the fall of '66 that the black leaders, along with some white leaders as well, formed the Committee on Open Housing. The leaders were, A. D. Williams King, who was the brother of Martin Luther King; Hulbert James; Leo Lesser; of course, Anne Braden was there; Lukie Ward; Charlie Tachau certainly. They set up this Committee on Open Housing, which was a coalition with representatives from a number of places, and I got on the committee by virtue of representing the KCLU.

So they decided they were going to put some pressure on the city administration to do something, and started marches. The demonstrations went on for a while, then the city went to the courts and got an injunction against the marches. It was when that happened that the spit really hit the fan, this was in April and May, end of March. The Committee on Open Housing had support from the Southern Christian Leadership Conference. We had access to them, their wisdom, their experience. Martin Luther King came here a couple of times. We had Hosea Williams, who was one of the chief organizers for Southern Christian Leadership Conference, who was here quite a lot and helped to develop strategy. We decided to march against the court injunctions, which meant, automatically, that we were subject to arrest and of course prosecution, all of that. We decided to do that, and strategically chose the South End of Louisville for the marches, which was really a very wise move because of the reaction that we generated. The more reaction, the more hostility we generated, the more the people on the fence and on the periphery of the movement decided, "Hey, this has gone too far, let's get this behind us."

We first went out and gathered, driving our own cars, but then the hecklers started to throw rocks and slabs of concrete into the cars and smashed windows and dented fenders and that kind of thing. So then we hired U-Hauls, and we all piled in the back of the U-Haul trucks and drove out to where we were going to march. Then they banged up the trucks in the same way. So finally we had to go to Cincinnati to hire U-Haul trucks. We would gather at certain places and we would be picked up and we would sit in the back of the U-Haul truck and we would go out to the South End of town, and then we would unload in the presence of police. We would line up and then we would start marching down between this gauntlet of hecklers, with the Confederate flags and so forth and so on. They were nasty and they were also dangerous. One night I was marching in back of Martin Luther King, who was hit in the face with a rock. A young, to-be mother was marching to my side and she was hit with a slab of concrete, there were cherry bombs exploding around. Like I said, we were grateful that the police were there. [The hecklers] were shooting off revolvers. It was spooky. It was scary.

Then, after a while, Bill Warner decided to try to stop these illegal marches.[10] Or maybe as safety director he was just concerned about our safety, or just the public peace. They started to gas and arrest people. When they started doing that, of course, they would arrest first the leaders, that is to say, the people who were on the front of the line. Then we started putting the leaders back in the middle of the pack, then they arrested everybody. We would exchange places, I would lead some nights, and there would be somebody else leading another night, and somebody else yet another night. But after a while, the police and the safety director knew who the leaders were. The arrests I remember were after we were tear-gassed and everybody was taken, I mean any number of people were taken.

Hal Warheim, Louisville

* * *

Cheri Bryant Hamilton, who later became a member of the board of aldermen and Metro City Council of Louisville, here recalls her participation in demonstrations as a teenager.

At the rallies they'd have speakers, they'd have singing, they'd talk about what was going on, they'd talk about strategy, they'd talk about trying to get an open housing law in Louisville. The board of aldermen was not in favor of that so we marched on the aldermen's houses. We'd go out there and we'd march on the police chief's house or we'd march on whoever the alderman was. We did a lot of marching out in south Louisville. We marched on Fourth Street. We had sit-ins in the middle of Sixth Street between city hall and county courthouse. I find it so ironic that during one of those open housing demonstrations we got thrown out of city hall, down those steps. I'm working in the same city hall in the same board of aldermen where I got thrown out of thirty years ago. But there was fear, too. Even though we were fueled with the passion that what we were doing was right, we were meeting hecklers out there wherever we'd go and they'd throw eggs, they'd throw rocks, they'd throw barbs at you, so they were heckling you. We just hung together and locked arms and sang. So you were afraid of physical violence. That's why the police were always out there. You didn't know whether they were to protect you or whatever, but they wound up trying to keep things from getting out of hand.

There were a lot of people that were not involved in the movement, I mean they thought we were shaking things up and should leave things well enough alone and "what are you all doing out there?" and "these kids shouldn't be out there!" There was one time my sister and I were out there and we had begged the babysitter to let us go. My parents were out of the country. That night we were down by Memorial Auditorium and we were having a sit-in out there in the street. The cops came and they're trying to get you to disperse and you don't disperse and you keep singing songs and we wound up getting arrested and we had to go to Children's Center.[11] My parents were coming back in town that night and they had to come down and get me out of there. Then we marched and demonstrated out by Central Avenue by Churchill Downs and I can recall my mother getting thrown in the paddy wagon and watching that and we're still locking arms and singing. I didn't get arrested that night. I think I only got arrested one time, but my father was, "Oh, I leave town and here you all go."

Cheri Hamilton, Louisville

* * *

Hamilton was the daughter of Ruth Bryant, an antipoverty and housing activist, who shares here her memory of her arrest.

I got in the paddy wagon. I was taken down to the police station. Then they put you in holdover. But on the way, when [the paddy wagon] was full, this white boy was thrown in. He was a heckler. He was thrown in with us. And he'd been calling them "niggers" and all kind of stuff before. Throwing rocks and all. The cops threw him in there. So I know he was scared. I know that boy didn't know whether he was going to get out of that wagon alive. So they took him on down. And you know what they made him sing all the way? "We Shall Overcome." He had to sing it, not in unison with anybody else, he had to sing it all the way down to this police station. He will never forget that. That boy will never forget that. Because he didn't know what was going to happen to him. I bet after that he never heckled people.

Ruth Bryant, Louisville

* * *

The open housing demonstrations brought leaders of SCLC, including Martin Luther King Jr., to Louisville. Here photojournalist Ken Rowland recalls another night King was struck by a rock thrown by a heckler.

I was shooting [film] at the corner of Taylor Boulevard and Central Avenue and they had a big crowd of demonstrators this night because Martin Luther King was going to speak to them on Central Avenue. I was standing at the corner of Central and Taylor shooting the wide crowd on the sidewalk—they were like eight abreast and it went forever—when a car turned off of Taylor coming the other way and turned down Central. On Central at that corner, out of sight of the demonstrators coming up Taylor, were two little girls about nine years old. King was sitting in the front seat passenger seat. The car stopped and King rolled down his window and spoke to the girls. I was far enough away that I couldn't really hear. To tell you the truth, I didn't even know it was King, until I got closer. But anyway, somebody was speaking to these kids, and the kids were listening and they were interested. Because it was obvious that they recognized this person. Then I saw it was King. Just then the crowd turned the corner and the kids became apprehensive at the crowd turning the corner. And all of a sudden, one of the kids spit at King. Little white girl. Neighborhood kids. And one little girl said, "I hate you." And I heard King say, "I love you." And then the car started up and went down Central and waited for the demonstrators.

That night turned out to be a very dramatic night, because where they were on Central Avenue there was a large crowd of whites. They were on the porches of the houses on the North side of Central. The rally ended. King had spoken, brief speech, invited them to come down to a West End church where he was speaking that night and where the rally would continue. He got in the car and all of a sudden, I tell you, it missed me by an inch. A huge rock, well, a rock bigger than my fist, was thrown at horrible speed toward King. It was meant to kill him. Instead it hit the divider, back in those days they had a divider on the windows. . . . .The rock, luckily, instead of hitting King in the head, hit that metal piece and just bent it inward like four inches, that's the speed that it was thrown. And the rock dropped into the car. Leo Lesser, he was a reverend from the West End. He was driving the car. He put that car into gear with screaming tires, he almost hit like two or three people, and sped out of there at high speed. [Later that evening at the church] he made a fabulous dramatic moment out of this. . . . He reached down and he picked up the rock and in his dramatic voice he said, "Upon this rock I will build my. . . ." And the crowd just exploded and drowned out "church." It was fabulous.

Ken Rowland, Louisville

* * *

In late spring 1967, after a controversy over whether to demonstrate during the Kentucky Derby, the Committee on Open Housing suspended marches and focused on voter registration and using the November elections to bring in a new board of aldermen.

These marches were going on as Derby Week was approaching. Hosea Williams came up with the idea of running a couple of black kids across the homestretch during the Derby. Well, this was quite a provocative tactic to be suggested, and it didn't fly exactly highly in the strategy meeting, as I remember. . . . [But] some of the core leaders, like Anne Braden, Charlie Tachau, A. D. Williams King, and a couple of others, had been arrested on contempt of court, it may have had something to do with the marches that were illegal and so forth. They weren't put in jail immediately, but strategically the city decided to put them in jail the beginning of the weekend and the first part of Derby Week. Consequently, the key leaders designing strategy were in jail on the Monday prior to Derby. Churchill Downs was having races, and while they were in jail, Hosea Williams got a couple of black kids to run across the homestretch on a race anyway. It was the Monday before Derby. Contrary to what the strategy group had decided, Hosea Williams, who was [a] really headstrong, independent organizer and strategist, decided he was going to do this anyway, and did it.

It exploded, and it exploded in our favor. Because that Monday night the church was packed full of enthusiastic people who, I guess, finally realized that we were for real, we were serious, we were damn serious, dead serious, and would go to any length to get this ordinance. It just mysteriously pumped new energy into the movement. Then, of course, the leaders got out of jail. I don't remember that they publicly criticized Hosea Williams, they may have done it privately but I didn't hear that. The ongoing demonstrations were just about petered out now, because we didn't have any more money for bail bonds. In fact, the demonstrations were, I think, finally defeated because the financial resources were depleted. But we practically closed down Derby Week. All kinds of events were cancelled. The parade was cancelled. They were so afraid of riots and demonstrations and so forth they cancelled the parade. They cancelled a number of other things where they expected trouble. Then Derby went on without any trouble, but they were scared to death about Derby. Soon thereafter, the marches were phased out.

Then, with the support of the Kentucky AFL-CIO, other black leaders, I think maybe Suzy Post was involved in this too, we designed a voter registration drive, and I was on the executive committee of that, along with a number of other people. As a result of that voter registration drive, I think we registered about five thousand new voters, particularly in the West End, particularly blacks. That seemed to make an impression on people, and particularly the Democratic candidates for aldermen, with whom somebody entered into a deal, that if these people, in the liberal community and the people who were now tired of all of this fuss and stuff going on, would support them in the election, if they would promise to vote for the open housing ordinance. So, when the election was held, the Republicans were thrown out, the Democrats went in, and we got the open housing.

Hal Warheim, Louisville

Kentucky's Fair Housing Act

Soon after Louisville adopted the open housing ordinance, attention shifted to Frankfort, where state senator Georgia Davis Powers, together with her allies in the general assembly, was pushing for a statewide law.

* * *

One of the first bills I introduced in the Senate was the open housing bill. My seat mate, who was returning from Paducah, Tom Garrett, said to me, you'll never pass that, and I said, well, watch me. I just got there, I don't even know the ropes yet, don't even know how to draft a bill. It so happens that the bill went into the committee that he chaired, judiciary committee. Every time I asked him, Tom, when are you going to get my bill out of your committee, he'd say every time I bring it up, I lose a quorum, I can't get it out. I said, but you will.

The most important bill to most of those men in that session was daylight savings time. That's all they were concerned about. The ones in the rural areas talked about how the cows wouldn't give the right milk in the right amount because of changing the time. When he came to me and asked me what I thought about time, I said I'm not concerned about time, I'm concerned about open housing, prohibiting discrimination in selling and leasing property, that people should be able to buy where they can afford. Well, my seat mate—he was for it—found out the opposition had nineteen votes opposed to daylight saving time, and that he had eighteen votes, but he didn't have mine. So you see how important, and I tell young people that, one vote is. So he came to me and he said, if I get your bill out of committee, will you vote with us? I said I don't know, you have to get it out with the expression that it should pass, because that would give potence to the bill once it gets the floor.

So, the very next morning, he met me at the capital door, and he said I got your bill out of committee, and I said, Oh, great, Tom, I said, let's check it at the Senate clerk's office, and we did and they had reported it out with the expression that it should pass. Now you going to vote with me? I said not yet. What's the matter? I said you take this roll call sheet, everybody you got committed to vote for your bill, daylight savings time, you check them off and get them committed to vote for mine when it hits the floor. Oh boy, he snatched the paper and took off. About two hours he came back with all the commitments.

Well, his bill came up first that week, for a vote, and of course it tied, 19–19; well a lot of the legislators came to me and said you didn't care what time it was, you need to change your vote, you're going to make it bad for Wendell, he's president of the Senate. He's going to have to break the tie. I said better for him, than for me. My commitment stands, so Wendell did have to break the tie, he voted for daylight savings time. Now a few days later open housing bill hits the floor. I got up and I was just speaking on it, why we should vote for it. Finally Tom pulled my coat and said, "Georgia, sit down before you kill the bill." [*Laughs.*] So I just moved to pass it as a bill. I had the roll call and was checking as they voted and that bill passed twenty-seven to three with eight abstentions. That's how big it passed in the Senate.

Then of course it went to the House and Mae Street Kidd and two other African American legislators with Norbert Blume, our legislator, who happened to be white, but he was always supportive. They pushed that bill through in the House and it passed. The governor at that time was Louie Nunn and of course he could do one of three things with it: He could sign it into law, he could veto it, or he could let it become law without his signature, and that's what he did. That's why we have an open housing law in the state of Kentucky. It passed in 1968, and it was the first one in the South and there were not many any place else in the country. So Kentucky's been ahead in some things.

Georgia Davis Powers, Louisville

Spreading and Enforcing Fair Housing

Adoption of the state law was not the end of Kentucky's open housing movement. In fact, the law spurred civil rights activists to fight residential Jim Crow in many towns and cities. The remaining stories describe how advocates secured passage and enforcement of those local ordinances, and how Kentucky's African Americans continued to fight for equal access to housing.

* * *

Our outlets were more in those days in getting these fair housing acts adopted in other cities. That's what a lot of our effort went into. See, Georgia's bill authorized local human rights agencies to adopt their own housing ordinances; and so that swept the state. One of these jurisdictions adopted it before they had the power. I think that may have been Bardstown in Nelson County. I'm pretty sure. We sent out a model ordinance and they up and adopted it. They adopted it prior to that. But then we got them adopted in Covington and Kenton and Fayette.

Galen Martin, Frankfort

One of the things that [the NAACP] worked on with the Human Rights Commission was the open housing ordinance, which was passed. Thomas Mitchell and I, our duty at the time was organizing people to go to city hall to try to get it passed. When we went to city hall to meet with them, we filled city hall. The meeting was taped, hoping, I guess, that people would not come back. But when we went back we carried more people. We had them out on the sidewalks because we had so many people. The ordinance was passed. We had help in that ordinance from people like William Natcher, and even the mayor, Bob Brown, was for it. But the city manager at that time was deadly against it, like the other people in the city. But it was passed anyway, it was passed on the second round.

Selvin Butts, Bowling Green

[The editors of the Lexington newspaper] were for an open housing law and said so. Well, everybody was talking about it: Louisville and even in Frankfort. Suddenly Joe Johnson, who was the county judge and a Republican county judge, who controlled the fiscal court, suddenly just put an open housing law through for Lexington and Fayette County.[12] It was a surprise to everybody, including me.

Don Mills, Lexington

In '71 here we passed this ordinance banning discrimination in the sale or rental of housing. And guess who proposed it? Officials of the City Human Relations Commission. That commission was a very helpful, that was one of the best things we came up with. This biracial commission handled problems of a biracial nature. And relating to this ordinance that would ban discrimination in the sale or rental of housing, let me tell you—I'm quoting from this '71 article—"this would be the first significant civil rights legislation against discrimination ever enacted in Hopkinsville."

Now this was enacted in '71. It wasn't unanimous. The vote was seven to four. So that shows you. We don't have unanimity at all on this, because it was controversial. They said the ordinance was drawn basically with the same provisions as the state open housing law. They copied it, basically.

Ken Litchfield, Hopkinsville

* * *

Once open housing laws were adopted in the state and in cities and counties across the commonwealth, the next task was enforcement. Here Galen Martin describes the development of the legal strategy to do so.

We did not at that stage do much testing at the state Commission on Human Rights. We advertised widely. We publicized the bill, and we encouraged people to file complaints and we aggressively went after those. But we immediately discovered that we weren't getting very good recoveries in our housing cases. Because with the state of the law, we didn't have any—you can't put fines into these things because that becomes repugnant, and you can't get the legislatures to adopt them. And so under the law, you can only get damages for out-of-pocket costs. So we weren't getting any recoveries. And the difference is important as compared with employment. In employment you have lost wages, so if you can recover lost wages, you can get a piece of change. Okay? But you didn't have that in housing. If they had to go and pay three hundred and fifty dollars, as compared with three hundred and twenty-five dollars, you might be able, in the right circumstances, to get that difference, but not otherwise. So whenever it was, I think roughly '72, to remedy that fact, we decided that we had to be able to get damages for embarrassment and humiliation. This was not a well-developed concept in the law. We went back to Georgia [Davis Powers] and we got her to put in this amendment that said they could recover damages for embarrassment and humiliation.

We were riding along real well at getting damages for embarrassment and humiliation. But then we had this case that Judge Meigs decided out of Frankfort. He was kind of a Bourbon. I mean he was from wealthy families, and I think he didn't fully appreciate these things. He and his wife, Sally, were very prominent socially. And that's all right, I'm not knocking that. But he decided this case and said that, "You can't get damages for embarrassment and humiliation," even though the statute was there. He essentially declared that unconstitutional.

So we set out to prove the importance of damages for embarrassment and humiliation. That case was coming on for appeal from the Franklin Circuit to the Court of Appeals. A lot of the reason we went to all this trouble was to build the background and the history for this type of damages. The reason we held the first hearing in Covington was so we could get this extremely prominent psychiatrist out of Cincinnati to just simply come across the river as distinguished from coming to Louisville or somewhere way down here. Come across the river and testify. He was the country's foremost expert on this matter of psychic damage. He had worked a lot on this case out of West Virginia. Offhand, I think it was called Buffalo Creek or something like that, where this dam, this sludge dam at the coal mines broke and killed all these people. He was an expert witness for the people that were trying to recover from the coal mines, the coal mine companies in that action.

It's the whole theory of compensatory damages and restitution. We knew what we were doing. The amazing thing about this is we developed this theory of the law, for damages for embarrassment and humiliation, because we saw the need in housing. But, it's had an even more significant national impact in employment.

Galen Martin, Frankfort

When I came back from Columbus we had a young attorney, and this young attorney goes in and he applies for an apartment in Ashland, the largest housing complex in Ashland, and was turned down primarily because he was an African American. We thought that there were some fair skinned couple of guys who lived there, and they were African American, but they were so fair skinned that this guy never knew that they were African Americans. Being the Director of Equal Opportunity Affairs, this guy came to me. So I go up to the chairman and told the chairman what had happened, and the chairman tells his boss to find them some housing. We found out that the utility, the Kentucky Electric Power Company, was the one who financed the whole project. They were interested in selling electric, you know, electrical appliances, electricity and they were financing projects at that time. Well, once we found out that, it wasn't very difficult for us to integrate. We just called the power company and said, "Tell this guy that he needs to do these kinds of things." So that happened.

In addition to that, the chairman, on his own, took out a full-page ad in the *Ashland Daily Independent*. This ad said that things were changing, that we were wanting to bring in professional African Americans to the Ashland area, and that we would pay for lawyers, whatever were needed, to pursue their rights. We would involve our attorneys, and he went on to say that even if somebody didn't work for us that we would use whatever resource we could to help tear down the vestige of discrimination in housing. He bought a full-page ad in the *Ashland Daily Independent* and had a lot to do with integrating housing.

So when I moved back—I never forget that—I went to look for a house, and a gentleman who had been an employee for Ashland Oil was running a real estate agency. He told this agent to show me an area where no blacks had ever lived. The guy who was standing there with us was flabbergasted that the agent had told him to take me to this area to look for a house. He just said, "Well, don't stand there, either you're going to work for me or you're going to go do something else." So he goes and shows me a house.

Then we had another agency that was, because he did a lot of work with Ashland employees, he was showing around. Then after he would show me a house, he'd go back and call up the families and say, "Now, you know, I'll fix it so you don't have to sell the house if you don't want to sell it to him"—to maintain his status in the community. Well, he goes to one family, and this family called me up. They were so incensed that he had come back and was kind of leading me around by a string. They called me up and said, "Do you know what your real estate agent is doing to you?" I had no idea that this gentleman was calling people up at night and saying you don't have to sell to me unless you wanted to but he had to bring me around because of their relationship with the company.

So once I found out that this was happening, well, I called up the owner of the agency, called him in and said this is what was going on. "I will see to it that you never get another dime's worth of business with Ashland." He apologized and said he wasn't aware of what was going on.

Charles Whitehead, Ashland

Now there were some housing problems here and I was involved in one of those things. I had a good friend, Brenda Stewart, and they went down to get an apartment down here and were told that they were full. Then she came to see me and said, "We think they are discriminating against us. What do you think we ought to do?" Well, I called Galen [Martin] and said, "What do you think we ought to do here?" And he said, "Have you got a white couple who could go and apply for that apartment?" And I said, "Yeah, I think so." I had Phil Summerland and his wife who had just joined the council staff. Now he's a Harvard Master of Theology or something, a good guy. He's from Texas by the way but a good liberal. So they went down and applied for this apartment, and were told that they could have it. So then, a big guy at the Human Rights Commission who was sort of their litigator or lawyer came down and met with the folks. I don't think they got the apartment or even maybe wanted that apartment at that point. It seems to me that the owner immediately sold the apartment building to somebody else, and they became more sensitive to this issue after that.

Loyal Jones, Berea

I think it became an acceptable thing. I don't know of too many instances where there was any overt resistance. There could have been, but if there was then nobody made any challenge. But with the city council passing the Fair Housing Act and with the NAACP being present. . . . Not that I'm saying that there weren't any. In a new development you might see one or two blacks or Negroes in what we call a predominantly white neighborhood. And vice versa, you'll see some whites that live in a black neighborhood. But it hasn't been any mad rush. . . . Now we've had cases where a white starts developing, and maybe it's a part of his development he can't sell for some reason, or there's something around over there that doesn't suit the white purchaser, he'll sell the rest to the black. We've got little spots like that now.

F. E. Whitney, Hopkinsville

Housing, which was passed in '68, was just paper. It had no effect, no meaning in the black community, or for the community as a whole. What really opened up housing in Bowling Green was General Motors, the Corvette plant that came here. That really opened up open housing. The blacks coming out of Saint Louis and Detroit and different areas had been used to a certain quality of living. They had been used to buying wherever they wanted to buy. As they moved in and began to challenge the housing—the realtors here in Bowling Green—the realtors really had to give in, because they could be sued. So, with people coming in from General Motors with expertise and knowledge as to how to shake the realtor, the real estate concerns, then that's the only time you had housing really being integrated in Bowling Green.

Some individuals had quite a few problems moving into white areas, all-white areas. But they moved in and persevered, others moved in. So the community became, after a number of years, adjusted to seeing blacks, maybe one black living in an all-white area.

George Esters, Bowling Green

In Paducah we didn't have a big problem with selling houses in the area. We're pretty much scattered, minorities on the south side, north side, west side, all over but in few numbers. It's just been like that. The majority did live "across the tracks," but we had them kind of scattered around. I only had one incident, it's been a number of years ago—I sold a house to a young couple and as they were moving in—it was on Estes Lane—guys came by in a truck and they were beginning to call them names. They said, "You better get away from here; we're going to be back tonight." It so happened that this young lady had a cousin that was a deer hunter, had all kind of rifles and guns. So she called him and he came up and parked his vehicle near the front yard, got a couple of his rifles out, on his shoulder, walked in the house. And he stayed there; they didn't have no more trouble. Nobody bothered them. But they was just trying to intimidate them. But we didn't—I never had any serious problems. . . .

I've shown houses all over this town and back as far as the '70s. Oh, they would be curious. I'd go with a minority couple in an all-white neighborhood and I'd see curtains go back, you know. Somebody come to the door and peep out the door, but no incidents.

Harold T. Alston Sr., Paducah

Now, another organization that I belonged to was the Human Rights Commission. I was interim chairperson during a time that they needed a director and I served on a couple committees, and one committee in particular was Housing. That was through some personal experiences I had concerning racism. My wife and I tried to rent some property, and that was part of our first awakening that racism was still alive. Most of these we were able to call, just to see if the property was available. Some people were just that bold to say, "Are you black?" on the phone. Of course I wasn't going to deny who or what I was. I would say, "Yes," and sometimes the phone would click there. One place we called, everything was fine, the rent, the accommodations, and everything, but then, when it got to who we were, we said, "Yeah, we're black." They said, "Well, we can't rent to you." I said, "Well, tell me why?" And this lady says, "Well, because I had a black man, and he was very demanding, and so on." And I said, "But you don't know me." "Oh, but no, we can't rent to you."

The one that stands out in my mind, was we went to see some property at the Plum Springs. Everything was fine over the phone, race never did come up. When we pulled in to the place, we were waiting, and the property owner drove up. He looked at us, and we got this unusual stare, as if to say, "You all are black!" Which, my wife and I, we had become accustomed to by this time. This was maybe the third or fourth incident where we had been denied property. At that time, we were talking, and we wanted to see the house, and he wouldn't even show us the house. He said, "You all need to go back into Bowling Green, and find some property there." But, my wife, she's normally a calm person, but this was the straw that broke the camel's back. He said, "Well, I'll rent it to you, but for an extra"—I think it was an extra hundred or seventy-five dollars during the time. And the rent from the place was only going to be a hundred and twenty five, so this was more like two hundred and twenty-five. My wife said, "Before I'll rent it I'll burn the place down." I said, "Oh, honey, don't say that." [*Laughs.*] I had to hold her back, because she was very upset. I said, "No, that's all right." I said, "We'll take care of this, we'll take care of this." "But you're not renting to us because we're black?" And he said, "Yes." He said, "That's the reason why." He said, "But if you all pay the extra amount," he said, "You can."

I went back home, and I was angry and upset. But I was trying to maintain some objectivity. So I started writing down the incident, documenting it. Something in the back of my mind told me here this was, it was at least the fourth situation, and I was tired of being confronted with it. . . . I think Mrs. Denny was the director [of the Human Relations Commission]. I turned in the complaint to her. I got the article out in the newspaper, where it'd advertised for a certain amount, and did all that. And she said, "Well," she said, "We are not equipped to do an investigation or anything here." So she said, "I'm going to forward it on to the State Human Rights Commission." So she did. They sent an investigator out, talked with me, and so on and various other things that went on to investigate the process. In the end, we were allowed to rent the house, if we wanted. At that time we had our first child, and winter was coming on, and not knowing what we were going to face, we said, "No, we didn't want to face the possibility of being out there, with the heat off, or something, and then the landlord not taking care of it." So we didn't feel good about it. So there was this small monetary agreement, and in the meantime found another place to rent. That got me a little more involved in the civil rights process and with the Human Rights Commission.

Ronald Lewis, Bowling Green

Chapter 5

Economic Opportunity

JIM Crow in employment, with its resulting economic inequality between blacks and whites, has been perhaps the harshest, most enduring problem confronting Kentucky's African Americans. Yet this issue also drew relatively fewer dramatic or unified protests, and is least prominent in Kentuckians' shared memory of the civil rights movement. Black Kentuckians faced serious job discrimination in all areas of the economy from the very beginning of the post-emancipation era. As in other former slave states, many African Americans in Kentucky started out as farmers, an occupation with which they were familiar from antebellum plantation life. Yet, according to the 1900 census, in the decades after the Civil War the majority of blacks did not own their own land and instead worked as low-wage laborers for someone else. Poor agricultural conditions, violence, harassment of successful farmers, and hope for a better life elsewhere contributed to the exodus of blacks from rural areas and out of farming.[1]

As Kentucky's African Americans migrated into towns and cities, they continued to find limited job opportunities. Most blacks found themselves employed as unskilled laborers or in service occupations. As George Wright asserts in his history of Kentucky African Americans, all across the smaller communities of the state, "blacks were hired to perform services for whites." Those services included domestic work inside white homes, but also quasi-domestic labor in such positions as waiters, hotel workers, chauffeurs, and barbers, among others. At the turn of the century, a few African Americans worked as clerks and salespeople in white department stores in Lexington. But the hardening of segregation closed off those opportunities, and by the Great Depression such positions were gone and forgotten—so much so that a later generation would remember the "first" black salespeople after World War II.[2]

A relatively small number of African Americans made their living in black-owned businesses or institutions. Following the exhortations of Booker T. Washington and other turn-of-the-century leaders, Kentucky's African Americans believed that black business development would lead to the advancement of the race and to the gradual integration of blacks into American society as equals. The number of black businesses in towns and cities grew throughout the post-Reconstruction period, reaching a high point in the 1920s. By that time, Louisville had developed a black business district, centered on west Walnut Street and anchored by the Mammoth Life Insurance Company, which was on par with African American commercial centers in other major cities. Smaller communities likewise had neighborhoods of concentrated black economic development. The Lexington African American community, according to one list, had at one time twenty-five barbers, eight physicians, three dentists, and enough black-owned shops to constitute a bustling business district. Henderson and Owensboro had similar concentrations of black professionals and entrepreneurs serving their own community. Many of these businesses were short-lived, served a small clientele, and did not survive the Great Depression. Ironically, those that did often suffered and failed after desegregation did away with the need for separate business districts or accommodations.[3]

One vital area of the Kentucky economy that was almost completely closed to blacks was industrial employment. As industry spread across the state, white owners and workers cooperated to keep African Americans out. At the start of the industrial era, for example, the Carrollton newspaper bragged that there were "no colored hands" in any factories in the community. There were some exceptions to this pattern. At the start of the twentieth century, as many as half of all tobacco workers were black, and they joined the Tobacco Workers International Union with their fellow white workers. Over time, however, both the union and the workplace became increasingly segregated. As machines were introduced, whites became operators and blacks were relegated to manual labor with little opportunity for advancement. In the union, workers separated into white and black locals. Similarly, blacks were pivotal but limited in Kentucky's coal industry. To a great extent they were recruited by owners who hoped to keep the workforce divided and thus docile. As the mines mechanized, the tobacco pattern repeated itself, with blacks being forced into unskilled positions, kept out of supervisory roles, and eventually pushed out altogether as machines lessened the need for labor. As a result, while 23.7 percent of miners were black in 1900, the proportion dropped to 13.5 in 1930, to 10 percent in 1940, and it continued to decline. By the World War II era, when industry boomed in the state, a survey by the Urban League showed employers even in the commonwealth's largest city still resistant to the idea of hiring blacks in industry above the level of custodial or menial labor.[4]

As was the case with other elements of Jim Crow, the first efforts to fight for economic opportunity came from individuals. African Americans demanded equal treatment from their white employers and fought their way into jobs and up economic ladders through perseverance and hard work. Occasionally, they would meet a sympathetic employer who would see the value of economic opportunity and make a change. But more often, it took organized action by civil rights organizations, unions, or ad hoc coalitions to push doors open. The roots of the modern campaign for equal economic opportunity were in the post–World War II era. At that time the economy was expanding and blacks wanted a bigger piece of the pie. Linking wartime rhetoric against fascism to American racism, civil rights advocates focused on jobs for returning veterans. After a failed effort to get local, state, or national permanent fair employment practices legislation, the NAACP and Urban League established industrial relations committees and began to pressure individual employers. New organizations such as the Negro Labor Council joined them. In Louisville the Farm Equipment Workers (FE) at the International Harvester plant pioneered truly biracial unionism, pushing for the end of both discrimination and segregation in the shop, and campaigning against Jim Crow in the community. These efforts focused on industry, and while there were some successes in getting promises of equal treatment, they did not change the general practice of most employers. Civil rights groups did have more, though still limited, success in gaining access to city jobs.[5]

As the civil rights movement arose in Kentucky, with pickets in small and large communities against segregation in public accommodations, employment discrimination drew the attention of movement organizers. Demonstrations by the NAACP and CORE followed a regional pattern of protesting not only segregation of customers by downtown department stores and restaurants, but the lack of black employees there as well. As Martin Luther King Jr. declared in Birmingham and at the March on Washington in 1963, the goal of the movement was both desegregation *and* jobs. Beginning in 1964, Lyndon Johnson's War on Poverty gave new energy to civil rights activists to campaign for better jobs. Though not specifically a civil rights program, nor aimed solely at African Americans, the War on Poverty was closely related to the struggle against economic inequality. The civil rights movement had drawn the nation's attention to the persistent problem of poverty. The language of community empowerment that was so integral to the rising black power movement now informed the ideology of the fight against poverty. And more specifically, many of the people and organizations that led the War on Poverty programs had their roots in the civil rights movement. The story of War on Poverty organizing in Kentucky, then, sheds light on how communities went beyond the more limited goal of guaranteeing job opportunity to tackle the intractable, systemic problems of poverty.[6]

Some activists worked at a grassroots level to organize poor communities, while others focused on securing laws against employment discrimination. The first statewide success came in 1960 when Governor Bert Combs pushed the legislature to adopt a ban on job discrimination in state merit jobs. At the same time, the state created the Kentucky Commission on Human Rights to "discourage discrimination." The lack of legislation against most forms of such discrimination kept the commission relatively powerless, however. In 1963, as pressure grew across the region and in Washington for antidiscrimination measures, Combs issued a "Code of Fair Practice," which banned discrimination not only in state jobs but in businesses contracting with the state. The code was continued by the next two governors, Ned Breathitt and Louie Nunn. Although it was effective against some discrimination, the code did not apply to the vast majority of African Americans because they were employed in the private sector.

The first major push for statewide civil rights legislation, which failed in 1964, would have covered both accommodations and employment. When the federal Civil Rights Act passed, however, and inspired Kentucky's civil rights leaders to try again in the 1966 legislative session, they succeeded in securing the passage of the Kentucky Civil Rights Act, prohibiting discrimination not only in public facilities but also in employment in businesses with eight or more employees [see chapter 3].[7]

The gap between policy and practice persisted, just as it had with open housing. The existence of a state law outlawing discrimination in employment did not end the Jim Crow practices that perpetuated economic inequality in Kentucky. Enforcement of the state law lay in the hands of the Kentucky Commission on Human Rights, which began investigating complaints almost immediately. In the first five years, the commission heard 185 employment cases.[8] Kentucky citizens also used a variety of other creative approaches for securing equal employment opportunity. Local activists launched boycotts aimed at individual employers. Black workers' organizations pressured companies to hire or promote African American employees. Communities recruited help from civil rights leaders to bring attention to particular problems. Local governments developed their own affirmative action policies intended to redress the many generations of discrimination. Yet it remained largely up to individuals confronting discrimination in employment to stand up and challenge bosses' policies, now with some support from local, state, and national laws.[9]

Recalling the fight for equal economic opportunity, Kentuckians tell stories of individual as well as collective struggles here, connecting 1960s-era employment activism to campaigns against poverty, and to battles still ongoing. This chapter begins with narratives of personal experiences with job discrimination. It moves then to stories about how individuals, black and white, and some organizations took action against discrimination. Included here are a number of stories about War on Poverty agencies or community organization strategies. What is mostly missing from the oral histories are stories of efforts to secure local or state laws to prohibit job discrimination. That omission is perhaps because such laws were not the result of distinct protest campaigns but often became part of statutes against segregation in public accommodations, which had been the subject of more sustained, dramatic, and focused demonstrations. The chapter ends with narratives of efforts to make anti-job-discrimination policies more than just pieces of paper. As these last commentaries make clear, the battle for economic equality in Kentucky is far from complete.

Experiences of Discrimination

The first narratives in this chapter describe general conditions African Americans faced in industry and business across the commonwealth.

* * *

The mines hadn't gotten fully mechanized at the time, they were just about to revert from "a strong back and a weak mind" to machinery. The mine we went to, it was fully mechanized. As time moved on and the mechanization increased in the coalfield, well, that pushed the black man back further, finally pushed him just about all the way out. When I first went into the mine, I went into a mule mine, where

I didn't stay but two weeks. The only white man you saw underground was the mine foreman, the entry foreman, and the man that rode the rope that's pulling the coal. All the rest of them under there were black men. You didn't see no more [white men] because they didn't want that kind of work.

David Pettie, Earlington

I think that blacks didn't have choice jobs, they had the lesser. If you had a job at the post office, a job at the railroad shops, those were the two choice jobs. Now when they built the atomic plant here, they called it KOW [Kentucky Ordnance Works] or something like that. But anyway, if you had a job there, period, whether you had a shovel in your hand or were a janitor or whatever you were—there was discrimination there—whatever you did there, you were going to bring home a pretty good paycheck. You were considered, in the black community, "Well, he's got a job at KOW."

At one time, you know, Paducah was a boom town; it was flourishing with money, and money was floating around. But blacks never did get their share of good jobs. The NAACP had to fight to get blacks on the job. Later, after we got the job, the fight became to get them in every aspect of the job market. But at that time, it was just getting into the door.

Gladman Humbles, Paducah

As I assess economic opportunity, I see it from the eye of a businessman because that was what I pursued. The barriers of finance, capital, location were all prohibiting factors for most aspiring black businessmen. If you conducted a service business that catered to blacks only, there was a fairly decent chance to make a profit. But, if you attempted to cater to the mainstream, as it's called, [there were] prohibiting factors such as location, they would not lease a building to a black person; transportation, which is another difficult one because even though there was no segregation on the buses, there were restrictions as to where the buses ran, people couldn't get to you. Of course there were taxis, but that was rather prohibitive to pay a taxi to take you to a particular store even if you could locate one. So there were a lot of prohibitions and barriers that were not artificial but real that deterred one from seeking to develop and pursue a profitable business. Out of the types of industry such as manufacturing or wholesaling or retailing, blacks stood the best opportunity or chance of succeeding in the retail end despite all the barriers. But in the wholesale end that was practically unheard of, even today, in the wholesale end of business operations. I know of practically no blacks because that's a distribution system and you have to have a connection with the manufacturer. And the manufacturer says, well, I would like for you to wholesale my goods but can you reach everybody in the market? Then you have to say, well, there are some whites that aren't going to buy it because of my color. So that's a limitation.

Jerome Hutchinson Sr., Louisville

* * *

The following narratives describe individual experiences with employment discrimination. Although the focus of these stories is on the discrimination, some narrators also allude to their efforts to stand up for themselves and others to employers or potential employers.

I had been searching for a job and [Berea] college had attempted to help me. I was accepted at one job. It was in the Appalachian area though. It was in a very small community and I was to live in with a family. Hearing the name of the place, and knowing the concentration of black people, I could say, I bet the family I am to stay with is not a black family, which wasn't a problem for me. I chose to call the family and say, "I'm to stay at your home. I need to know if it makes any difference to you that I'm black." It made both a difference to them and the people hiring me, because they had assumed that all students were white. So I always regretted telling them that. I wish I had appeared without having said that. I was told not to bother to appear.

Jessie Zander, Berea

I wanted to be an artist and everybody said no. But I was always a very determined person. I prepared myself to do that. I used all the methods to go and get the job. They didn't say no, we don't hire black artists. I read enough to know you could get a job as an apprentice. I kept getting shafted and getting the run-around. But it made me better each time because they would give me polite criticism. "Well, you can't do this." So I learned to do it. I had taken a correspondence course. "Well, you need to take some courses." So I got some courses in town. I came to the Arts Association. Then the last guy said, "Well, do you have a degree?" I said no. "Well, you need a degree." I realize now that all of those things were designed to stop me. They'd say, well, he'll go and he won't come back.

I went to a place down on Sixth Street. It was a print shop. The guy was delighted with my work. It was a big printing place. He said, "Man, I need somebody right away. If you can do this you've got the job." So I sat in there all afternoon, probably from about 12:00 on. I sat there and worked all day and had a job. I went home, because by that time I was married, had one child. So I had a job. But the next day I went back he said, "I'm sorry, I can't keep you." I said what's the problem? He said, "Well, the guys in the shop refuse to work in the shop where a Negro has a professional job up in the front office. They said you find a white artist or we are going to leave." So they forced him.

Robert Douglass, Louisville

I was the first black on the Paducah Fire Department. I was like the fly in the milk. The fire department was an all-white outfit. It had been kind of a political plum for whites and here I come on the scene. In fact, there were only two or three people that spoke to me for a long time. I slept with one eye open. We slept dormitory style and they had a special bed for me. We worked twenty-four hours on and forty-eight off. We had three crews. So somebody had to sleep on somebody else's dirty linen. But for me, they had this special bed. I had my own linen so no one slept in my bed. That was fine with me.

When I first went there, they were having union meetings and they told the chief they didn't want me eating with them. I've never wanted to eat with anyone that didn't want me to eat with them. That's kind of a private matter. So my wife was bringing my meals. So one day I was getting transferred to another station and the assistant chief said, "We've all decided we're going to start treating you like a man. We want you to come eat with us and be one of the guys." I was a bit reluctant to go but I went. He sat at the table and he started telling [anti-] black jokes in a very derogatory manner. One of the guys came down and apologized for him. So when I made assistant chief, and we had privileges of coming home to eat, I came home. Then they started teasing me about how I thought I was too good to eat with them. [*Laughs.*] So it was kind of a no-win situation.

Gladman Humbles, Paducah

I was in insurance and I was doing pretty good. I was earning a better-than-average income. But I had to travel a lot. My brother-in-law had applied for a job and got a job at the post office. He was encouraging me to come on down and get a job since I wanted to quit traveling so much. I had a family, I'd been in service. I went to Ohio to get a job out at Wright-Patterson Air Base and I was qualified for a job there and just had to wait for my turn though. So he said, "Why don't you just get a job at the post office?" I said, "Well, I may go down and talk to them."

By this time, I've advanced to district manager of the insurance company. So I always felt comfortable with a shirt and tie on because I'd worn it so much. So when I went down to talk to the postmaster about a job, I had on a suit, shirt and tie. This didn't sit too well with him. He'd been accustomed to hiring minorities that looked more like they were working people. He told me, "I don't think you want a job down here." I said, "Sure, I do." He'd looked at my application. He said, "We don't pay as much money as you're earning." I said, "There's other considerations too. I have to do a lot of traveling. I want to stay at home. I think I'd like it down here. The pay, I think, will be all right." He discouraged me from taking the test. I took the test anyway. I passed the test but I couldn't get hired.

I left insurance and went to work as a carpenter because I could get in a carpenter local. I couldn't get in at an electrician local. So we got rained out one day. I had on boots and muddy overalls. I drug all that mud in [the post office]. I knocked on the door, and he let me in. He looked at me one time and he said, "Well," he said, "We may have something for you." [*Laughs.*] "But we don't have a carrier's desk. We don't have any openings for clerk/carrier, but we do have an opening for mail handler. Now if you want to take a mail handler's position, we'll let you have that, and then when a clerk/carrier job comes open, you can have that." Now, remember I passed the clerk/carrier test. So I said, "Yeah, I'll take that."

It was temporary employment—I knew that. I started in about the fifteenth of December. I had to leave my job that I had working as a carpenter. I was making much more money, but I knew that was temporary. It wasn't going to last and I needed something more stable. So I went to work there as a mail handler. The man just lied to me. He said, "We're going to get an opening pretty soon." He didn't know that young men talk. The white fellows that I worked with, they had taken the test and failed it but they were hired anyway as a clerk/carrier. I passed the test and I couldn't get a job as a clerk/carrier. I didn't tell them what had happened to me. They just talked. But I knew what had happened. Well, the postmaster, who was white—a very fine person, fair person—we were talking and I told him what had happened to me and I told him what I was going to do about it. I was going to [the] fair employment officer in Cincinnati. So he said, "Oh, you might not have to do that." So the next day—after I told him I was going up there—the next day the postmaster came by and said, "We got an opening." [*Laughs.*] But he said, "I wouldn't advise you to take it though." He said, "You get all the time you want now, but if you take that position that's a carrier." I didn't want to be a carrier because I'd never worked outside. I worked on the inside. "We don't have any clerk jobs open but carrier job." He said, "The weather is very nasty here. You'll be working out in all kinds of weather. In here, you're where it's nice and dry." He just discouraged me. He said, "I know you've got a family and right now you're getting forty hours a week. But you may be getting twenty hours or twenty-two hours a week. I don't know if that will be enough to take care of your family. But you think about it. If you want it, we can give it to you." So I talked to my supervisor, a person I had known because this person had traded at the grocery store I worked at when I was a kid. I knew him fairly well. He told me, "Oh, don't pay no attention to him." He said, "You go ahead and take the job." He said, "You'll get plenty of time." To make it brief, I told him I would accept it. I accepted the job as a carrier and I worked for the post office for twenty-seven years. I retired in 1979.

Later, I was a civil service examiner. I got the job as examiner—giving tests, all kinds of tests, civil service tests. I held that job about three years, and the job was abolished. So I had to revert back to carrier. I tell you, I've had so many problems, you wouldn't believe it. At the time I took the test for the civil service examiner, they gave it to a white person. Of course, they had a less[er] score than I had. I wrote to the fair employment officer in Cincinnati, and I really didn't want to pursue it because I don't like disappointments. I said, "I'm just going to prepare to leave." I was going to leave, but I got a family. I can't just walk away, you know. I got to have something to do. But the fair employment officer came down and he wasn't very helpful. And he was black. But after he talked to the postmaster, he left without even talking to me anymore. I had that happen on two occasions.

Harold Alston, Paducah

When I went to work for the railroad, we reported to work in the same building, but the whites were on one side of the building, in a small square building with a wall partition. They were on one side of the building reporting to work, and we were on the other side of the partition. We would go out on the same yard and do the same work. Terrible, terrible. . . . In the department that I worked in, they literally had two rosters of employees. They were listed on that roster by seniority. They had one roster that all the blacks were listed on and another roster that all the whites were listed on. The railroad was very, very segregated. African Americans did not get opportunities for jobs that paid higher levels of pay. For example, the railroad had a lot of craft workers, they had machinists, they had boiler makers, they had blacksmiths, they had pipe fitters, they had locomotive engineers. They had a big office in Paducah. The only black person in that building was doing the cleaning work, while they had a large office staff there. People doing just basic clerical work, but we had no opportunities for any of that. And the craft work, like machinist, boiler maker, blacksmith, pipe fitter, these kinds of jobs young white males would come to work for the railroad, and they would on many, many occasions, depending upon the need, assign them as apprentice tradesmen. They were in the process of learning to become a machinist, in the process of learning to be a blacksmith, in the process of learning to become a boiler maker, in the process of learning to become whatever type of skilled trade that required a period of training. Black employees were not assigned to these apprentice positions. Apprentice boiler maker, apprentice machinist, apprentice blacksmith, whatever that craft trade, they were not given those assignments.

[That caused] the most glaring form of inequity. The white employee, a young man, would be assigned to a machinist apprentice. He would ultimately become a journeyman machinist, a journeyman blacksmith, a journeyman boiler maker, and his salary would rise accordingly. He was able to support his family at a higher standard of living. He was able to send his sons and his daughters to college. The African American never reached that level with the railroad. The white employees were able to raise the standard of living for their families, give their children educational opportunities, and therefore place them in a higher level of achievement and in a position to subsequently support their families. It was passed from one generation to another. Because John's son was able to go to Paducah Community College, and Joe's—who's black—son couldn't go, when John's son finished two years, and wanted to go to Murray or University of Kentucky or whatever college, his dad had the money to send him, because his dad drew more money from the railroad because he had a better job that Joe's dad didn't have. Not only did Joe's son experience the segregation of society in Paducah's schools, he couldn't even afford to go beyond Paducah.

Robert Coleman, Paducah

I went to all the places like IBM and Xerox and places like that and I had a satchel full of qualifications and everything else. But the reality then was that Xerox and IBM and even GE were not hiring African Americans! In other words, you'd go in and they'd give you the interview and then they'd tell you, "We'll give you a call." And you never got the call. They were taking whites and they were sending them on to schools somewhere, and I had more training than they did. So I started drawing unemployment and put in applications everywhere. They even cut my unemployment off and said I wasn't actively seeking employment. I challenged them because I said I seek employment where they're hiring. I think it was better off when they used to advertise "for white only" on jobs. That had stopped, but the reality of it is that they were still doing the same thing. It would have been better to say white-only, then it would have kept us from even going there and wasting your time and people smiling in your face, but they wouldn't give you a job. As a last resort I took the exam for the fire department and the police department. I passed both of those and I even took the test for radio dispatcher or something. I was ready to go back in the service because I just couldn't get employment. Then they called me with the police thing. But even then, to show you about the racism, I think I had made seventh or ninth highest score of anybody that took the civil service exam. So I was supposed to get hired anyway. It wasn't no case of where you're doing something special for me as a black person. But I still would not have been hired had it not been for Dr. Johnson, who was a black dentist who was a good friend of my parents who knew the safety director at that time. He went to his friend and more or less said, "Well, he's a good boy, can you all hire him?" That's the reality of how I got hired even though I should have been hired anyway.

I got hired as a police officer in 1961. I went into the police academy and at that time there was just two of us in the class, two African Americans. Historically there had never been more than one or two or none, most of the time there were none in the recruit class. That was the history even after I got in there until we started to initiate lawsuits to change that. I went through the police academy like I say. I did well in the police academy and graduated from the police academy. Again I was faced with the same kind of racism. Even though I had been to college, I had done well, I had scored well, and did well in the police academy, when I came out of the police academy I had to walk a beat. Eleven at night to seven in the morning, ten below zero, the elements, and if you can imagine that's thunder, lightning, snow, whatever it was. I had to walk and all of us had to walk because we were African Americans. They didn't let blacks ride in the police cars at that time. Here you had all the training as a police officer but then you didn't get to operate as a police officer because you had to walk.

Now what I was able to do is to, and like we've always been able to do, is to take something that you considered a negative [and make it] a positive. It caused me to really know the people that you were working with, because we had to depend on the people. I walked in an area from Sixth Street west to Fourteenth Street, which was the area where we had black police officers. In that area we had the good people and the bad people. We learned the good people from the bad. We had to rely on the people to help us because we didn't have any radios, we didn't have any call-in boxes. We had to call in by phone. I've been in the situation where I would be in an alley and have five people I locked up for gambling or whatever it was. I've handcuffed two of them together and then I'm bluffing the other three and telling them what I'm going to do if you try to run and stuff like that—I wasn't going to do none of that stuff I was telling them. I would be there and have to wait until somebody walked through the alley and then I asked them to call the police! That's the kind of situation we were in. It's just like we wasn't the real police. They would call and then we'd wait until the white police officer would come with the wagon or with the police car to put the prisoners in their car. But it caused us to be better police officers because we never were disconnected from the community.

I was one of the first to ride in the police car and to ride in the integrated police car with a white partner. I was asked if I wanted to work, I think it was about '68, in homicide. There was a white lieutenant, James Garrett, who observed how I worked as a beat officer. They would come out to investigate the murders and stuff. We'd find bodies sometime in garages or whatever it was like that. He was impressed by the kind of job I did so he asked me if I would be interested in working up in homicide. That's when I went to the Southern Police Institute and got all of the training that other blacks had not. They hadn't been through that process. So I graduated from the Southern Police Institute Homicide Investigation School there and I worked there in homicide I think for about four years. I also graduated from the National Crime Prevention Institute, which is out there at Shelby Campus out there. Before I went to homicide I was assigned to the two-wheel motorcycle. I was the first black assigned to that.

Shelby Lanier, Louisville

Fighting Job Discrimination

The following section contains voices of those who fought job discrimination alone or collectively, including those of white employers who decided to go against the grain.

* * *

There were people in the neighborhood who were getting calls from my father's job asking if he was white or black, white or colored they called it at that time. They would say, we don't know, you'd have to call their home and find out. Of course they never called. There was a problem there because for five years they thought my father was white and they had given him "a white man's job." But one of the workers saw him one day with a car full of little colored children and went back and told it. They got together and said they were not going to work with him any longer because he had this colored family. So the president of the company—that's American Radiator and Standard Sanitary—called them together and he said, "I understand there's a rumor going around that some of you don't want to work with Darren Montgomery. Those who don't want to work with him, you stand over here. But I want to tell you if you stand over here you can pick up your paycheck today. Those who are willing to work with him, you can stand on the other side." He worked there forty-two years and never had any more problems after that. I use that very often because if a leader stands up and makes a decision, the workers, the constituents will follow whatever the leader says, whether it's the president of a company, president of a institution, the president of a country or wherever. You set the tone. Very often I think about governors of this state, who could have done a lot more than they did if they had not been worried about getting re-elected.

Georgia Davis Powers, Louisville

People could get jobs at Fort Campbell. Our people were working here on farms and as maids and chauffeurs. They found they could get a job at Fort Campbell. There was a little protest from some of the people in the county that went to the general and talked to him about hiring all of their blacks down there, and they were having a hard time. He told them, "Well, you pay them more money and that wouldn't happen." Some did that who wanted to keep the black help, because they figured that was the only way they were going to get their maids and their cooks and their chauffeurs. They'd have to pay them. I think that's the impact that Fort Campbell had on the community.

F. E. Whitney, Hopkinsville

* * *

Here Joe Graves, a white businessman from Lexington, describes how he integrated his own family store and thereby put pressure on other employers to do the same.

My family had a clothing store here with the Cox family. It was called Graves-Cox and Company. It was a fine men's specialty store and it was started by my grandfather and his partner. When I got there after graduating from Transylvania in 1952, we had some black people working there. But they weren't working as salespeople. There were no black salespeople in Kentucky in conventional retail stores. We had an exceptional man there. One day he told me that he was going to have to leave and go to work for the post office because they had good opportunities for black people. I was just devastated. So the next day I talked to my father and his partner and I said, "You know, we're about to lose this man." They were just thunderstruck because he just was so exceptional. So we decided in 1957 to promote him to salesman. I'm sure he was the first black salesman in Kentucky in a major retail store. His name was Ferdinand Garner.

I remember the conversation when my father and his partner and I were talking. Father's partner, Leonard Cox, said, "Well, do you think we ought to ask the other salesmen how they would feel about this change, because it is quite a change." I remember suggesting to him that we didn't ask our salesmen when we promoted white people, and it would be better [*laughs*] not to ask them because we would surely get some who wouldn't like it. So we just announced the promotion, and within six months, he was our third leading salesman. The word really got out. We already had a lot of black customers because we treated people well. But he not only was extremely well received by the black community, but the publisher of the newspaper at that time, Fred Wachs, who was a very conservative person in terms of race relations, he just was delighted to have Ferdinand wait on him. He just was such an excellent person.

We probably did lose some business. There're always wins and losses in every change. But it made me very proud of our organization. I can remember that we had some other really qualified black people, and we started also promoting them into sales positions, where they could make more money. I had two men come to see me who ran a department store here in Lexington. They were people I'd known all my life, went to the same church. They said, "Joe, we just wanted to tell you that we are kind of unhappy with what you're doing because it's upsetting our employees. We've got some black employees and we're fond of them, and they do a good job. But they're not qualified to be salespeople. They've heard that your store is promoting people to commission situations, and they expect us to do it. And they just are not up to it." So I say, "Well, that's an interesting situation." I said, "I was in your store a couple of weeks ago and I was on the elevator, and you have an elevator operator there. She did a terrific job of explaining to the people on the elevator what merchandise is on each floor as she went up. She was friendly and outgoing and she's a great ambassador for your store. Now you say you don't have anybody who's qualified to be promoted to commissioned salespeople. We have a position open on the third floor in the boys' department, and I'd like to get your permission to talk to her because I could put her in a situation where she could make a lot more money than running an elevator. And we would love to have her because she's just the kind of person I would want." They kind of looked at each other and they said, "Well, we hadn't thought about her." I said, "Well, I'd like your permission to talk to her." That was about the end of that conversation. We continued to be friends, and I think she was promoted by them. But you know, you got a little of that kind of feedback.

Joe Graves, Lexington

My father grew up during the depression and he was thought by some people to be highly intelligent. He basically as a young man made his own money. . . . He joined the labor union movement. It was sort of a radical movement in the late '40s and the early '50s. When International Harvester came, they actually were probably the first persons— and this is really in the South—to effectively implement integration. The [union leaders] convinced the white workers here in Louisville not to accept a higher wage than the black workers. The argument that they had was that the bosses were dividing them and that they had what they called the southern differential, which was that they paid workers in the North greater than they paid workers in the South.

Sterling Neal Jr., Louisville

They had this line, the FE [Harvester union] did, that black and white workers had to unite because that's the only way they could win. This was in the interest of white workers just like it was to the black workers. They preached it all the time. They really did, the organizers that would come. So they created a different atmosphere in that union hall . . . where if you were white and you came in there, you were accepted if you weren't biased. That was the atmosphere. That was what you were supposed to do. Whereas out in the street, out in the world, out in the white world, you were accepted if you were antiblack. It makes all the difference in the world in the way people behave. So what the FE organizers preached constantly was the self-interest of the white workers, that we had to have black/white unity. They always bragged that the International Harvester plant had the hiighest wages in the South. They said the reason they had it was we wouldn't let them divide us by race. That's what has kept us down and all that. So it was in the self-interest of the white workers.

I remember vividly one night some black worker had been fired for no good reason. So they were going to walk out the next day for that department to support him. I remember this white guy got up and said, "This just isn't fair. We're not going to put up with it." He didn't talk about this isn't in my self-interest. It's not fair. Which has led me to believe—I think it is in the self-interest of white workers—but I don't think it's the only appeal. I think there's a sense of fairness in people if you can appeal to it. Organized labor knows inherently that if you're going to be strong you got to be fair. That you're not going to have a strong union if there's favoritism for this person or favoritism for that. That destroys you. It's a sense of fairness but also this is a way we can fight.

Anne Braden, Louisville

[After the public accommodations ordinances] young people began to work on employment opportunities. Stewart's had the big store downtown then and they realized that Stewart's didn't have any clerks who were black. They felt that if blacks were buying products there, there should be blacks employed in positions other than janitor, elevator operators. And so they did picket that.

Abby Marlatt, Lexington

We decided that our first project for community involvement was to get clerks in the neighborhood groceries. The NAACP took that on as our main project. The young lady [Julia Lewis] who became president of CORE was also a member of the NAACP, so she and I kind of worked together. There were three target groceries, because they had to depend totally on the black population for their existence. We sat here in the middle of this floor and made posters and things that night, and it rained the Saturday that we were going to do this. I said, "Well, let's just cancel it." So we started calling some of the people who were planning on walking the picket line. They said no, we are all ready for it. "Can't we put some paper or something over the signs and try to save them?" I said, "If you're willing to march in the rain, I'm willing to march in the rain." So our first day of picketing was in a hard, hard rain. But everybody stayed all day long. When it was their time to relieve us, they showed up.

It took quite longer than I would have thought that it would take for us to get them to change. We had to do that for about three Saturdays. One reason was because the people still went in, crossed our picket lines. Some of the ministers came to the groceries and told the owners that they would put a stop to that. One owner ran out, "Oh, you're not supposed to be here." I said, "What do you mean we're not supposed to be here. We're on the sidewalk." "But Reverend Jackson told us that he would take care of it." I said, "He doesn't even belong to our group, so he can't make those decisions for us." So that's how we found out that the ministers were going behind our backs doing this. It disturbed quite a few of them.

But anyway, we were successful. We had talked to the store managers before we did any picketing, asked if they would hire. Many of them said, "Well, we hire them." Of course, yes, they hired them to clean the floors and had one young man working at the vegetable and fruit counter, which was fine. But we want somebody to be on that cash register as well.

Audrey Grevious, Lexington

The War on Poverty

While many black—and white—Kentuckians focused on the issue of equality in employment, some activists turned to a broader attack, envisioning an end to poverty and linking antipoverty efforts with the civil rights struggle. The War on Poverty began in 1964 with the Economic Opportunity Act, which created and funded a wide variety of programs and established the Office of Economic Opportunity. Local governments and organizations received grants from the OEO to run their own initiatives, such as the Model Neighborhood Employment Service described below. The most creative part of the War on Poverty, and the component most closely allied with the civil rights movement, was the Community Action Projects. Under the CAPs, community organizations received contracts to hire organizers who would then work in poor communities to identify and begin to address problems on a grassroots level. These projects brought together civil rights and antipoverty activists in community work.

* * *

So we had a program that I first got hired [in] that was a combination state government/model cities program. It was called the Model Neighborhood Employment Service. I was on the ground floor of getting that started. It was right down on Second and State Street. It's still in Bowling Green. The idea for Model Cities was to find folk, train them, do some job development for them, and work primarily in the black community. Model Cities was a federally funded program. For about two years, it ran real well. We had an outreach program. We brought people in. We tested them. After testing them we sent them

to vocational schools or did direct job development. We worked with
the Youth Service Bureau. I was hired by the state as what would have
been an employment counselor, so that is where my salary came from.
But the operation of the program came through Model Cities. When
Model Cities funds started to dry up, then a lot of folk were pretty
angry. You talk about wanting to do something for the people. Here
we are doing it. But it means very little.

Don Offutt, Bowling Green

I had some theories about how I was going to organize the community. I realized all the great movements are grassroots. You need the
masses to make the changes, but the masses don't have time to organize themselves. The masses understand what they're up against, but
they don't understand it collectively. So what all the great movements
have done is they brought the masses together and gave them that collective consciousness. Made them aware of that collective consciousness about whatever their problems are. Because they all suffered from
them. They're all poor.

The idea was to have a community organizer and three resident
people. Hire one over in the Southwick and one in Cotter Homes. So I
got the two ladies who were most vocal over there. They hired me and
I hired my helpers. Then I trained them. What we did was go door to
door with a number of questions. How do you feel about so and so?
Then you ask them, would you come and meet with the group? You
find somebody who will have it at their house. In any block only one
or two would want to do it. But the others will come. So you organize
them around what they see as their most basic needs. If it's a sewer,
how do you go about finding out whose responsibility it is. You write
those people, then you go visit them. Then you have people to call.
They don't do anything. Then you have the right to demonstrate. You
do it that way because then no one can accuse you of being provocative. You have the masses, you have the large community on your side
because you have exhausted all of the steps that a reasonable person
would pursue, and you've shown that the people who are leaders aren't
reasonable. Once you do that, you publicize it, politicize it, you talk
about it. Then you demonstrate. You talk about all the things you've
done. I had this area down here the most organized.

When you're organizing, the first thing you do is you're pleasant.
How are you doing? And you always ask them, well, who else you

think might be interested? Have you talked with anyone else? Have meetings talking about some of the problems. How do you feel about this? How do you feel about the government? Whatever it is. It will be no problem to politicize this, because none of the people in that area have been treated correct. The reason why they would be involved in it is because they have been left out. They didn't leave themselves out. Someone pushed them out. Blacks have been left out and excluded and set aside from people in society. What we did over there was the Park Duvalle Center—that was a result of my organizing. The first thing I did was to force public housing to give us an apartment so we could help these people over here. I realized that there are family problems. So we got somebody from the Children and Family Agency to come in. Then some of the employment people to come down. You couldn't get a doctor to come down so we had visiting nurses. We established the visiting nurse concept and the employment people came out and the women came over. We'd put out the information, if you have a community problem, you could come in. The idea of the organization was to help people help themselves. You got to help them help themselves. I had to convince those agencies to come down. I had to say, either give me the funds to get them on the bus to get them there or give me funds to pay her babysitter because she can't take the babies with her to see you. Or else, let me have a place where I can bring someone in. So I went to the agencies and said, look, this is what we're facing down there. Would you be willing to come down one day? So you can convince people and you can convince the agencies. So we did that.

Robert Douglass, Louisville

I was approached by the head of the Community Action Commission staff person, who asked me, "Father, can you work full time in this? We're going into a new program year and we're going to have coordinators of all these areas: Russell, Manley, Portland, so forth, and you would make a good leader of one of the areas." So I go to the bishop. By then I was turned on. Oh, yeah, this is going to fulfill a dream of working in the poverty program, using my skills to serve maybe the downtrodden, the poor. What was going on behind the scenes in church circles and with pastors was, why don't we get into some positive action? Why don't we turn this around? Why don't we address the issues of poverty and housing, why don't we organize the neighborhoods? Across the country I later found out there were probably fifty priests that did this. I was hearing about bishops allowing the priests to jump into a new work, a new ministry other than teaching, other than pastoring a church. They could get into this and make a difference. So I said yes. They interviewed me and very quickly said, "You're coordinator for Russell area and there's going to be seven other coordinators and you're going to form a group and there are going to be community organizers. We're going to teach you community organization." The concept in the beginning was to be with the community, develop leaders.

So the issue that started coming was jobs. So we pressed to get a job coordinator in our office three days a week. People would come in off the streets and apply for jobs and this helped them, rather than going downtown to the main office. There was a need for basic skills like typing, so one of the teachers at Trinity would come down nighttime and we got some typewriters and just started teaching people how to type and write and do English, basic skills.

A lot of these folks that I worked with in the War on Poverty moved into the existing establishment. The skills and development that they experienced or learned, they began to use in other agencies. A number of them got a degree, started working on different degrees. Some of them became teachers. Some of them became members of the school board staff, the central office staff. Some of them got into banking or their own private business. Quite a few, as in the white world, got interested in politics, and I still hear names every once in a while of somebody running for alderman or alderwoman that started way back in this War on Poverty. The War on Poverty is always condemned, pretty much. It was a waste of time, a waste of money. But it's hard to measure what Ms. So-and-So learned or Mary learned or Yawanda. What did she learn or why did she change? It's hard to say. Maybe it was because they were in the Neighborhood Youth Corps. Maybe it was because of that crazy job she had working for Parks and Recreation in the summer of 1969, that motivated her to think of her own education. She didn't want to be in that position for the rest of her life. A number of folks, I know, it made a difference in their life, even though they were only in it a short time. I think the biggest thing was awareness was raised. The whole idea of self-determination was taught and learned in this experience called the War on Poverty.

Tony Heitzman, Louisville

Enforcing Nondiscrimination

In the mid-1960s, the pressure from civil rights organizations for policies banning economic discrimination bore fruit. Governor Bert Combs's fair employment codes in 1960 and 1963 opened some doors in state government. More significantly, however, the federal Civil Rights Act of 1964 made employment discrimination by private businesses illegal. The Kentucky legislature followed suit two years later, including employment in the state civil rights law. Yet even after Kentucky's Civil Rights Act outlawed employment discrimination and charged the Kentucky Commission on Human Rights with enforcement, African Americans had to continue to push as individuals and in organizations against the barriers to full opportunity. Some used the new avenues of enforcement available on a state and national level, others used familiar and more direct protest strategies. As many of the following stories attest, the success of these efforts was partial.

* * *

I went to work at LG&E August 10, 1960, as a laborer at the Cane Run power plant. Later I transferred up to Seventh and Ormsby in the storage department of LG&E as a janitor. So as time went along we was doing both janitorial work and any other type of work, labor, running jack hammers, painting, etc. In fact, we were doing the work of other white employees in higher classification. They had no blacks in none of these departments. Had black linemen and line crews, but it was a black foreman over a black crew. No integrated crews. No meter readers. No blacks in none of the managerial positions. They had one black supervisor, he was over the black crew.

So myself and a fellow worker, Edwin Hill, well, we got tired of it and we filed a complaint with the United States Civil Rights Commission. They delegated it down to the Kentucky Human Rights Commission. So it was settled in May of 1967 with Kentucky Human Rights Commission. That is, LG&E settled with the Kentucky Human Rights Commission. But they didn't settle to our satisfaction. We took it beyond to the United States Civil Rights Commission. It was token changes. They made some changes but they weren't to our satisfaction. We asked for things. They were doing it, but they were doing it slow. Like posting the jobs, they were supposed to stay on the board for a week. You go there and they put it up on the board today and tomorrow that job was gone, not because it was filled. They just removed it from the board. So if it's not on the board then people that were interested had no knowledge that the job had been posted. So these are the things they were doing. We brought that back to the Kentucky Human Rights Commission's attention and they took it and said that's the best they could do. So we went on to the EEOC and from there to the Justice department.

Well as time went along we prevailed at getting meter readers, getting the line crews integrated. We also got the locker room and rest facilities and the eating rooms and those facilities integrated and as time went along we got other departments. Where they wanted to concentrate blacks right in one department, the Human Rights Commission saw a pattern of discrimination. So if you find that pattern, then that would open up the whole company to be looked at. It's when they looked at the overall picture that they found it lacking in so many areas. They appeared before the United States Civil Rights Commission. The official from LG&E was saying that blacks enjoyed doing this kind of dirty and menial labor.

I was called a communist because I was involved in trying to change things. Incidentally, we had one white employee join with us. Blanford, he joined in because he saw what we were saying to be true. Now he had no other whites that would come forth and stick their neck out and say, "Well, what these two black guys are saying, it's really true. This is what's going on here." But he did and I appreciated it.

James Kiphart, Louisville

Lorillard had a tobacco processing company at Twenty-ninth and Muhammad Ali, which was Walnut Street. There were black folks hired there. Not as many as there should be, most of the workforce there were whites who did not live in the area, many of them coming from Henry County and Indiana and other places. [The members of the Black Workers' Coalition] felt as though many blacks in the community should be hired, particularly with a company in the community. This company, not only did it have only a few blacks hired there, the blacks that were there had the hardest jobs. One of the jobs was upstairs, feeding tobacco down on the conveyor that went into processing the cigarettes. So there were a few meetings of a few of the blacks who worked there who were upset about this. Some of them had been there a long time and they hadn't been able to get advancement or get out of that black department where they worked. That's what it was, it was a black department where only black folks worked, with the foremen all being white.

These people who worked in this place up here with hot, hard work, getting the tobacco down to the belts, had a few meetings outside of the plant and decided to shut off that section one day, a work stoppage. One of the guys was Moskoe Rapier. He was an official with the Black Workers' Coalition. So they closed off this upstairs, locked the doors, and had a work stoppage. Without these guys the whole plant had to shut down, nobody could work. Oh, God, the plant went crazy. The big wigs who run the plant, they called the police. You would have thought that the whole West End was being seized by police. These guys would not come out. They locked the doors upstairs and stayed there maybe for hours. Although they were few in the plant, these guys were able to close the whole operation of the plant down. Now this is big money that they're losing every hour that those guys don't let that tobacco hit that conveyor belt. Anyway, they called the police, the police didn't know what to do because they couldn't get up there. If it had been our plant they would have burned it down, but they couldn't do that so they didn't know what to do.

They tried to get the guys that were locked up. They finally got rid of most of the guys who were part of the work stoppage. In the process black folks was called in to work in all parts of the plant. Black folks who work there today, and I'm not sure they make cigarettes any more, but who work at that place today probably don't have no idea how they got there. Moskoe Rapier was almost run out of town. Tarred and feathered. He could not get another job, so I understand. But in the process of doing that, many other folks have gone there and retired there, and gotten a job because of what these few little guys did.

Bob Cunningham, Louisville

When I went in the legislature, employment with the state government was only 3.4 percent African American. When John Y. Brown became governor, we went to him and told him we wanted a minimum of the African American population in the state, which was 7.8. At that time the employment increased for African Americans to 8 percent, and that has been the level that they have tried to keep. Now there was nothing wrong with going to 10 percent or more, but they haven't done that. They used that as a benchmark and they have continued to use that. Then of course we have the affirmative action law, so that's been effective also in Kentucky, and we still have it. . . . The key thing that we always told them was we don't just want African Americans at the bottom of the employment barrel, janitors, and those people. We wanted them in higher echelon jobs, in management jobs, and we do have them there now, management and cabinet level jobs. As far as I know they've maintained that [percentage], but I suspect that if I checked it thoroughly, they could do better, [*laughs*] they could do better, yes.

Georgia Davis Powers, Louisville

In later years, after affirmative action came on the scene, I got discouraged when I found out that, "Well, this is not worth the paper it's written on for places like Harlan." We learned that you have to hire a certain number of employees *before* you're required to hire a black person. We didn't have employers here that hired in that volume. The school system and the hospital would have been the ones that was hiring the most people, and they were hiring black people. We had a man that was seeking employment in one of the programs, and they didn't want to hire him. Of course, if you don't want to hire him, you don't say, "It's because you're black." But they'll say, "It's because you're not qualified." White people are hired all the time that's not qualified for positions, but they train them. So this is when I got involved. I contacted the affirmative action office and I contacted some more folks, and this is when I learned that there was nothing that we could do. This was in the late '70s. There was nothing we could do because they were not employing a certain number of people. So I said, "Well, this—as far as Harlan is concerned—affirmative action is not worth the paper it's written on."

Nancy Johnson, Harlan

The Bowling Green NAACP wanted to address some problems in housing and employment and in education. Those were our main thrusts. At that particular time, there was information on affirmative action. That was our initial thrust, to bring affirmative action to Bowling Green. We had to educate the city of Bowling Green, because city officials were unaware as to really what affirmative action was, and so was a lot of the community. We met with officials from the city, and they were under the impression that affirmative action was just quotas. We said, "It's more than that. It's a force to bring equality in education and employment, and equality in housing and in other areas, by taking some positive and forceful directives." We tried to educate them on the fact that quotas were only brought in after an entity like the government, or agency, or company failed to actually implement their equal opportunity programs, or, they'd made little effort. After they'd been given the opportunity, then the courts actually ordered quotas. Many of them had the wrong impression, again. Affirmative action—they thought you just had to put a minority in that area whether they were qualified or not. That was another reason why affirmative action did not go well and it got a bad reputation.

Ronald Lewis, Bowling Green

We did get involved with getting some blacks hired when they opened the tunnel over here to Cumberland Gap. When they first started the procedures for the opening, they had no blacks in their employment. I didn't get deeply involved. I couldn't because of my job and stuff like that. But I did play a role in getting them some of the information and the people and things that they needed to do and know, in order to do what they had to do for getting someone hired. We did get in through the Democracy Resource Center—John Cleveland used to work with Democracy Resource. We did get Reverend Louis Coleman, who's an activist in Louisville, to come to Middlesboro and give us instructions and directions and information on what we needed to do.

I talked with John Cleveland and he got in touch with Reverend Coleman, and we set up a date and time for him to come. We just got the word out that he was going to be there. We had a very good turnout. We did telephone, door to door. . . . Word of mouth type thing. I think since then there may be, there has been three blacks or maybe four hired over there. Maybe there's three or four working there now. I'm not quite sure.

Esther Costner, Middlesboro

* * *

The civil rights movement in Kentucky achieved significant gains in the form of state and local policies against employment discrimination. Nevertheless, many African Americans in the commonwealth see the persistence of discrimination as the fundamental problem facing the community, as summed up in observations from Louisville's Joseph McMillan.

The main issue as I see it is economics. The black community is suffering. It really is like colonialism is taking place here. They suck the blood from the black community. The black community suffers because there is no economic development in the black community that's worth anything and the few jobs that come up, the city jobs and the other jobs, there's discrimination. . . . I think the little people are the people that we need to be fighting for and to fight for jobs and job opportunity and for businesses and minority contracts and sub-contracts and all, I'm in for that.

Joseph McMillan, Louisville

Profile

Julia Cowans

JULIA Cowans's narrative offers a window into what it was like to grow up black and poor in an eastern Kentucky coal camp. Cowans was born in 1925, in an era when the coal economy was still in a "boom," drawing African Americans to Appalachian Kentucky as an attractive alternative to the harsher field labor options available to blacks farther south.[1] Yet the hardscrabble upbringing described here suggests just how limited African American choices were in many rural areas in the early twentieth-century South, including Kentucky. Cowans's recollections of race relations in the Bell County coal camp of her childhood also suggest the variations racial hierarchy could take in different segments of the commonwealth. Although it would be a vast oversimplification to conclude that impoverishment unified Appalachian blacks and whites, Cowans's understanding of racism clearly took shape in the context of coal-mining poverty that encompassed whites too, while still allowing them some structural advantages over African American mining families.

Cowans's experiences are fascinating, but it is important to note that they are far from representative of African Americans in Appalachian Kentucky. She went from being a young girl so frightened of trade unionism that she threw rocks at United Mine Workers organizers who tried to enter the coal camp (an episode she recounts here) to becoming a dedicated trade unionist who married one of those organizers, Hugh Cowans. Such working-class activism inspired only a minority of miners, white or black, and the Cowanses frequently found themselves the only African American leaders in union drives.

In the longer interviews from which this selection is drawn, Julia Cowans recounts her experiences more thematically than chronologically. Her

177

narrative weaves back repeatedly to her move from fearing the union to embracing it, and it is apparent that this coming to consciousness represents a significant turning point in how she reflects upon her life. Although Cowans's understanding of oppression arose from being both poor and black, her trade union activism predated her civil rights crusades of the 1960s, '70s, and '80s. Her experiences highlight overlaps between the civil rights movement and other types of social justice crusades, and her support for trade unionism seems to have predisposed her to become a leader herself in later civil rights drives. Both workers' rights and civil rights campaigns evoked Ku Klux Klan activity in Harlan County, and Cowans's recollections of those conflicts suggest that for her the two struggles were not separate, but intertwined.

The narrative of Julia Cowans is also one of the more unconventional in terms of how it came into this collection. The story she tells here is stitched together from a series of interviews she and her husband, Hugh, did jointly over a period of years in the 1980s with Alessandro Portelli, an Italian scholar whose pioneering work on Harlan County, Kentucky, helped to popularize oral history and to demonstrate its significance both as a method of inquiry and for the insights it could yield into culture, communication, and how people make meaning of their experiences. Portelli generously allowed us to edit and include this narrative drawn from those interviews. His sessions with the Cowanses took place, as he has described it, in a "context halfway between a formal interview and a social visit, culminating in a dinner of fried chicken," and evoking a story in two voices, one hundred pages in length, that was much more stream-of-consciousness than the KCROHP interviews.[2] It is important to note that Portelli's oral history interviewing style with Cowans was quite intentional, forming an integral part of his attention to process, sound, and people's interior worlds. Readers may note that Cowans's narrative contains words and phrases that are unfamiliar to some, yielding a lyrical style of speaking that uses repetition for dramatic effect. A few of these phrases are explained in the endnotes. Her speech is unique in this collection, reflecting African American and Appalachian dialects. Our decision to maintain it with relatively few changes here serves to affirm her fierce working-class identity and the rich cadence of her storytelling.

* * *

I was born [on May 5, 1925] and raised down there in Cardinal, Kentucky, in the mountains there, Bell County. That's the only life that I

knew was coal mining. My father, grandfather, great-grandfather, they
all were coal miners. You had to be, or you didn't live in that community, and when I was growing up, the coal mining was just very bad.
You didn't really live, just existed, just existed. I can remember so many
times when we were girls that it'd be dark when the [men would] go to
the mines, and we'd be in bed when they'd go and we'd be in bed during the time they come in and rest, and they'd be gone again. Sometime we didn't see them 'til on Sunday, and I can remember waking up
sometimes during the night and going in the kitchen and I'd see my
uncle laying on the floor. Be laying there sleeping and just get up and
get some food and go back.

I was the oldest [child] there in the house. My mother would send
me to the store to draw scrip, and I never remember axing for but a
dollar.[3] One dollar. I've never gone to the window and say, "Two dollars, three, five dollars." Yeah, there would never be any money. Never
be any money. Everything that you wanted, you would have to go to
the company store and buy it. You did not leave off that company
property, go to the next town to buy anything and bring back in there.
No, you didn't do that. And especially if you had a family of any size,
that kept you in debt all the time. Work a lifetime and be in debt to the
company, and some of the old coal camps, they had fences. They had
guards to let you in there and guards to let you out, and if you tried to
go in there and you didn't live there, you had to get away from there.
If I lived in here and was expecting some of my relatives, I had to go
down and report it so they could get in. Like a concentration camp
or something of that sort on a lot of those coal camps that I know
about.

We grew up under those conditions and when my husband was
talking about when I threw rocks at him—see, [we all] were ignorant
of the fact of what this union would do. Whatever the company official said, that was the law. [They would tell you that] if you let this
union in here, you're not going to have a job. So the men were frightened, and that's why it was hard to get [a union] organized. It was very
hard, and we were little children at the time he was talking about us
throwing rocks at them. And [to] stand and see all those pickets coming, it scared us to death. All we knew was they were coming to stop
the men from working. That's all we knew about it. So I used to get
a bunch of kids and we'd line up and get us a pile of rocks, and we'd
see them coming and we'd start throwing rocks at them. [*laughing*]

We didn't know [things could get better] once they got organized. . . . before they got organized in Harlan County, blood ran like water. Many a man lost their lives. When they find out all of this benefit that was for them, they was willing to fight for it, and they started fighting for it and, oh, they were slaughtered like hogs. I can remember right there in Cardinal, Governor Chandler, A. B. "Happy" Chandler, sent those tinhorns in there, to guard those what they called "scabs" in the mines and out.[4] My mother used to take in washing and ironing, and she used to do the laundry for those soldiers that were there. This was during the time of the organizing.

And [later] we had women picket lines.[5] I'd gone on the picket line after growing up and knowing what this was all about. After they organized and the [company was] still trying to break the United Mine Workers back up in there, well, I walked on the picket line many a day. And we've taken coffee and donuts and things to the men. It was pretty bad for a long time, but after we were organized, living was somewhat better, somewhat better. See, before they were organized, if a woman had a house full of children and her husband died or was killed, I've known women had to give they children away to other people to raise because they couldn't make it. And the company, the coal operators, if that husband was killed in the mine, they had lawyers that would beat that widow out of her money. They would bury him and give her a few dollars but beat that lady out of money that was rightfully hers and her children's.

[The camp had] separate sections. You came to the white camp first and then over on the hill, that's where the blacks were. I would say it was more white than black. But at that time, far as I remember, it was a lot of blacks too . . . just say, for instance, when my father came from [Alabama], he come to the coal mine, then they would run what you call "transportation." They go back [south] and get they people and bring them up to the coal mines, you know? . . . I heard them talk about, how if when one brother came up, and he's working coal making good money—or whatever money they were making, it was better than what they had—and they go back home and they had to . . . what do you call it? Sneak them away? Steal them away? Or something, because down there on the plantations where they were, if the plantation owner knew that they's coming around, sneaking them families away, they couldn't of done it. I used to hear them talk about that, and they migrated from down south—Georgia, Alabama, places like that—up

into the Kentucky coal mines. I think that was done just about everywhere [there] was coal mining carrying on.

My great-grandmother, she ran a boardinghouse. Black men come
there and get jobs, they didn't have furniture. No, they would live at
the boardinghouse. She ran that boardinghouse for men that would
come there and get jobs that would stay there until they moved their
families there or maybe just leave and go elsewhere. I grew up in that
area, went to a one-room school. The grades went from what we used
to call "primer" to the eighth grade, and all that was in one room, and
all the black children went to the black school, and white children
went to the white school. 'Cause wasn't no such thing as integration
[at that time] down in that part of Kentucky. My gosh, I guess I would
be safe in saying there were maybe forty-five or fifty children in that
one room.

Where I grew up, it was segregation, all right, such as white
school, black school, white church, black church. But they all did the
same work, coal mining. They did different levels. My great-grandmother, [besides running the boardinghouse] she was a midwife. And
she helped deliver or delivered most of the white and black babies.
Everybody called her, white and black, either Grandma Casey or Aunt
Casey. You go in her dining room, you see them children around that
table, you see just as many whites [as] you see black. If they was out
there playing at meal times, she make everybody come in there, wash
up and eat, sit around, and honestly, I didn't even know what integration or segregation was all about til [I was a teenager].

[That] great-grandmother was a slave's daughter and I'd sit and
hear her tell things. Oh, she used to tell about how the blacks were
treated. It upsets you. I don't even like to think on them, how, if one
black did something [wrong], they'd bring him out and call out all the
other blacks. Hang him, tar him and feather him and burn him and,
oh, just terrible things. She always had a motto: stay in your own back-
yard, and then as I grew up and grew older, I don't know what you'd
call it. I wouldn't say it was a hate, but I resented the way that blacks
was treated, and that's why Reverend Cowans and I was involved in
these struggles. Uh-huh, we fought for the miners down there. We
went on the picket lines, [and then we] sat on the national board of
the Equal Rights Congress.

My mother and father separated when I was too young to know
him, but she was married to my stepfather—Will Smith, that was his

name—up until he died. . . . The best a black girl could hope for in those days was to be a schoolteacher or maybe, possibly a nurse. And I wanted to be a schoolteacher. That's what I wanted to be, but during my eighth year of school, see, my stepfather died. In those days there wasn't any, in Kentucky anyway, what they get now, child's welfare, to help a widow with her family. And my mother was about six months pregnant when he died. I had to come out of school, and I went working in the white boardinghouse scrubbing floors, and washing windows and walls, and washing clothes on the washboard, just whatever we could do to try to survive. That's what I did, and I was the sole source of our income. My mother was real sick. She could not work; there's days we thought she wasn't going to even live, and I worked for $1 a day. At this boardinghouse, see, they had two shifts: night shift and day shift, and I'd have to be there like, what, 5 o'clock [in the morning], and sometime it would be 6 and 7 o'clock when I come back home in the evening, for $1 a day. . . . There was five of us. That was the income for the whole family. But in those days you could take a dollar, you could go get five cents worth of beans. You get a bag of beans. Things was just cheap 'cause money was scarce, and let me tell you this. In the mining community, jobs are limited: ain't no work. Everybody's poor and striving and trying to make it. And when they changed the boardinghouse, they got some more people that took over and they had their own help. So then I didn't have a job—the [mining] superintendent down there, he gave me a job cleaning up the big office every afternoon, $10 a month. Whenever I would get that $10, my sisters and brother, [w]e had a little wagon that my stepfather had made. We'd take that wagon. Groceries was cheap down at Blackmont. That was about a mile or so from Cardinal, at Black Mountain. We'd go around that hill with that wagon, go all the way to Blackmont and spend that $10. I can remember, get a big sack of flour, big sack of meal, a bucket of lard. Flourmill then cost ninety-eight cents for a twenty-five-pound bag. Stuff like that, and we'd get that and bring it back around that hill in that wagon, and nothing else came in that house till we got the next $10. That's the truth. That is the truth.

I tell my children that I've never been young. I've had responsibilities all of my life and [when] I married the first time, it wasn't a man that I loved. It was a man that I was forced [to marry for financial] security, a coal miner. He was twenty-eight years older than myself. And I'd always taken care of my mama's children, worked hard for the family, and I didn't want children, period. But time I married they came like clockwork. . . . In those days, back up in the mountains, we didn't know nothing about no birth control. Never even heard of [it].

We stayed together twenty-two years. Had ten children. We ended in divorce. . . . By this time, we was living in Harlan County. [Then] I met Hugh Cowans. I knew his mother, years before I even knew him, because we were real good friends. She helped me with my kids [while] I worked. [Hugh] and his wife . . . used to come from West Virginia over to Harlan to see his mother, and eventually, their marriage ended in divorce. But by this time he was preaching, he'd been called into the ministry. Before they divorced, he went blind. He say they told him when he come out of the Army that one day he might lose his sight because of war injuries [from World War II]. He'd come out and worked twelve years before, and went fishing one Saturday evening, come back, backed into his garage, went black. His sight went just like that. And so he went to a school for the blind, and learned Braille and everything, and he come back, and he stayed with his mother. I used to help him, and so eventually we got married. We had one daughter, Sylvia. We were married, oh, about thirty-two, thirty-three years, before he died [in 2001].

Evarts, that's the first place we lived in Harlan County. Reverend and I, we had become members of the NAACP. I [signed] up the first white man in Evarts in the NAACP. He was our police chief! He sat down, we talked to him, and told him the nature of this NAACP. It ain't white against blacks against white. It's about equal opportunity. . . . I said, "Marvin, it's not about sex mix[ing]." I said, "No, I don't want my son to have your daughter, any more than you would want your daughter to have my son." I said, "But it's equal opportunity," . . . and he said, "That's what I'm for." We all called him Gunsmoke, and I wrote him up first before I wrote anybody else up as a member.

In Evarts they had . . . open counters where they served [all]. Black children go in there, sit by the white children, order what they want. We had no problem to confront us that we had to have meetings and things [about]. My husband and myself set up a Junior NAACP. We schooled them on what it was all about. Our children got along fine. Those kids [black and white] were raised up together right there, and they would fight for each other. [She recalls one exception in which a white boy threatened her nephew with a knife at school.] . . . My husband and I, we won't have this. We went to the chairman of the school board that ran a hardware and furniture store there in Evarts. We sat down and talked it out. He said, "Well, I'll tell you, Hugh," said, "Don't worry about it. [That white boy] will never go another day in that school." And he didn't. Now that's the only . . . incident that I can remember we had in Evarts.

At Harlan, which was the little county seat there, now I didn't live down there, but we lived about eight or ten miles up, and we started encouraging the children to have sit-ins. 'Cause there were some who wouldn't serve you in Harlan, which was no trouble in Evarts. They'd start let[ting] the children sit-in. It was one drugstore that had a restaurant in there, and he said, "Before I would serve those people, I'll shut it down." That's what he did. Wasn't no hey, or yea, or nay, or nothing about it. He closed it down. But I know it didn't happen in Evarts 'cause I was right there and involved in community services.

* * *

Julia Cowans's story encompasses seven generations: from her grandparents, through her own two marriages that produced eleven children, and on to several great-great-grandchildren. But her memories return frequently to the centrality of the union and of equal rights movements that brought vast social changes but left many wrongs still to be righted.

Anyway, we've fought for the United Mine Workers. That's our life. That's our life. My husband left home many a times going to West Virginia, different places, to speak out for the United Mine Workers in his blinded condition. As he said, he had to face the Klan. . . . So this [white] girl told me, she said, "That's no husband. In the first place, he's black. In the second place, he's blind." And I said, "A black blind man going out hunting the Klan—that takes courage." And I'm just like him. I'd rather die than go back to what I come from, and if I have to die standing up for what I believe in, then that's just the way it'll be. 'Cause fear—see, that's what it's all about anyhow. They rule you with fear. When you lose that fear, they ain't got nothing else to hold against you. I would rather be dead than to live under the oppressive conditions. I don't want my children and my grandchildren to come under what I did, suffer the way we had to suffer. [But] we got so many people that don't feel that way. They want to reap the benefits! "You can go out there and get yourself killed and beat up and knocked and kicked around, and I stay in here with the shades down."

That's why things're no better than they are, and I'm going to tell you something else, too. It wasn't only the black people that caught the devil during the time of the struggle in the coal mines, organizing. There were white people who went through hell, too. But even the worst condition for the white man was better than the best for the black man. But they went through hell, too, yes they did. . . . Any time that [the Klan] wanted to bring trouble [between the races], they'd use a black man and a white woman, and don't care how much this white man said he loved [blacks], they don't want that black man fooling with that white woman, see? The Klan knows this. Whether it's true or false, they bring up this issue, go to insinuating things, and that starts ill feelings, and starts putting [black and white] at odds with each other when they're supposed to be together . . . that's just the way they operate.

Even in our own community, we got a lot of opposition even from blacks because they were afraid, and they said that we, Reverend Cowans and I, would get them killed, get their houses blown up, and we've gotten up a lot of mornings. Where we live, cars just come right by our house, and we found Klan leaflets that been thrown in our yard and stuff like that. But they couldn't stop us.

Chapter 6

Black Consciousness, Black Power

IN the mid-1960s the cry of "Black Power!" resounded throughout the nation, destabilizing the nonviolent civil rights movement of earlier in the decade and generating a new kind of militancy among African Americans.[1] By the latter years of the decade, the philosophy of Black Power began to gain a following in Kentucky, sparking a variety of new initiatives. The central ideas of Black Power were not new. Several of the key elements—including black nationalism, the desire for economic self-sufficiency and independent politics, and the promotion of pride in African and African American history and culture—had been significant forces in the black freedom struggle for generations. Now, however, these ideas coalesced into a new Black Power movement that galvanized young African Americans to take the fight against racism in new directions, challenging the goals and tactics of the earlier postwar civil rights movement that held up racial integration and even color-blindness as a desired outcome. An early Black Power icon was Louisville native Muhammad Ali, the boxing champion who upon winning the heavyweight title in 1964 publicly acknowledged his allegiance to the Nation of Islam, discarded his birth name (Cassius Clay), and came to symbolize a new era in black pride.

The most well-known of the organizations to emerge from this challenge was the Black Panther Party, which took its name from a 1966 struggle in rural Alabama but evolved as a primarily urban phenomenon. The BPP's controversial public image gave it a high profile in the mass media and resulted in its becoming the leading target of government surveillance of the new black militants.

Yet Black Power was ultimately much larger and more diffuse than simply the Black Panthers. Across the nation and in the commonwealth it found a range of expressions. For some African Americans, Black Power meant economic self-sufficiency and self-help, leading—for example—to the expansion of Nation of Islam businesses and the creation of Black Panther free breakfasts and other economic aid programs. In a move that raised the most controversy, some Black Power advocates rejected non-violence and promised to defend themselves and their communities with arms if necessary. While not alone in their rhetoric advocating armed self-defense of black communities, the Black Panthers in particular became iconic for their militaristic dress, brandishing of rifles, and upraised fists.

Perhaps the most enduring element of the Black Power movement was the focus on celebrating African and African American culture. The anti-colonial movements unfolding simultaneously with the U.S. civil rights movement heightened African Americans' interest in the African side of their heritage, and released a broad stream of black consciousness that was expressed not only politically but culturally. African Americans began wearing fashions such as the dashiki (a long shirt), sporting "Afro" hairstyles, and reviving African spirituality. Some adopted new names and naming practices, individually but also collectively, choosing the self-description "black," for example, and rejecting the use of "colored" or "Negro." This assertion of black pride and identity led to the black arts movement and ultimately to an embrace of multiculturalism in American society more broadly.

Another emphasis for African Americans influenced by the outpouring of black consciousness involved separation from whites into black-only organizations and institutions. This move questioned integration both in society and in the movement, leading to extended debates as to what role, if any, whites should have in the civil rights movement. That questioning process led in some cases to whites being asked—and not always politely—to leave and to go organize against racism among other whites. The most notable case in this regard was the Student Nonviolent Coordinating Committee (SNCC), which had become famous nationally among 1960s activists for its militant, youth-led leadership of the sit-ins, freedom rides, and voter campaigns in the Deep South. Later in the decade it was SNCC's Stokely Carmichael (later known as Kwame Ture) who popularized the slogan "Black Power!" with his fist in the air. But the same phenomenon of insisting on white members' resignations occurred in Congress of Racial Equality chapters in Kentucky and nationally, and in other groups in the state.

The spread of Black Power politics also coincided with rising racial tensions and repression of activists. African Americans were increasingly frustrated with the slow pace of change and the seeming inability of new civil rights laws to overcome the systemic racism that undergirded black poverty and powerlessness, especially in urban areas. Civil rights activism often led to other forms of social protest, especially against poverty and the Vietnam War. In each of these cases, what many young idealists thought of as the "establishment" proved intransigent to the fundamental policy shifts the movement sought. Meanwhile, a conservative white backlash against further racial and social change produced increased resistance on the streets and in the halls of government, including stepped-up measures to repress black activists. Such measures included arrests on questionable charges, harsh sentencing, and the infiltration of movement organizations by government agents posing as supporters.

This combustible combination of frustration and repression produced a wave of race riots in the summers of the later years of the decade. In the public and official imagination, these riots were inextricably linked to, and thus blamed upon, agitation by black militants, leading to conspiracy charges and legal harassment that often turned out to be either baseless or at least widely overblown. The level of government repression eventually beat back the more radical challenge of black power, causing the movement's decline in the early to mid-1970s.[2]

Across the country, the Black Power movement was primarily, though not solely, centered in urban areas and on college campuses.[3] Because this was also true in Kentucky, most of the expressions of Black Power activism could be found either on the campuses of the state's institutions of higher learning, or in its main cities, primarily in Louisville. Although interviewees recall black student organizations at the University of Kentucky, Western Kentucky University, Eastern Kentucky, and Berea College, narrators from many parts of the state make few or no references to these philosophical changes of the late 1960s. As a consequence, more of the stories here than in other chapters of this book focus on Louisville. The narratives make clear that Kentucky Black Power advocates focused on promoting cultural pride and providing services for the African American community. Like cities in the North and West, however, Louisville suffered its own racial "disorder" in the spring of 1968, which led to one of the first sets of conspiracy charges in the country against black militants, the Black Six trial. That trial, and the later prosecution of the Louisville Panthers, sapped much of the energy from the movement, with Black

Power advocates who remained moving into less provocative channels of action.

Cultural Pride

In Kentucky, the most visible expression of 1960s black consciousness currents was a widespread flowering of black arts and culture. Several individuals and organizations promoted African American and African history and culture through artistic expression and the creation of new programs or the reorientation of existing ones. In this section narrators describe some of those efforts and the ideas behind those initiatives.

* * *

Since I was a music major, in terms of my student activism, I just jumped all over the [Berea College] music department. Of *all* the things in America, even with racism just spewing out of your veins, of all the things that happened in America that we can identify as African, music is at the top of the list. Yet the music department did not in any way reflect [that] African music is the source of the music. It had impacted on everything. So one of the things I remember doing was trying in class—our classes were very small; three, four, five, music majors—to interject some of my musical experiences growing up in Birmingham. My teachers had not a clue.

[Then when I moved to Louisville], the big thing we did in the summer was not to just have a regular summer camp, but to have an African village camp. Can you imagine? This was '70, '71, '72. We were going to have this African village camp. Well, I was just so excited about this. We had heads of the village, families. Everybody had to study their name, had to create a name. I mean, these simple things were so profound. The whole sense that the community has so many things it can learn and teach itself. There were also teachable moments in these kinds of things.

Ann Beard Grundy, Berea

Louisville was producing significant African American artists. We had a group and we all painted together. Bob Thompson was a significant artist who died at a very early age, about twenty-seven. He just had a couple of retrospective shows last year, and was in the

Metropolitan. Sam Gilliam, who is known all over the country as a significant artist. You had G. C. Cox, who recently died in Louisville, who was our godfather, and who taught all of us there. Then you had Fred Bond, who is a wonderful potter. He's dead now, died of cancer. You had Bob Douglass, who teaches art at the University of Louisville, [who] just completed a book on another artist and is on his second book. He's a fine artist. Ed Hamilton, who just did the latest thing in Washington on the Civil War African American soldiers. We all painted together.

It was wonderful what we did. We couldn't find white galleries to show us. So we showed anywhere we could, oftentimes that would be at a bar. They'd give us a space; we'd re-decorate the bar for them. Or a church basement, the YMCA. We went out to St. James Court once, strung lines up and hung there. The next thing you know, St. James Court is the major art event. We were there first. We finally bought an old Mom and Pop store in the African American community. We formed an official group called the Louisville Art Workshop. Fred and his wife lived in the back of the store. It was our gallery.

Then we began to use art as a political statement. Everybody has always used music and art and writings to deal with the times. It was during those times that we were very busy making our statements. We did it by creating events. We would have an open show for the community, no charge. As part of the show we would have dance and poetry and essay readings. I've still got some of the old programs. Those readings gave us a chance to voice our indignation at our condition, or to voice the good and the bad, the sensitive and the not so sensitive. It was a way of expression among ourselves.

Mervin Aubespin, Louisville

The '60s had a very special kind of aura about them. I was young and wanting to see things happen in this community that weren't happening. I look at other places and I know things that are going on. I have friends in Chicago, in New York. I go up and visit with them. One of my friends from Chicago, as a matter of fact, had a shop. I haven't really come down on what you call that type of shop now. I opened a shop [called "Corner of Jazz"] at 28th and Greenwood. Prior to its opening I had gotten these huge posters, H. Rap Brown, Stokely Carmichael, Malcolm X, Muhammad Ali, all the "radical" black leaders. I had them in the window prior to opening. So everybody who passed 28th and

Greenwood could see that something is getting ready to happen here. When I opened it up, my friend from Chicago, I called him, he came down. He brought me sculptures, he brought me African clothing and jewelry and all that kind of stuff. A friend whose dad owned a record distributing company in New York—a Jewish guy, who was living here who was married to a black girl, working the poverty program. His dad sent me a bunch of dynamite LP's at the time. So I had music. Then we hooked up with certain black book distributors out of Chicago and New York. I just started making contact with so many different sources. So we opened up. We had books, we had music, we had African clothing, we had African carvings and paintings and artwork and all of that. It was a fantastic place to be.

What happened was that guys—I would say guys mostly—but the community started coming by after we opened up. I would introduce people to certain books to read, or certain music to hear. They would come back and stand in my store, talking about these books. A lot of people were really getting turned on to it. I guess something was going on across the country. Black folks were becoming interested in black life. So they would come back for conversations and so forth.

Ken Clay, Louisville

We were all about trying to find something to alleviate problems that black folk were having and at the same time trying to identify with the movement that we saw swelling across this nation and across the world, particularly Africa. I think the anti-colonialism movement in Africa had a lot to do with what we were doing here. I think those of us who somewhat kept up with what was going on in Africa began to associate differently with Africa. See, there was a time when black folk in this country were somewhat ashamed of Africa. We knew Africa through Tarzan movies. I hate to say it, but I'm almost sure that as a young boy when I'd sit in there and look at Johnny Weissmueller, who played Tarzan, I would be rooting for him, "Kill those Africans." That's sad to admit but I'm almost sure that was happening then. So when we began to hear about the striking down of colonialism in Africa and the people, Jomo Kenyatta and Patrice Lamumba, that we were hearing about, it woke something up in us and we began to identify with things that came from Africa. . . . To identify with Africa wasn't that we hated white folk, it was trying to find our roots; something that said I came from a little more than a cotton plantation. Or that

I had a beginning and there was more to me than what you saw; that there was a history about me, around me that was being suppressed by somebody who didn't want you to know really who I was. We must begin to know ourselves. I think that seeing Africa in a new light began then, and all the African art began to be something that we had in our houses. I think that what we saw in Africa is something that inflated the pride in black folks here in this country.

In 1972, my son was born and I named him Lamumba, and people would say, "Was that his real name?" Well, we as blacks were beginning to name our children something African rather than Benjamin Franklin Jones or George Washington Green. So there became a whole new breed of black folk at that time who wasn't being understood by the whole of white America. I can remember vividly a white lady telling me that the people she feared most at that time was black people who had afros, the afro hairdo. . . . The emotional chemistry was so different until what we were doing they didn't even understand.

Bob Cunningham, Louisville

What about Whites?

The new primacy given to black pride and identity raised a major question: what was the role of whites in the struggle against racism? In the mid- and late 1960s, civil rights organizations began to debate this issue, in some cases leading to pressure for whites to move out of black-led organizations. Here a number of activists describe this conflict, while others dispute the extent to which black power meant black only.

* * *

[At the University of Kentucky] it was very hard to try to help people understand that we needed to take seriously the Black Power movement and the concerns for black people to define their own terms for doing things. Because integration, in most of our minds, had meant come in and join us in our house, do things our way. [We needed to] try to learn how to have a reciprocal kind of relationship. I don't remember the particular discussion now, but it was pretty difficult in terms of whites seeing things one way and blacks seeing it another. I can remember so well when we finished up that evening how we went our separate ways. The black participants went one way and the whites went another to kind of heal our wounded selves, and then came back together the next day. But I think that we were committed to coming back together.

Betty Gabehart, Lexington

What happened to CORE was Black Power. This came in nationally, and in 1968 I remember very distinctly a meeting at which there were probably fifteen or twenty people and there were probably three or four of us who were not black who were at the meeting. We were told that honkies were no longer [*clears throat*] accepted and we could leave, thank you. Well, I thought, we've done our best and if they don't want us, then all right. That was a very angry meeting. We just left.

Abby Marlatt, Lexington

The Kentucky Commission on Human Rights was sponsoring a meeting and the discussion turned to whether or not whites should be excluded. So most of the people who were there voted to exclude whites. So I left. You know, I think that is a pile of crap. Here we are. This is government money that's paying for a government-sponsored conference. Okay? I am not for allowing any citizens to be excluded on the basis of their race from anything that is government-sponsored. So I think that was wrong.

Galen Martin, Louisville

There were those people in Louisville who felt as though the black movement needs to be led by black people with the help of white people. But, as far as saying we can't work with white people, we don't want to live with white people, I don't think you saw much of that during that period. Now it was fashionable to be super black. Super black was being nationalistic, "Down with white folks, man, I can't work with white folks." Everything is black. But that was only black folks finding themselves and beginning to appreciate something that they had long been taught to ridicule, which was themselves. So I think that wake up of, "Yes, you are somebody," that we heard from Jesse Jackson or that cry of "Black and Proud" that we heard from James Brown woke us up inside. So it wasn't that we hated somebody else, it was that we began to straighten our backs. When you straighten your back, it's pretty hard for people to ride on it. You heard a lot of that. But I don't think it was ever that white folks were not [welcome]. The Nation of Islam, who we called the Black Muslims at that time, weren't that political, more religious. They were somewhat nationalistic in a sense. What I mean is they were more about working with black folks than white folks, but I don't think there was any hatred of white people. We didn't quite have the time to hate white folks, we had to try to do something for our own, for ourselves. Everything that white folks perceived as far as hatred towards them, I think they were internalizing their own feelings of what they thought about black people. It was always the fear of white folks that we were trying to get into position[s] where we could do to them what they had done to us. That never was our feeling, that never was our position. We never wanted to enslave white folks. We never thought about raping white folks or lynching white folks. That wasn't what we were talking about at all.

Bob Cunningham, Louisville

Of course SCEF always supported Black Power, I mean the whole Black Power movement.[4] I still think we were absolutely right. It was a real step forward, it really was, and that was the time for it. It wasn't really anti-white, it was pro-black. Now some people, I mean a lot of blacks just naturally are going to be anti-white for many reasons. But the movement itself was pro-black. They said, "This is our movement. We're going to do our own destiny." They were coming to feel like whites really had dominated the movement in many ways. . . . There was a lot of white monied influence, white liberals and people—and some of them very good. Some of them risked their lives. Some gave their lives, I guess. But people didn't feel like it was theirs! So that was [SCEF's] position and everybody knew it.

Anne Braden, Louisville

Black Power on Campus

Outside of Louisville, Black Power currents were most evident on the campuses of the state's colleges and universities, where Black Student Unions organized African American students to press for more recognition and better treatment. J. Blaine Hudson tells the full story of the University of Louisville BSU and its confrontation with school authorities elsewhere in this volume. Here, narrators recall their own student days and activities on other campuses.

* * *

We had no clue about how to start a black student union. In fact, part of the aggravation was, when you said BSU, the local white kids would be upset because that was the Baptist Student Union. How dare we? So that was a struggle all the time, which we enjoyed. So we put a sign up. There was a student, Kenny Miller, from Louisville who had come to Berea. We wanted black students to get together for something, and one of us went up in the student union there, in Berea, and put up a sign: "All blacks"—and by this time we were using the word "black"—"all black students need to meet in such and such a room at 6:30 this evening." Right where everybody walks right past that bulletin board going to the dining room so we knew everybody would see it. Well, one of the people who saw it was the dean of women, Ann Marshall, who came along, saw that sign, "Oh, why God hath made of one blood all nations and men. We can't have separate meetings" and stuff like that. So she did what we say was the most profound thing she could do, she ripped our sign down. Thank you, Ann Marshall, 'cause that just lit us up. How dare you tell us that we can't see ourselves as a community within a community! So, Kenny went back and put another sign up; and it was so funny. It was an "in" joke, and every black kid got it. It was coded language. "All ye who use Peach and Glo, Royal Crown Hair Grease"—and he went through all of this stuff, you know—"Press and Comb," please meet in the Ballard Room. At 6:30 we were all there, every black student on the planet.

Things had started to roll then. That was about the time period most BSUs around the country were rolling. . . . At the heart of it was a sense of we wanted to have an organization that met our needs as African people, cultural needs. That was the first part. The second part was we wanted to change Berea College. We were very clear about that. Berea had sent out this mixed message. Berea's motto is: "God hath made of one blood all nations of men." Now, having grown up in the Christian church, I clearly knew what that meant in terms of how the church interpreted that. But when you take that statement and you put it in its broader human context, it became things that Berea didn't want to talk about: the fact that it had a lily-white faculty, the fact that it had denied its own African heritage and roots.

Ann Beard Grundy, Berea

Jeffery Weathers burned a Confederate flag at a bonfire, I thought we were really going to have to fight our way out of there. Nothing happened. Jeffery would remind you of Jimi Hendrix, so he was plenty black, with a plenty big afro. Jeffery was one of the baddest guys I ever saw. At the bonfire he walked up, held the flag up, walked in front of them and threw it in the fire. We all went because we thought we were going to have to fight, and nothing happened. I was glad when we left. I was kind of glad nothing happened. Not long after that a couple of the athletes decided that they didn't want to hear "Dixie" played for the fight song. From there Western became a pretty good place, started to have some reasonable access to all the things available to all of the students. The other major time came in '68 with King's assassination. They brought in the police and the National Guard to set up a perimeter around the campus so folk couldn't get on or off. But we did go in and what would have been an attempt to take over the Administration building, that kind of fizzled out. The president came down to talk to us. Had he not, it probably would have gone bad.

Don Offutt, Bowling Green

I would say by the fall of '67, the [black students'] agenda was pretty clear, and it was to open up Eastern in a variety of ways. Efforts were begun to start a black student union. I remember being on the edge. I'd go to the meetings but really wouldn't commit. I wanted information but was not willing to make a commitment in any significant way. There were efforts then to petition the institution to bring in some black speakers and that type of thing. Entertainment was an issue. The social life there at Eastern was geared primarily towards the white students. There was this fellow, he must have been the student body president, who was sensitive at the time. He was friends with a number of the black athletes and so he began talking some to the administration on behalf of the black students' needs. So the BSU was organized. A while back I was going through some papers and I ran across a 1969 edition of an Eastern newspaper. It was an April date [or] early May and there was a record of some of the demands that we had made for adding some black history and black literature classes into the curriculum. But also we were asking for black teachers. This article was a summary of the gains that had been made during that year and one of them was that Dr. Cheaney had been hired to teach and was going to start the fall of '69. Henry Cheaney at the time was a full-time professor at Kentucky State. Bob Martin had contacted him and ultimately gotten him to agree to come to Eastern and teach a black history course. And so he did so the fall of '69 and the spring of '70. . . . It was a four-hour course on a Saturday morning.

But I remember at one time that we didn't seem to be getting anywhere with our demands. A fellow by the name of Eric Abercrombie, who was from around Covington, Ohio, emerged as one of the more outspoken leaders. This Raymond Clay who had kind of taken me under his wings the first year was very vocal about some issues there on campus as well. There was a history professor, and I cannot think of his name, who was interested in black students and this Eric Abercrombie was a history major, and I can remember him passing on to us discussions he would have with this professor basically encouraging us to go on [with our] efforts.

It was at Eastern, and during this time, that a political consciousness began emerging in me. . . . I was at a point where I could begin to make sense out of the way the world and society was organized, and also was beginning to learn about resources and acquiring some tools. I remember just being taken with this job that I had at the library because of the exposure, okay? *Ramparts* magazine. Boy, oh boy, I mean it was just like second to nothing, no experience up to that point. Got to read then a lot about the Black Panthers and what was going on there. Very struck with the community programs that they had, particularly the Feed the Children or Community Breakfast programs and so on. And it was at that time then that I began to get a sense of some things that I could do. This involvement in tutoring children after school was one of those. By this time also I'm becoming more aware there was a very large proportion of the students, the black students, who were there were from Louisville. Sons and daughters of people who were aldermen and that type of thing. So I began getting a sense there are some people in Kentucky who are making changes.

Anne Butler, Richmond

[In] '68, the year we started the Black Student Union, I was the secretary. Part of it was because of all this kind of newfound activism. A lot of us decided that, well, we couldn't complain about not being able to participate in things that we didn't try out for. So some people tried out for cheerleading. I tried out for the drill team and actually was the first African American drill team member. I was selected as an alternate at first, so I didn't actually get into uniform till the second semester, which was actually okay with me because it was basketball season then, and indoors.

I remember the Kappa Alpha men's fraternity had this annual Old South Week where they would basically be like the Old South, antebellum stuff. They would parade though campus on horseback and with the Confederate flag, the whole deal. We decided to stop that. So we linked arms, and blocked the passage, and that was kind of a brouhaha then. They couldn't pass. So they had to turn around and cut their parade short. They were saying that, well, we could be a part of that if we wanted to. And we were like, "Well, what roles exactly would we play?" [*Laughs.*] From then the Black Student Union was pretty active during that time. We also had a Miss Black Eastern pageant. Things like that went on for several years. We were a pretty solid group. I think the '68 class was the largest group of blacks at one time that came to Eastern. Oh, it had steadily been increasing, I think the year before, in fact, there were a lot of people that had gone to Male High School with me that were graduating in '67 that were there. I think collectively, from all over, '68 brought in a big group. And so we were all pretty cohesive, for the most part. The meetings were pretty well attended.

Michelle McCrary, Richmond

The thing that I had to come to grips with was if I was going to stay here and survive, I was going to have to find a way to cope [with] being black and being at UK. All of us were kind of struggling with this and we dealt with it in different ways. But you know, it was clear to me that I was going to have to be reminded that I was black every day of my experience here. For some people . . . it really took a toll. I mean, there are some people who I know are dealing with it to this day, their experience here at UK in 1965. But I think I was fortunate. I did meet some people who I saw as my support system. This guy, Major Jones, was one and then there were a group of guys from eastern Kentucky, and there were some other people in the community who I really connected with immediately. We found out that as long as we bonded around that experience of being black and being at UK, maybe we could do something about it. So for me it was like my kind of coming to awareness about who I was as a black student.

Initially there was no Black Student Union. But we did have a group that we called Orgena. This says everything about where we were in terms of our sense of identity because this organization, Orgena, was primarily a social organization and was just there to give us a social outlet. The name itself is "a Negro" spelled backwards. I mean, we talk about it now, it's like we were a bunch of backward Negroes, but [*laughs*] that's what we had and that's where we were in our thinking. So we relied on that for a couple of years to give us some kind of an opportunity to have some parties and socialize a bit.

[The BSU got started] about 1968, and the development of that really did parallel the events around Dr. King's assassination. So then the Black Student Union movement across the country was really picking up momentum. We were very much in tune with that. We had people on campus who were doing some traveling and moving around other campuses and they would bring us back information about what was happening in other places and what we ought to consider doing. University of Louisville [had a BSU], in fact we used University of Louisville as almost a reference point for us. . . . Berea did too, but we didn't have as much contact with Berea as Louisville. We were up and down I-64 a lot.

Recently we did a panel that was kind of retrospective of that period. It wasn't until the four of us sat down and started talking that it occurred to all of us that we were really pretty forward-thinking. I don't know what our source of inspiration was except we did know what was happening around the country. But we were dealing with things basically like, well, recruitment and retention. I mean there was our own situation that was sort of a problem, but we knew too that if we were going to improve things that we had to have more of us here. So we were as students developing recruiting programs. We would go down to local high schools and visit with high school seniors. Talk to them about what it would take to prepare for UK as best we could. At the same time we were trying to put programs in place on this campus to recruit some of these students here for kind of summer preparatory experience. We were lobbying for hiring more black faculty and we were lobbying for creation of courses. We were back in that period pushing for either a black history course or a black culture course. And it was really interesting reviewing some of these old *Kernels* [UK newspapers]. We were pushing this black history course, and the chair of the history department responded to us by saying that that would be much too narrow. That would be like asking for a woman's history course. [*Laughs.*] So we were lobbying for that, and as things intensified around the country we stepped up our agenda so that some of the stuff became nonnegotiable.

Oh, but let me tell you, too, this transition from Orgena to BSU was not without some conflict, internal conflict in the group, because there were a number of students who really felt that we didn't have to take on this political agenda. That it was really risky and that if we would just work within the system and work with people who were sympathetic, that things would change. . . . The environment at that time varied from indifferent to hostile. . . . But the thing that I recall about that period was we knew, even though we were small in number, that we really weren't alone. Campuses at that time were fairly—there were a lot of influences coming through here. So we had a chance to meet students from other places. We had a guy from SNCC who was in the graduate school here who was kind of our liaison. We met people like Fannie Lou Hamer, who told us we were doing the right thing. We met, oh, all kinds of people, the Deacons of Defense from Bogalusa, Louisiana, came through—[this] was like the forerunners of the Black Panther Party. It was heady times and we were just ready for it.

Chester Grundy, Lexington

When I came to school here in 1967 there was a black student group here called Orgena that in the spring of 1968 led to the establishment of what's called the Black Student Union. The BSU, like Orgena before it, was very much concerned about the life of black students on campus, the academic life, the social life, the cultural life, the entire experience. Being concerned about that, we felt there was a need to take on certain kinds of responsibilities ourselves as students. We recognized that some students needed help with classes. So the Black Student Union began organizing a tutorial program where students could help other students. We pretty much knew the students who were doing well in school and who weren't doing well in school. We hooked up those individuals. We recognized that there was a need to provide a cultural experience that was meaningful to black students. The university-sponsored activities were geared toward white students. So BSU began to develop programs that would get black students an opportunity to witness, to get a better sense of our own black culture. Out of that need came Black Voices, which was a committee at first within the Black Student Union to provide a black cultural experience.

We also began to develop programs primarily around what's called black history month, but we also held programs around, say, birthdays of particular black leaders or black individuals who had in our mind played a role in the history of black people in the United States, such as the birthday and death of Malcolm X, Harriet Tubman. We also began to try to bridge some of the gaps between black students and African students, recognizing that if we wanted to provide cultural experiences for black students we had to include programs that would present various African cultures, be it through dance or song or sculpture. I recall that we approached student center people and asked about having an art exhibit in the student center art gallery. We got art from the various black students who were in school at the time and also we got art from the African students. So those kinds of things developed during those first couple years during the development of the Black Student Union. It was black students trying to meet the needs of ourselves.

James Embry, Lexington

BULK, the Black Six, and Civil Disorder in Louisville

One of the most important Black Power organizations in the state was the short-lived Black Unity League of Kentucky, formed in 1968 in Louisville. BULK grew out of the community organizing efforts of the West End Community Council. Its first programs focused on education about African and African American culture for high school students, but the group also traveled around the state to help organize black student organizations. BULK became embroiled in controversy for its role in organizing a rally against police brutality in May 1968, which ended in a mass uprising that lasted four days. Key figures in the organization were tried for conspiracy, which caused it to decline and eventually disband. Here BULK's story is told by the white executive director who helped to found the group, Charles Tachau. His story is followed by descriptions of the riot and the Black Six trial.

* * *

In 1966 and '67 I became quite active in the West End Community Council. In the summer of '67, I accepted the position of executive director to succeed Hulbert James. In my own mind I had in mind to do it for about a year, which was what I did. With some encouragement from Hulbert and others, I decided that one of Louisville's biggest needs was some kind of an organization that young blacks could belong to other than the NAACP or Kentucky Christian Leadership Conference. The West End Community Council was perceived as a good organization by most of them, but it was seen as a largely adult organization and had always insisted on a goal of integration and mixed racial membership. Well, that was right at the period when black consciousness was becoming very big, and there were some young blacks that you could not attract to an organization that had any whites connected with it. So I got the idea that maybe we could get VISTA to employ a few local young blacks to kind of organize a black group. I got two young men to be taken on as VISTAs and assigned to the council, one of whom was Sam Hawkins, a local man who had been very active in the open housing movement. Another one was Bob Sims, one of Dr. King's organizers who had been sent here to organize in that and had done so. They proceeded to organize the Black Unity League of Kentucky. It was always referred to as BULK. Their first efforts were to organize in the schools and colleges.

Then this incident occurred between Manfred Reid and the police which stirred up a lot of excitement in the black community. It looked like for a while it was settled and then it turned out it wasn't. The chief of police disciplined the cop involved and the Civil Service Board reversed him. Anyway, after three or four weeks it flared up again. Well, BULK, of course, got very caught up in the agitation respecting that. I was kept pretty closely advised about what was going on by both Mr. Robinson, who was the chairman of the council, and also by the two VISTAs. They had a big meeting over at Reverend Hodge's church. He was the president of the local branch of the NAACP. The NAACP and the KCLC and BULK and possibly some others, they decided to have some kind of a big rally to protest this.[5] A VISTA told me that they wanted to have it there at that church, but the older leadership insisted that they couldn't get enough people in there and it needed to be out in the street. The VISTAs claimed that they thought that was dangerous to have it out in the street, but they were overruled.

Well, anyway, then they set up this rally to happen at 28th and Greenwood. In the meantime the Poor People's March on Washington had occurred possibly a month before. These two VISTAs as well as a number of other people from Louisville had gone there and they had met this man named Cortez in Washington, who claimed to be a member of Stokely Carmichael's organization, SNCC. Maybe he was a member of it. I don't say he wasn't, but they never really checked it out. But anyway, in casting around for a speaker to come and address this rally, these VISTAs said they thought maybe they had a connection whereby they could get Carmichael to come. So everybody said, "Fine. Fine. Do it." And so then they contacted this guy Cortez who had promised he would help them any possible way. Well, his way of helping them as it turned out was to say that Stokely would come.

It was my impression, which I will go to my grave believing, that if the police had stayed out of there another three or four minutes, nothing much would have happened. The speakers were on the top of automobiles parked in the middle of the intersection. The police had it all blocked off about a block away in each direction. There were a lot of people there, true enough. There were a bunch of kids, as far as I could tell, that were up on a roof of a one-story building there on a corner. I was sort of standing under the awning of that building. So I couldn't see what was going on there too much. But there was, of course, a good deal of excitement and a lot of things had been stirred up and people yelling and so forth. And these kids commenced throwing bottles off of the roof and there were lots of adults in the street hollering at them to cut that out and I think in a few minutes they would have. But instead of that the police kind of panicked and roared in there with sirens and lights and things and they started throwing at the police and, of course, the police were outnumbered and the police were looking around trying to see who to grab. They had their guns pulled out but they were helpless. As soon as everybody realized that they really had the police where they wanted them, the whole thing escalated in a matter of just seconds.

Charles Tachau, Louisville

Then things started like crazy. The rioters just went up and down the street, breaking windows and going into businesses and things of that nature. Ironically, they didn't touch my business [the Corner of Jazz]. I was inside. I didn't go out. I didn't know what was really going on outside other than chaos was taking place. I looked out and saw that car, the police car, burning. I said, "My God," and that was it. I was inside along with some other folks. There was a reporter, David Diaz, who was a *Courier-Journal* reporter, he was in there, too. There was a couple of other folks. Suddenly, things kind of subsided. It was very quiet on the street. I decided to put on the speaker out front, "Respect," Aretha Franklin's "A Little Respect." When that music hit, people came back out and just started dancing and having that kind of thing. It was really kind of nice.

The next night, the next morning actually, the National Guard was called in. I went over to my store to just see what was going on and the National Guard was there. I couldn't get to my store. I had to stand over between two houses. I was standing there with a guy named Neville Tucker who was an attorney. Bill Warner and some other city officials were walking down the street and the National Guard was all over the area. In the meantime, the guys on the street were just playing with the National Guard. They would go up, and the National Guard had their bayonets out, and the guys would go out and play with them and talk to them. The National Guard was at attention. There were a couple of black guys in the National Guard and I saw one of them, tears were just coming out of his eyes. He didn't want to be there at all. But while I was standing there, a couple of kids were playing, running around. One of them threw a rock and the rock came right down in front of me. Now, right on the porch next to where I was standing was a county police officer with a double-barrel shotgun. When that rock hit that ground in front of me, he turned around and put that gun up in my face. All I could do was look up to him. Neville saw what was going on and he saw Bill Warner out in the street and he went to get Bill. And Bill Warner came over there and got me out of that situation, for which I am ever indebted to him. But I saw hate. I mean, I saw hate, I saw fear. I was just glad that he didn't pull the trigger. But it was just so—and I wasn't fearful. I guess looking at him made me say, "Damn, I've never seen hate like this before." But that was an experience I had and that's one of those personal things. But the guys stood in front of my store protecting it. They said, "We're not going to let them mess up your store." I think mine was the only store that they didn't touch. It meant something very special to them.

Ken Clay, Louisville

[After the riot, Bob Sims, Sam] Hawkins and Cortez, Manfred Reid, Mrs. Ruth Bryant, and a fellow named Pete Cosby were arrested. It was claimed that they had formed a conspiracy to cause a major explosion down at the Louisville Refining Company on Southwestern

Parkway. And Cortez, who was, to put it mildly, an ambiguous kind of a character, had apparently claimed this while he was in jail. He had been arrested, I guess, on charges of starting a riot, which he had. He also claimed that he was an undercover agent for the FBI, or at least so the prosecuting authorities of the police alleged. Now he always denied this to me and denied that he had told them any of this stuff. But I don't see how they could have made it up. Anyway, most of them got out on bond, but we never could get him out. Eventually there was a trial and they were all acquitted. They didn't really have any very substantial evidence against them.

Charles Tachau, Louisville

The thing that was so stark about the Black Six case was that they arrested black leaders from all different segments of black society, so that they were sending a message to the entire black community, "You have to stop this stuff." Black leaders like Ruth Bryant, she was a prominent civic lady and her husband was a very well-known doctor. Then there were street activists, Bob "Kuyu" Sims and Sam Hawkins. Sam had been an antipoverty worker. Pete Cosby was another activist. They really targeted, it seemed like they targeted the entire black community strata to send a message to—a chilling effect.

Dan Taylor represented James Cortez and I believe Ben Shobe represented Ruth Bryant in the Black Six case. Cortez was kind of the central person in terms of why the case got as far as it did. The police alleged that he said certain things after they took him into custody. He denied saying those things. Then the police used that to then arrest people and charge this conspiracy, of which there was no evidence whatsoever other than what the police alleged Cortez told them! The case, unheard of, was moved on the motion of the commonwealth attorney to Hart County, which in my recollection the prosecutors didn't even have the legal authority to do that! Only the defense had the authority to ask for a change of venue! But that happened. In the climate of what was going on, if you can imagine a prosecutor saying we can't get a fair trial. So the case was moved to Hart County. Then eventually the case was moved back to Louisville!

Judge [S. Rush] Nicholson was really kind of one of the more interesting persons. You know it's very unusual for a judge to direct a verdict of acquittal in a criminal case and that's what Judge Nicholson did. This case was a political football for so long and finally when it did actually go to trial, a couple of years after it happened.... Then for the judge to direct a verdict of acquittal was quite, quite interesting.

Bill Allison, Louisville

The Diversity and Demise of Black Power

In addition to BULK, there were a number of smaller Black Power organizations in Kentucky, most of which were in Louisville, where they focused on black community self-help, economic self-sufficiency, and empowerment. These groups included local organizations like Our Black Thing or Black United Brothers. They also included local units of national organizations, most importantly the Black Panthers. One particular concentration was an effort to fight the rising drug problem in the black community. These narratives describe some of these projects, and groups, as well as the unraveling of the Black Power movement in the early 1970s.

* * *

[In Louisville at Plymouth House] I was youth director. It began to hit home to me how much poverty so many people in America live with, especially black people. The Settlement House was kind of the watering hole. One of the things that [Morris] Jeff instituted shortly after we were there was—I'm sure it was a spin on the Black Panther piece—we started serving hot meals after school. We could easily have three, four, five hundred children who would come into that center every day. As youth director, I was trying to work with the kitchen staff, the volunteers, to organize around this and then to do programming afterwards. First thing Jeff told me when I got to Plymouth Settlement House was, "Spend a little time just going and just sitting and talking." He said, "You're southern, you know what to do. Go sit on the porch and figure it out." And it hit me really hard, because what he wanted me to see was that [poverty] in almost every home that I visited—and I came to know all these families.

Ann Beard Grundy, Louisville

I worked with two groups. I was in an organization that nobody's heard of—except those that were in it—called Our Black Thing. We went to Reynolds Metals Company and told them that there was a house at the alley near Twenty-eighth and Grand, they owned the house, and that we wanted to use it as what we called a black house. And we told them that no wasn't an option. So they gave us the use of the house. We had enough black paint to get half of it painted and we tried community level kinds of things out of there. We were trying to develop a free university, just a whole bunch of stuff that we were doing in those days. We were trying to stir up the awareness and the consciousness of the people about the oppression that we saw. . . . We found out that a woman and her family had been burned out and we tracked the woman down and we thought it was proper to give the woman five hundred dollars. We found her in some little church on Eighteenth Street. It was kind of real funny because we were at that time armed. We carried .45s and really were paranoid and would have opened fire on the police if they had jumped too fast. When we walked in the church this minister probably thought some hoodlums were coming in. We asked for this woman by name. He said, "There she is!" We gave her the money. And then she said, "Well who are you?" And we just walked on out of the church and he prayed while we were walking out.

We were trying to create a new kind of society, we had a real serious kind of effort to do that. We decided that we were going to get the two housing projects to develop into a commune and divorce themselves from the city of Louisville and create a healthier lifestyle. By that time we had developed into a new form of organization called Enterprises Unlimited. We started a program called the Stop Dope Now program because we perceived that the government, starting in 1960, had begun pumping drugs into the black community as a way of smoldering the social agitation going on at that time. I witnessed that myself, bringing drugs at a real low price, two dollars, and just spreading it all around. Then the susceptible individuals got addicted to it and then the police didn't mind or the FBI either. They could use these people as informants. We saw that as a strategy to destroy the community. So by the mid-, late '60s we decided to step in and do something ourselves, so what we did was started a corporate firm. First we rejected all formal kinds of things, and then found out that we couldn't raise money without it. So we created an organization, got a 501(c)(3), went to various community, so-called leaders. There were about seventeen of us initially, all black men. . . . In 1969 Enterprises Unlimited started a drug abuse program that had a methadone component to it. We started a youth center called the Masters of Reality in Old Lucky Morris's pawnshop on Twenty-eighth and Greenwood. We had a motto that came from a 1926 article: you can either be a dupe of reality and sink, a slave of reality and drift down the stream, or a master of reality and chart your course. . . . We had a factory that we were going to take people that didn't have job skills and try to get them into to have to come to work on time. We had a bunch of sewing machines and they were making garments and all this sort of thing. We had those components to it. At first we raised probably about a hundred thousand dollars just by going from place to place. At first we had a staff that was volunteer, then we worked out a contract with River Region—what they now call Seven Counties—where we did drug abuse sort of thing.

Sterling Neal Jr., Louisville

I became a Panther when I seen a six-year-old black boy eating out of a garbage can in Cincinnati, Ohio. I was attending the University of Cincinnati taking some courses and was working at Christ Hospital. I was on my way to work and I seen this little black kid eating out of a garbage can. I stopped my car and he said he was hungry and I remember that I said, "Take me to your house." I went to his house and his family didn't have any food at all and there was a whole family there, mother, father, grandfather, great-grandfather, kids, and everything. So I took the mother to the store and I had some money. I wasn't rich. I was a poor person myself, still what I did I took her to the store and I got her beans, got her some pork chops and things like that. She was so happy, you know. The garbage can was right next door to a building, and there was a picture of [Black Panther leader] Huey P. Newton in the window. I stopped in there before I took the kid home, because I was new to Cincinnati, to find directions to where this kid lived. And they told me, "Well, you go over there and do what you got to do but come back." So I went back and I joined there, right there.

Then I got sick with bronchitis. So I came back to Louisville to rest. Then I met, quite by accident, Ben Simmons, George Thomas Alexander, Judy Simmons, Yvonne, John, Carol Morse, Herbert Jones: these were the core of the Black Panther Party here in Louisville. They were spending a lot of time trying to organize. I didn't say anything for a month or so and then I told them, I said, "Well, what you've got to do is get officers, then you've got to get a location of an office," and I said, "Then you've got to have a program, a social program." "Carrying guns is one thing. You don't want to hurt nobody, you don't want to murder nobody, you don't want nobody to murder you." I said, "But what you've got to do, you've got to get social programs."

So the party started a program up in the West End of Louisville, a breakfast program. Then we had a clothing program. We had a program where we went from door to door and we assessed the needs of the individual black person. It took time. To cover two blocks took two days. If a person didn't have food we got the food, we went and bought it, took the food. If they needed something, clothes, even if they needed a pack of cigarettes or whatever, we helped them get it, or if they needed to get on Social Security we took them to the Social Security office. We were trying to serve the black community.

We didn't have the money to buy bacon and eggs and bread and milk for our breakfast program. We went to stores and a lot of times they throw this stuff out, but as opposed to throwing it out they would give it to us. Then what began to happen was we would go to different places and there were different white merchants who didn't want their names to be known who would give us food, good food.

Carol Morse and I went out and walked around and did this and we also talked to them about voting. We assessed the needs of the people. See, we knew that you can't talk to hungry people about ideas, no matter what race. Sometimes we accidentally ran into white people who were incidentally hungry and didn't have any clothes or sometimes they had social problems in their house and we would get them the necessary help. We would help the white people as well. Quiet as it's kept, the Black Panther Party helped a lot of white people, too. Here in Louisville I'm talking about, when we started going down in Portland, for example.

They were willing to accept our help. They were willing to talk to us, although they were leery of us. They had this pre-conceived idea of how we would act and what we would do, and then half our time was spent in breaking down a wall of fear. We spent a lot of time breaking down a wall of fear.

I told the Louisville Panthers, "The best thing to do is to try to be involved in the black community, and the way that you are going to have to do is you're going to have to avoid, if possible, any confrontation, but if you can't avoid it then you will have to stand up to it." What happened was that Ben Simmons and I, we located an office on south Eighteenth Street and it was near Eighteenth and St. Catherine. So anyway Ben Simmons and I were walking back to my mother's house. The police were occupying the filling station at the time and what they did was they shot guns in the air. They knew we were Black Panthers and they were trying to get us to shoot so they could kill us. Ben was getting ready to shoot and I said, "Look, don't do it." So we began to travel by car then, we stopped walking except when we got further down in the West End.

In the end, people in the party became paranoid. There was more infighting in the Panthers here in Louisville. We had gotten to the place where we had a considerable number of Panthers. What we didn't know was that a lot of them were agent provocateurs. They were there to stir up trouble and trouble is what they did, they stirred it up. They had us fighting amongst each other and everything. As a result we were not attending to social programs or anything. We were barely hanging on with meetings. You know, interestingly enough, these agents were black, they were not white. You know, I have come to the question today of how could an African American sell himself out like that?

Nancy Pollock, Louisville

The Louisville Seven case really seemed to me to be kind of on par of the Black Six, there just was no evidence to link them to this crime. It was the climate of the times. Right here in Louisville people were so afraid of the black movement fighting for civil rights that they had to frame these people and put them through all this horrendous turmoil for several years. It affected their lives, the rest of their life. The Panthers were, from what I can tell, the same way. There was no evidence really.

What actually happened, Laird's Tourist Home was a nightclub in the black community where drugs were readily available, prostitutes were readily available; and white and black mingled there. Then on Derby eve, it was known as the place to go among high rollers, you know, underworld type figures, shady type folks who would come into Louisville for that whole week and they would know they could have a good time at Laird's. That Derby eve there were all the folks from all over the country there. At two or three A.M. in the morning some folks who had been at the party opened up their jackets, pulled out sawed-off shotguns, and said, "Okay, everybody take your clothes off and get down on the floor." They proceeded to take rings and jewelry and cash, and left. The police immediately pinned it on the Panthers, charged them with all of these robbery charges.

There just wasn't any evidence. I think one of the Laird's employees said, "I recognize one of the Panthers as being in the group that night." It was very vague. The Laird's people were very shaky. They all had criminal records. They all were under enormous pressure. When we got the list of witnesses who showed up for the indictments, they were all over the country, Detroit, L.A., New York. It's all these high rollers with big money, none of whom really wanted to come back and testify! They all had questionable backgrounds. . . . Maybe some did come back and testify, but nobody picked out any of the Panthers, except there was this one employee at Laird's who did.

Now the judge was again Judge Nicholson. He directed a verdict of acquittal for five of the seven Panthers. They had all been in jail for like six months on high bonds. I guess this is why I'm kind of favorable towards him because he had guts. Two of the Panthers went to a jury trial and Ben Simmons was acquitted and Darryl Blakemore was convicted by that one person who worked at Laird's and indicated that he was in the group. Darryl was also convicted of possession of a sawed-off shotgun, a federal charge, so he did some time in jail. But it was extremely shaky, particularly in the climate. This is now 1972 when I think they were arrested, in '72, and the trial was that fall.

Bill Allison, Louisville

I believe that by '73 the mood of the country shifted. I think Spiro Agnew did a real assault on the university and that had implications for the street level kind of stuff. The Black Panther Party had fizzled out. As a matter of fact the Black Panther Party here, we supported them even though we thought that they were about a couple of years behind the times. By that time we had moved into what we called institution-building, and it was kind of clear to us that what you need are resources. . . . By that time the idea of armed defense became more of a vulnerability than it was an asset. When we were there they didn't have some of the laws that they have now. Law enforcement, which used to form a fascist kind of connection with paramilitary groups, had shifted so that they were neutral, I mean as neutral as they had ever been. A person really could seek justice with calling the police for instance, whereas before the police officer might have just been part of the Ku Klux Klan.

Sterling Neal Jr., Louisville

* * *

By the mid-1970s the Black Power movement nationally was dissipating. As Sterling Neal points out, it was in part a victim of government repression and white backlash. But the movement, like the struggle for racial equality itself, did not die so much as move into new channels of activity. Just as nationalist sentiments and efforts to promote empowerment through solidarity had not been born with the 1960s, they continued to live into the next decade and beyond in new forms of cultural pride, economic development, and African American political power.

Profile

J. Blaine Hudson

J. BLAINE Hudson is an author, scholar, university administrator, and Louisville native whose activism in the latter phases of the 1960s civil rights movement helped to usher in major institutional changes at the University of Louisville. Born in 1949, Hudson grew up amid the massive social upheavals of the 1960s, and he came of age when the slogan "Black Power" was replacing the early-1960s vision of a nonviolent "beloved community."

Hudson's narrative situates his civil rights activism and his becoming an educator within the influence of family—especially his grandmother—but also in the movements that brought sweeping social changes to his home city during the years of his youth. Hudson grew up during the first wave of school desegregation in Louisville in the 1950s, but he himself attended racially integrated schools starting only in high school. An academically gifted student, his intellectual prowess opened multiple avenues of opportunity, but he also faced dogged discrimination in desegregated schools. Hudson's youth unfolded along with the flowering of the Black Consciousness/Black Pride cultural movement of the late '60s, and by the time he entered the University of Louisville, he was both politically active and a prolific poet whose works reflected the currents of Afrocentrism in his midst.

As a cofounder of U of L's Black Student Union, Hudson lost his National Merit scholarship and was suspended from the university in 1969 after the BSU occupied an administration building to demand a Black Studies program. He returned to the University of Louisville a year after his suspension and earned a joint undergraduate degree in history and counseling, then later received a master's degree from the College of Education. Following his passion for African American education and history,

Hudson went on to the University of Kentucky for a doctorate, which he received in 1981 after completing a dissertation on the history of the Louisville Municipal College for Negroes. Ironically, since 1992 he has been a professor in the Pan-African Studies program he helped to establish. And in 1999 Hudson became an associate dean in the University of Louisville's College of Arts and Sciences. His first book, *Fugitive Slaves and the Underground Railroad*, came out in 2003, earning him considerable accolade and public interest regionally. A year later, he became dean of Arts and Sciences. In that role Hudson has continued to steer the University of Louisville toward fulfillment of its urban mission through new initiatives to attract and mentor minority students, faculty, and staff, and through institutionalizing adult education programs like the ones he had developed in his youth.

* * *

When I was born, our household consisted of my mother and my father and my grandmother and my grandfather. . . . My grandfather had been a principal of the Scribner High School, the black high school in New Albany, Indiana. My grandmother had been a teacher there until her retirement and then they moved to Louisville basically to live with my parents. . . . My mother was working for Municipal Housing or whatever it was called at that time. My father was a pharmacist and at times would have his own business and other times he would be working as a pharmacist in other people's businesses. My parents had been married since 1937, so when I was born in 1949 I came as something of a surprise. My mother was actually thirty-eight years old when I was born. That's pretty old in those days. My father was forty-four, almost forty-five, which was old. One of the interesting things that dominated my early years was [that] beginning in 1950, 1951, we began to have a series of deaths. So by the time I was twelve years old, I was the oldest male in my immediate family, and our family had undergone a transformation from being a family that was pretty solidly middle class at least in terms of resources to a family that was on the verge of poverty, if not all the way there.

I won't say it was a good experience, but it's an experience I learned a lot from. The person who seemed to really step forward in my family at that time was my grandmother. My grandmother really became the central person in our larger family and probably the most important influence on me when I was very, very young. She was in her mid-sixties by the time I was born . . . a bright woman, well-educated, well-read, been an educator all of her life, had a very open and receptive mind for someone that age. She was always reading something new and always willing to encourage, and particularly me because I was the oldest grandchild, to do things that weren't necessarily the norm or weren't necessarily popular. She encouraged me in my writing, my poetry, in many of the interests that I had. . . . Much of my early education came from her. I can still remember to this day shaping my letters in clay on a mirror that was on the top of a table when I was, like, three years old with her. She lived to be almost 101 years old so . . . I would have been almost thirty-seven when she died.

My father suffered a devastating stroke when I was six years old . . . so he couldn't work and many of the insurance and other kinds of arrangements that exist now were certainly not in place then. So not only did we have to find a way to take care of him, but we had to also find a way to compensate to some extent for lost earnings. He had friends who were doctors that he had gone to school with who gave us free medical care. . . . Of course, my family was part of Louisville's old black middle-class. The man who was at one time president of Mammoth Life [Julius Hankins] would take me out shopping a couple times a year and buy me a couple of new suits. . . . So even though my own father wasn't there, I . . . had a lot of male role models to choose from. . . . It turned out to be a very rich childhood.

[I] went to a number of high schools. I started off at St. X. . . . I ended up going to Atherton in my sophomore year . . . [that's] a high school in the East End of Louisville, generally in an area that's sort of upper middle class, predominantly white. There were probably about ten black students at Atherton when I was there. . . . I had a couple of interesting run-ins with white teachers there. . . . I took chemistry in my first period. [The teacher] had a picture of a chimpanzee on the inside of his cabinet behind his desk. It's early in the morning, right, and anytime someone would yawn he'd open up the door and point to the picture of the chimpanzee. Well, he and I got along okay until I got an "A" the first grading period.

This is something I've run into a lot. A lot of white Americans are willing to concede that a black person may be able to run faster or jump higher than they can, but they have a real problem if you're smarter than they are. . . . But [after that "A"] it seemed like he was determined that I wasn't going to get two "A"s in a row in his class. We had an examination and I think there were twenty-five questions on the examination. I got twenty-four out of twenty-five right, you know, my math tells me that 96 is an "A." Well, he decided that instead of getting a 96, I got an 88 or something like that. He took points off because I didn't start my answer on the top line of the paper. So I questioned that, and the next thing I know, I'm being sent to the office and I'm on the bus going home. So my mother had to come back out there and [straighten things out].

Then I had a Latin teacher. [*Laughs.*] This is sort of funny. I've been writing poetry since I was eight years old, and I enjoyed Latin, but Latin was enough to keep you busy about twenty minutes of the hour. So when I finished what I had to do, a lot of times I would look out the window, and I'd be writing something. This was one of those teachers that you just sort of knew that [even my] being in the class was a problem for her, just body language, facial language. . . . Anyway, one day I was just writing some stuff while . . . other students were still working. I was through, so I wasn't doing anything disruptive. Well, she decided she was going to come by and throw my stuff on the floor and then tell me that I was supposed to pick it up. I didn't pick it up, so I'm going down to the office again and I'm on the bus coming home again. After that I didn't want to be there anyway, [so] I went to Male the next year. What makes it so interesting is that when they made the announcement that I was a National Merit semi-finalist, at the beginning of my senior year at Male, there were some people out at Atherton who had the nerve to talk about how they basically had made me what I was. That was the damnedest thing I've ever heard! I didn't really . . . have a bad experience with some of the other teachers at Atherton. I didn't have a bad experience at Male. But . . . to some extent, at Atherton certainly, I was a stranger in a strange land.

I also recognize that I've had some experiences that a lot of other [African American] kids of my generation had not had because from the time that I was five or six years old, I was involved in academic competitions. At the time those competitions were just beginning to desegregate so I was in the little spelling contests and the little math contests with kids from all over the county. Of course, by being able to do well in those kind of competitions, my attitude towards whites was always very different from the attitudes that a lot of my contemporaries and my neighbors had.

Segregation in American society was so complete that it literally created two separate worlds. You could be a part of one of those worlds and not have much of a clue as to what was going on beyond its boundaries. I can remember . . . my mother taking me downtown sometimes when she would go shopping, because after my father got sick we didn't have the use of a car anymore so we would have to ride the bus. All of a sudden there are these crowds of very, very white people. Now, of course . . . I had seen white kids at these academic competitions and so it didn't seem all that unusual to me. But African Americans had to be very much aware of the boundaries because if you guessed wrong about one of those boundaries you could end up in big trouble, you could end up dead. White Americans didn't necessarily need to be as conscious of that, but African Americans did.

It was a different kind of society. I can remember when my father was sick and he couldn't drive anymore and they got me into Cub Scouts. We'd ride the bus sometimes. Buses coming out of the West End, back in those days, went all the way down to Shawnee Park. Well, that was white, and so you would have [white] people on the bus coming out of the deep part of the West End going through the black part [farther east]. So you get on the bus, the folks just assume that you're supposed to sit in the back part of the bus or at least not in the [very] front. . . . Of course, as you became more and more aware of those kinds of things, it was very easy to understand what it was that you were fighting against, the barriers you were fighting to break down.

[Resistance], in my case, was a matter of timing. Louisville was not a big place for having separate fountains and that kind of stuff that you would find farther south. By the time I was really old enough to do a lot of traveling around on my own, a lot of that stuff was illegal. . . . I can remember when we had the demonstrations here in '60, in the winter of '61, the Nothing New for Easter campaign. I remember wanting very, very much to participate in that. I had an older cousin who was involved in some of that. By that time, many of us were beginning to get a sense of what a movement was and that this was something that was important to relate to. But generally, my life was pretty much contained in the bowels of the West End, of Louisville's black community, and when I went outside, it was usually under conditions that were pretty well controlled.

[After high school] I came out here to U of L. I had taken classes at U of L in '66 and '67 and enjoyed it. With me being an only child . . .

the decision to come here was an interesting one. I had thought a lot about going elsewhere. I'd had a lot of offers with this merit scholarship business. . . . But I decided to stay here. . . . Woodrow Strickler, who was then the executive vice president of U of L, actually recruited me directly, had my mother and me into his office. Of course, my mother was sold right at that point. . . . One of the consequences of the circumstances of my early life: the age of my parents when I was born, what happened to the men in my family, was that whether I liked it or not or whether I wanted it or not, there's been a degree of responsibility for the older folks in my immediate family that's just been there. There hasn't been anybody else to do that. . . . Plus, when I was eighteen years old, my attitude basically was, give me a little quiet time and a good library and I'll learn no matter where you put me.

* * *

Hudson's political commitment continued to evolve at the university and he became part of a group that coalesced as the Black Student Union, or BSU.

Much of what happened at U of L, in terms of the development of the Black Student Union in '68, grows out of the open housing movement in Louisville, that really goes back to '66 and '67. This is the same time you've got the emergence of the Black Power movement, the Panther Party, other groups like that on a national basis. . . . King's assassination was a powerful catalyst for our group, as it was for many, many other groups. And we tended to become more and more radical after that. Of course, the riot here in Louisville, in May of '68, and all those things kind of feed in together. Much of this goes back to the Black Unity League of Kentucky that rose out of the open housing movement, as a kind of radical, black nationalist group. Many of the folks in BSU had been involved in BULK, as it was called.

[For] some of the younger ones, like me, that was kind of the framework that was there for us [as we came of age]. . . . We became more and more convinced that . . . gradualistic approaches were not going to work. Holding hands and singing songs was not necessarily going to work, although that was a good tactic up to a point. But we became much more insistent, much more unyielding, and were willing to take greater risks to try to force change. . . . We saw ourselves very much as being part of this national movement. By the time I started at U of L, there were black student organizations all over the country. The fact that we organized one . . . was not as revolutionary an act as it might seem. . . . Movements like that are always minority movements, but what made it seem more like a movement in those days was that there was a degree of sympathy for what we stood for and what we tried to do among people who would not have taken any kind of overt role or marched or demonstrated. So even if you were in an organization that might be fairly small, you didn't necessarily feel yourself cut off. . . . We probably had twenty to thirty active people, maybe half of that when it came down to folks who were really willing to take some sort of risk. On campus, there would have been maybe several hundred African American students. Now a lot of them came [to school] at night, and so they were kind of an invisible population to many of us, but they were here.

* * *

Here Hudson describes the network of which the University of Louisville's BSU was a part, as well as the objectives that most animated the group.

In the earlier days [of the civil rights movement], you had SNCC, the Student Nonviolent Coordinating Committee, pronounced "Snick," that had a kind of unifying force. But once the whole Black Power issue came up, SNCC split and . . . in a way just sort of dissolved. The Black Panther Party was becoming very well known at that time, but . . . Panthers tended to be strongest in areas that didn't have strong pre-existing organizations. Louisville was one of the areas where there was a lot going on, so the Panthers were here but they were never a real force here. But . . . when you get right down to it, a movement is more like a loosely defined network than it is a big formal organization with dues and by-laws and a building and that kind of thing. In Kentucky, there wasn't much going on outside of Louisville, quite frankly, and so part of what we did as a BSU was we tried to start BSU's on other campuses. We traveled around the state to Eastern and Western and UK and Berea and places like that. We tried to plant BSUs in the high schools locally around here.

A couple of things that were very important for me during that period in a sense shaped a lot of my later work. One, I became editor of our newsletter, which was our propaganda sheet. The other, I became the head of the tutoring program for BSU because we set up little tutoring centers in different parts of the West End. We had somebody from the admissions office that helped pay us for doing some of that. What that did for me—because I was about the youngest person in the organization—it helped establish the link between political activism and working in a real tangible sense for a constructive social change. You've got to do more than talk about the ways in which a society should be changed, you've got to get involved in changing it. . . . It's easy to say what somebody else ought to do, but it's not that easy to get the knowledge base and the skills that are necessary to make those changes happen yourself. That was a very good experience. Of course, we got progressively more radical. We developed a proposal during the fall of '68 and it was presented in early March of '69, a "recruitment proposal," we called it, but it had a little bit of everything in there, including the creation of [a Pan-African Studies department].

When some of us still get together, we really take a lot of pride in that because in some respects we were a lot more forward-looking than many of our contemporaries were, largely because so many of the things that we envisioned really did have a niche. They really did have a purpose. And PAS is still here. The great irony of all is for me to end up working in this [framework]. I never would have thought that would have happened.

Anyway, we presented this proposal the early part of March and got into about a six-week negotiation cycle with the administration. The university gave us a fair amount of ground, so we knew that some good things were going to happen. . . . They had agreed to establish an Office of Black Affairs, they had agreed, I think, to create the [African American] collection in the library, they had agreed to what we called the Martin Luther King Scholarships. We were still haggling over how many, but they'd agreed to create a fair number. . . . Some of what we did in BSU taught all of us a lesson that we couldn't have learned anywhere else, and that was how power works. Not that we had it, but how power works and what you can do to make power respond to you, and what can happen if you miscalculate too. It was a really interesting experience for someone who was nineteen years old to have.

[When] negotiations broke down over who the director of the Office of Black Affairs was going to be, we took the next step, which was to take some illegal action on campus. We had held a couple of different kind of demonstrations. The first day we demonstrated was April 30, 1969. Then May 1, 1969, we came back and took over the building that was the Dean of Arts and Science's office, and if you go north on campus where Parrish Court is now is where that building used to be—they tore it down years ago—we took that over the second day. That was the day the police ended up breaking in, and we all ended up going to jail. The week after that, there was almost a star chamber hearing out here, and most of us were kicked out of school.

There were about ten people altogether [who occupied the building]. Then people like Gerry Neal and Claude McCullum and some of the rest were out in front on the steps. They didn't get arrested because they weren't breaking the law, but they were out there. Because there were a bunch [of] real crazy whites who wanted to break into that building, a lot of the big black football players and [other black athletes] formed a little line in front of the building. So they weren't in the building but they [became] part of what we were doing. . . . We were in there a few hours. I forget just how long it was now; we had to write press statements and all that stuff, so I spent most of my time doing that. We had some younger students in there that I had to try and calm down, so Bob [Martin]'s job was to guard the door and my job was kind of to try to keep some sort of order with everybody else inside. We had people stationed around campus, on top of buildings, just to let us know what was going on.

There was supposed to be a lot more people there that day. Most folks don't realize that the dean's building of A & S was not our goal. We had planned to take over the whole student center that day, but there were a lot of folks, and some of the community groups that we had alliances with, that never showed up. [Later] we found out that the police were picking these people up all over town. So there was an informant [who] let the police know what our plan was because when it came down to it we just didn't have enough people to take control of a large building like the student center.

As I look back on it, we kept our focus on issues pretty well. . . . Our agenda was a pretty radical agenda, but our methods were not unusual for the time . . . we had a fair amount of support. . . . The campus was a lot more liberal then, too. There were a fair number of folks on campus who were SDS-type characters, so we had a fairly broad base of support among that liberal to radical group of whites. . . . Louisville was never a real liberal city, not now, wasn't then. But Louisville's always had a segment of its population that's been pretty progressive, [and] we had a fair amount of support, I mean, this is where I got to know people like Suzy Post . . . like Anne and Carl Braden.

[After the arrests] there was a hearing. We'd been found guilty but we were out on bail on appeal. All that happened real fast and the case itself didn't go back to court again until the winter of 1970. Now we had one person who got arrested with us who had no business being in that building. Lord knows why she was there, but she testified . . . she wanted to claim that we forced her to stay in the building, which was not true. But to make a long story short, it turned out that by the time that we did go to court . . . there were a million different laws they could have charged us with violating and we were guilty of those. But the one they charged us under was this anti-riot act that they had passed in Kentucky right around that time, a year or so before that. Under the provisions of the anti-riot act, the police had not done what they were supposed to do. In other words, they couldn't make it stick, so ironically we got off. . . . They [were supposed to have given] some kind of notice to "stop doing whatever you're doing and vacate the premises." They hadn't done that. Even some of their own people testified that . . . all they saw was just people bust down the door.

We were [eventually] represented by people from Legal Aid. But interestingly enough, when we went to court the first time right after we were arrested, the person who helped us make our case more than anybody else was a [conservative] district attorney, J. Earl Dearing. But Dearing was black, and he was the one that questioned us, and since he saw that we didn't have competent representation at the time, Dearing brought out in his questions the issues that eventually got us off. . . . You could tell the judge [was] just seething, but it was within [Dearing's] right to do that. He put all the stuff on the record that needed to be in the record that would eventually get us out of going to jail.

There was a sense of who the ringleaders were. Bob and I were the main ones that kind of got as close to a "death penalty" as you could get. . . . It was illegal for me to come back on the U of L campus for a period of time. . . . I never thought I would come back here [to finish school]. Honestly, I think deep down inside I always felt that I would complete my education, but I was looking at a lot of options. One of those options was a more full-time involvement in the movement. Of course, this was the period of time when the movement itself begins to unravel, and there wasn't going to be anything to be involved in full-time before long. There [came] a time in the early '70s when the movement as we thought of it was pretty much in shambles. Then I thought very seriously about going to Africa. A friend of mine and I thought very seriously about trying to move to Tanzania, because I always had a lot of respect for Nyerere and what he was trying to do—African socialism. But it's the same battle wherever you go, and you can always fight that battle close to home, but it was a very attractive idea given where the country was going then.

Let me go back: for someone who was nineteen, almost twenty years old the day we walked out of court in the spring of '69, most of my life had played itself out against the backdrop of the civil rights era, and then the immediate aftermath of that. I mean, all of my experience had been rooted in the time when this nation, however grudgingly, was making progress in the area of race. Now, of course, I can look back now and understand that around '66 or so, that progress stopped. But there was no reason to believe in '68 or '69 that that was as far as we would get, or that some of the other ways in which American society needed to change would not actually happen.

We were prepared to live in a very different kind of world . . . the problem came in when that different kind of world didn't come into existence. Initially, if you think back . . . after King gets assassinated, after Kennedy gets assassinated, for a little while, [movement] people felt that, well, if we just try a little harder, push a little harder, we can get this whole thing back on track. Then it began to dawn on people after Richard Nixon got comfortable in the White House . . . that there really was a systematic effort in play to suppress the movement, not to fulfill the movement but to suppress it. What that did [was to] leave a lot of us with some real, real nasty choices to make. People who were involved in [activism] back then will tell you that some of the most interesting material is what people never talk about—all the emotional and psychological turmoil that people went through. How many people got strung out on alcohol, or on drugs, or crazy relationships? Reactions to the stress, you know. How many people joined the movement for therapeutic purposes, anyway? . . . All the worst sides of it [began] to bubble to the surface in the early 1970s, and it got to the point where you didn't know who you could trust.

In the civil rights era, if there was anything that people underestimated, it was probably the extent to which, once things changed to

a certain point, there would be tremendous resistance to them changing any further. What that would leave us with is a revolution that
was only half finished. . . . So what happens when you stop halfway?
Where we are right now is a real good example of what does happen.
Some people move forward, and life works out reasonably well, but an
awful lot of people get left behind. . . . But I don't think [the move-
ment] was shortsighted. If all segments of American society had acted
in as much good faith as people like Malcolm X and Martin Luther
King did, this would be a very different country today.

Chapter 7

Black Political Power

IN many ways the defining feature of the modern civil rights struggle was the effort to secure the right to vote and political power for African Americans. After the brief democratic promise offered during Reconstruction and despite the Fifteenth Amendment's guarantee of the right to vote for African American men, governments of the former Confederate states devised myriad mechanisms at the turn of the twentieth century for denying that right—including the poll tax, white primary, grandfather clause, and literacy tests. When those were not enough, white mob terror visited upon black political activists intimidated potential voters and leaders. As a result, across the South only a tiny percentage of the eligible African American population could register or vote, and for all practical purposes black political power was eliminated.

Perhaps the most distinctive element of the struggle for racial equality in Kentucky was that African Americans in the commonwealth did not face these legislated restrictions on the vote. Although Kentucky did not vote to ratify the Fifteenth Amendment, once it became law there were no further efforts by the state legislature to deny blacks the right to vote. This was at least in part due to the dominant Democratic Party's recognition that because of the relatively low proportion of African Americans in the state, their political power was not large enough to be a threat. There were some attempts at the local level to restrict black political participation, such as city poll taxes or property ownership requirements. And in early elections African Americans were often delayed at the polling places or challenged to produce proof of their right to vote. Despite these routine and bitter reminders of their inferior status—which included segregated voter lists in most parts of the state—black men (and eventu-

225

ally black women) in Kentucky for the most part faced no legal barriers to voting.

In the early twentieth century, African American voters with few exceptions supported Republican candidates. This resulted in part from loyalty to the party of Lincoln and from the identification of the Democrats as the party of white supremacy. Indeed, in turn-of-the-century campaigns Democratic candidates regularly used racial demagoguery to whip up white voters by threatening that a vote for Republicans was a vote for black domination. Meanwhile, Republican activists tried to strengthen their party's chances by courting black votes and securing African American loyalty. In early twentieth-century Kentucky this custom primarily took the form of promises to protect blacks from mob violence and to support some limited rights, such as desegregation of public transportation.

What African American voters also strove for, at least in areas in which they were most numerous, was patronage and support for black candidates. After World War I raised Americans' hopes for the promise of democracy, blacks became more assertive in pressuring the Republican Party to deliver in exchange for their loyalty. In Louisville, for example, one group of political activists broke from the Republicans and formed the Lincoln Independent Party. Though they won no elections, they succeeded in convincing the Republican administration in power to hire the first black city employees.

With the coming of the Great Depression, New Deal, and World War II, the national Democratic Party under Franklin Roosevelt began to attract black supporters, and enough Kentucky African Americans switched their loyalty to produce for the first time a party competition for their votes.[1] As a result, at the dawn of the civil rights era African Americans at least in the urban areas of the commonwealth were poised to gain political influence through their role as potential swing voters. To be successful in that approach required racial unity that at times outstripped any party allegiance.

The first black elected officials in Kentucky were in Hopkinsville and Christian County, where in 1897 Edward Glass, James L. Allensworth, and John W. Knight won local offices. The early 1900s also saw other African Americans elected to city council positions elsewhere in the state. Their numbers were small, however, and in many places there was a complete absence of black public officials until well into the civil rights era. Like the early black retail employees, the story of these first officials is largely absent from the modern collective memory of African American political participation in the commonwealth. The interviews with civil rights leaders rarely name these early pioneers and instead recall a series of "first" elected officials in the 1960s and '70s. One of the most significant firsts in the state was the election of Charles W. Anderson of Louisville to the state legislature in 1935. Anderson was a prominent Republican Party activist who was the first African American Kentuckian to be elected to statewide office since Reconstruction. He served as a representative in the general assembly for ten years. During that time he introduced a long list of proposals that benefited African Americans and aimed to chip away at segregation in the state. Over the next several decades he was followed in Frankfort by Dennis Henderson, Jesse H. Lawrence, and others, including Amelia Tucker, the first black woman in the legislature, and Georgia Davis Powers, the first black woman state senator, all from Louisville.

The story of the struggle for black political equality in Kentucky thus diverges from that of its sister states in the South. Where other African Americans fought to obtain the right to vote, black Kentuckians' challenge was to translate the vote into real political power.[2] Here the Kentucky story provides a useful lesson for social movement history. It is not enough to have the franchise; African Americans have had to fight to overcome informal barriers and white citizen opposition to black candidates as well as institutionalized party resistance to the integration of blacks into positions of power. The interviews in this chapter shed light on this complex and ongoing story.[3]

Political Life under Jim Crow

In this opening section narrators recall political conditions in the period before what is commonly regarded as the heyday of the civil rights movement.

* * *

Fifty years before the Voting Rights Act, during the administration of Woodrow Wilson, my grandfather paid his poll tax and he registered, and he voted. I still have his voter certificate that goes back to the time. I believe that Woodrow Wilson was elected. . . . Now let me be clear, this voters' certificate [is] dated in 1916, eighty-four years ago. I never experienced this kind of a condition. This was a condition that my grandfather experienced, and my grandparents back in those days. I do not recall violence in Kentucky to discourage the African American vote. My experience as a youth was limited to western Kentucky, and I never heard of violence. I never heard of anyone who went to the polls to be turned away if they were registered. What happened was, there was no encouragement. All of the elected officials were white. Society was controlled by whites, school systems, everything was separate. It was not until actually my teen years that I began to experience things that indicated that there was some power in voting. Once in a while I would hear the black people saying, "Well, let's try to get some of the streets in the black neighborhoods paved; let's try to get a street light here or a street light there. Let's try to get some of these jobs." It was not until past 1950 that African Americans got anything other than common labor jobs in city government, although we were taxpayers. I say it proudly, my family has been paying taxes in the commonwealth for over a hundred years, and I got the evidence. I have hand-written tax receipts over a hundred years old. Yet we could not experience the fruits of being law abiding, tax-paying citizens.

Robert Coleman, Paducah

We've had two blacks from the beginning of the city council. That was back in the '40s that the city council started. They worked it out so it wouldn't be a problem on election day. You say, well, how in the world did the blacks manage to gain election? Okay, we divided the city up into twelve wards and you only voted in your ward. So we had two wards that were almost all black, and so naturally, you see, their councilmen were blacks. Now we have a twelve-member council, and we have three blacks now. But there have been two or three all the time on membership. That's why we didn't have such protests and so forth. You can see that in this community, we may have had the southern habits, but you can see the difference. We were enough on the line between North and South. We weren't deep South and we weren't deep North.

Ken Litchfield, Hopkinsville

The blacks voted here, always. They were segregated on the ballots. If you wanted to look at a voters list, you looked at the black list and you looked at the white list. Even taxes were segregated on the tax rolls. If a lawyer were examining a title to property that was owned by blacks, he went to the black indexes; if it was owned by whites, you went to the white index. There were very few appointive offices for blacks, up until fairly recent years. And no elected black officers for many years. Blacks were a comparatively small part of the population, and by and large they were undereducated. They didn't have the finances to run for public office. And face it, there were a lot of people who still had severe prejudices against black people. They believed in segregation. The governor of Alabama had a lot of adherents here, so I can understand why they didn't run for public office.

Morton Holbrook, Owensboro

Prior to 1953 blacks weren't encouraged to vote. I can remember as a little boy when voting day was, the farmers would come up here with wagons and pick the fellows up and take them back in the country to pick strawberries or do some kind of work, so they wouldn't be voting. They weren't encouraged to vote. In 1953, when we got the NAACP and the incident at Fort Campbell, we got the people concerned to wake up, so that they can become a part of this thing. Voting became a big thing for that generation.

F. E. Whitney, Hopkinsville

* * *

Frustrated with the lack of real power won by their access to the vote, African Americans at times organized both outside and inside of the dominant party structure for change. Here narrators describe two attempts by blacks and civil rights advocates to assert themselves politically, first in the Lincoln Independent Party and then after World War II in the Progressive Party, as recalled by Woodford Porter and Joseph McMillan. The Progressive Party was organized around the 1948 presidential campaign of Henry Wallace, former secretary of agriculture and vice president, and standard bearer of a progressive labor and civil rights coalition challenging both segregation and the hardening of the Cold War.[4] Despite these two bolts from the two-party system, most African Americans continued to work within the Republican or Democratic Party to encourage black voter participation and gain political influence, as described here by Loraine Mathis and Ben Shobe.

In the 1920s, the Republican Party had almost sole possession of the black vote every election because blacks were taught to believe they should vote Republican because Abraham Lincoln freed the slaves.

There weren't any blacks involved in government or doing anything for the government or the city or the county. My dad said there was one man down at city hall who was a janitor and some woman who was a maid. Those were the only two blacks employed by government. There were a group of men, one of them was an editor of a newspaper, couple of doctors, one was a banker, and my dad, and some black women who were involved who tried to get the Republicans to agree to hire some blacks in government positions. There were no policemen, black policemen, no black firemen, no black nothing other than these two servants. The Republicans refused to do this.

That's when they decided to form this Lincoln Independent Party. They knew they couldn't win an election, but they would try to establish the value of the vote. That's when my dad ran for mayor. Evidently the Democrats had started gaining some foothold in the city and the Republicans got upset really. They thought they might lose an election and they tried to buy my dad off. They offered him a sum of money which in those days was astronomical, something like ten, fourteen thousand dollars. He refused to do it and that's when they say, "Well, okay we'll break you," and they eventually did. They did with the help of African Americans. But I have no animosity because they didn't know what my dad and them were trying to do. Some of them were taking the money from Republicans. They're just people, that's all! I don't think they got too many votes. My dad said they took their ballot boxes and threw them in the river where they couldn't even count the votes. Politics was a pretty dirty thing back in those days. Well, after the crash and during the big depression and the advent of Franklin Roosevelt, all of those people who were Republican became Democrats. I guess you would say for a while my daddy was the leader of these people. At the end of the '20s you saw the crack coming and they hired a handful of black policemen and they established a black fire squadron then. That's when the crack came.

Woodford Porter Jr., Louisville

When [my classmate] John Stubbs came back from the service and got involved in this civil rights thing, he got involved with a group of people in the 1948 elections. That's the first time I really got into politics. They had picnics over at Clifty Falls, Indiana. I attended one of those over there. Then a man named Henry Wallace ran for president. My mother was a staunch Republican because in those days most blacks who had sense, or people who thought they had sense, voted Republican just like most blacks now who think they got sense vote Democrat. . . . But I got involved with Henry Wallace's election. I was only eighteen years old and I was going around registering people to vote in my neighborhood against my mother, who was a Republican and was a precinct captain. In those days they picked particular blacks and they would make them in charge of getting the black vote out, and my mother was one of those people. Here I was her son in school pushing Henry Wallace in her district. I was for Henry Wallace because he was the closest person for equality. I mean his platform spelled out equality and so I just went around and worked for him, actively worked in that campaign. I couldn't even vote!

Joseph McMillan, Louisville

I was a member of the Democratic Executive Committee for twenty-eight years and I was taught how to do voter registration and then I taught many other people how to do voter registration. And W. C. Young and I would work extensively with the young people, especially after I became advisor of the youth in the NAACP. We would work with the young people and teach them what they could do. We would go door-to-door just before election day and put out the literature. We would go door-to-door to get people registered to vote. We would go door-to-door in the predominately black communities because we wanted our people to register and vote. Now we would work with white people, too, if they were in that area. But we really wanted our people registered to vote because we told them it is important that you vote. We worked with the NAACP. . . . We wouldn't tell them who to vote for, we would just ask them, "Will you please consider voting because it's important that you vote." Then on election day, we would have the young people to man the telephone, and then if we needed them to help babysit while the mother or father would go to vote, they learned how to do that. We just felt like it was important that they learn the political process.

Loraine Mathis, Paducah

In 1946 there was a Black Democratic Club and there was a Third Ward Republican Club. It had people who were involved in trying to change things politically, like Charlie Anderson, like Jessie Warders, Joe Ray, who was a real estate man. The Third Ward Republican Club was composed largely of precinct captains and the legislative district chairman in the black areas. They also would call upon any people who had political jobs who happened to be members of that particular party. They met monthly and discussed what areas they thought they could help themselves in. They were people who thought they could prevail upon the mayor or prevail upon the county judge or prevail upon the people in charge of the main political parties. We had political bosses back in those days. I remember the Democratic Party particularly had strong political bosses and they ran everything, Johnny Crimmons and Ms. Lennie McLaughlin. The black clubs would try to impress upon people in that position like Ms. Lennie and Johnny Crimmons their need for jobs or business opportunities that could be advanced and so forth. They were pretty active.

Ben Shobe, Louisville

Fighting for Political Power: Individual Struggles and Movement Strategies

In recalling the struggle for black political power in Kentucky, narrators most commonly remember the story of election "firsts"—that is, the first African American elected in a particular place or office (often, the narrator him- or herself). This section includes stories of individual political careers and descriptions of the various strategies employed to open doors to political office for African Americans.

* * *

We had been trying for I don't know how many elections to elect a black person to the school board. We hadn't been successful. We had some people run that we thought were pretty popular people: G. W. Jackson, who was one of the most popular teachers at Central High School, Hortense Young, who was very active in almost everything black around here. She tried and she never made it. We called a community meeting one night up at the Chestnut Street Y and they were talking about running somebody for the school board and they named people and that person would say, "I don't want to run." I just sat there and listened and finally I said, "What the heck, I'll run!" Well they settled on me because I was the only person who wanted to take this thing on because they thought you'll get beat again.

Lyman Johnson and Maurice Rabb were my confidants and we got together on a campaign strategy. I had a very good friend, Charlotte Smith McGill, whose mother was very active in Democrat politics. Louise Reynolds, who was a future alderman, was very active in the Republican Party and they were my friends and they worked with me and we formed a strategy. It's been called single-shot voting. There were three openings on the school board that year, and when you get the ballot they say vote for only three. There were twelve candidates but you can vote for only three. We organized Democrat precinct captains, Republican precinct captains who were black—this is in the black wards primarily—with instructions to tell their people, "Don't vote for anybody but Woodford Porter. Don't you vote for but one person, not three people."

The community was good to me, as far as money for getting placards and getting letters out and all that sort of thing. They gave me the use of the second floor of the building up on Chestnut Street. They just said here you can have it for the campaign. That's where we had headquarters. Charlotte and her mother helped devise the campaign by knowing where the precincts were that we had the majority of the votes, black votes. We organized those. It was really, really well done. We got the precinct captains, both Republican and Democrat, in those wards to commit to supporting me. I went to all those meetings they had, the debates and whatnot. I think I came off pretty well in the debate. I organized a platform of the things that I advocated, of course desegregation was one of them, I'll be honest with you. I knew I wasn't going to attract many white folks, although I did get some. The election went off and I got elected! Took my seat, served eight years, chaired the board two or three times in those eight years.

Woodford Porter Jr., Louisville

In 1966 I asked my representative, who was Norbert Blume, to find me a job in the general assembly so I could be there every day and promote the [state civil rights] bill and still have a job that paid. So he did. He found me a job in the bill room at the House of Representatives. And what that meant was placing bills in folders for the legislators and put them on their desk every morning. So as I would do that, I would talk to the representatives. They were very arrogant. They were not very kind to employees. It was like they were too important to talk to the employees. Anyway, I said to one, it was a prophetic statement—he said he couldn't vote for it and he was telling me all the reasons—and I said, "Well, I think what I need is my own seat up here. If I get a seat up here I'll know how to vote and I'll vote right." Of course, it passed in '66.

Then in 1967 I was reading the paper one morning and I saw where the senator was moving to the East End. One thing I learned while I was working there, that you had to live in the district that you represented. So I said to my husband, "I think it would be a good thing if I filed for the seat." He said, "Yeah, if you want to. Fine with me." So I called a couple of people and asked them to meet me down at the courthouse. I was going to file for the state senate. Nobody thought I could win, but I thought I could win. By that time, I had worked for candidates for five years. I had been involved in politics politically and civically for five years. I had learned how to organize precincts, I learned how to get endorsements. I had learned how to win and I didn't see any reason why I couldn't win. So I went to the courthouse the following day and I invited two women who were in a club called Charity Pity Club. It was a church club. This group had asked me to speak to them at their club. So I asked a couple of them to sign my papers. The next day when I got there every member of the club was there. Well, I only needed two signatures. I just took an extra sheet and got them all to sign. So that was the beginning of my campaign.

The first thing I did was, I arranged to meet with the executive board of the AFL-CIO. I had a friend who was on that executive board named W. C. Young, who was from Paducah. He was a unionist. So he arranged to get me an appointment with several of the board members. Well, they endorsed me right away. That endorsement meant money and in-kind services. They had a big operation up on east Broadway. They had a printing machine, all kinds of equipment. So I could get all my printing free, and access to telephones, plus money, because I didn't have any money personally. So they really furnished just about all that I needed. But others endorsed me too. The civil rights groups endorsed me, the Louisville Education Association, the Kentucky Medical Association, and the Kentucky Educational Association. I was endorsed by a lot of groups. When they endorsed me and they gave me money, I told them that I appreciate the money but I wanted them to understand that that money would not give them my ear. That it would not influence me in my vote or any legislation that

I might promote. So I made that clear. So they said fine and they gave me the money anyway.

I had two opponents, actually. I had one official one, Dr. Charles Riggs, who was a chiropractor, was white and Catholic, lived on Northwestern Parkway, had been raised in that area all his life. The makeup of the racial population was about 65 percent white at the time. The district was the entire West End, west of 22nd Street. But, they had a poor voting record. Norbert Blume, the same representative who got me the job in Frankfort, endorsed me, although he was a member of the church that Dr. Riggs was. I think Norbert saw the handwriting on the wall, because the West End was in transition from white to black. Plus, I think he did it probably because he wanted to help me. In '63 I was his campaign chairman for Congress. He was defeated, but it was like, I helped you, now you help me. So he endorsed me and he gave me a lot of tips on what to do and how to do it. He'd been in the House for a number of years.

I did win the primary. What happened is, the local Democratic Party said that they were not going to make an endorsement in that race. There were thirty-six races on the ballot in the primary. They said they would stay neutral in this race. But Norbert put me wise to that. He said, you be prepared. On election eve, I received several calls from precinct captains telling me that they had received their material from Democratic headquarters and my opponent's name had been stamped in his block, hand-stamped. So the next morning, Raoul Cunningham, my campaign chairman, he was director of the youth choir of his church. About seventy-five young people were in his choir. So what we did was utilize his choir. We had them to come to the headquarters on Broadway, 30th and Broadway, after school, and we'd have plans for them. . . . We used them to pass literature out from door to door. They were very helpful.

Election night, I just stayed home. Raoul went to the Armory, and he found out I had won, so he called me back and told me. I got dressed, he picked me up, and we went to the tenth floor of the Seelbach, where they were having a Democratic party. When the elevator door opened and I stepped out, it was just like I had won the governorship. There were not too many Democrats won that year, statewide. They were telling me that I was the highest office that won. Said I should have been running for governor instead of the State Senate.

Georgia Davis Powers, Louisville

In 1979 Mr. Crafton had to quit the school board because of his job. So they asked about different people and they called me and asked me if I would be interested in taking his place until his term was up. I told them yes. I had no earthly thought about being in public office. There was this white girl that came to me and she said, "You know, I don't think you should even try to run." She says, "Because they're not really ready to accept a black to a board." I said, "Well, why not?" She says, "Well, Owensboro is still prejudiced." I said, "You know there is prejudice everywhere." There was another woman that was running which was a good friend of hers, but see, I didn't know that. So I came home and I told my oldest daughter that and she says, "Well, Mama, you always told us don't be a quitter." I said, "Well, you're right." So I just started talking to different people and I ran and I won. I was really surprised.

Jean Higgs, Owensboro

Harry Sykes was not born in Lexington; he had moved here. He had played for the Harlem Globetrotters and was about six-eight, so he was truly a commanding figure. I'd gotten to know him some way. I was very interested in elected office because I could see it makes so much difference who you have in there. So I told Harry that I wanted to work for him. I worked for him in the precinct around Meadow Lane. I had some things to hand out as people walked to the polls. I remember handing this brochure, had Harry's picture on it, to somebody, some man that was walking to the polls. He looked at me and threw it down on the ground. And he put his foot on it, pushed it around. Said, "I'd never vote for a nigger."

What the black community did, which was very smart—they were very organized, and they used kind of a single shot system. You're supposed to vote for four commissioners; they just voted for one. That was organized probably by the black churches. The black population maybe was only 20 percent of registered voters. But by single shotting, they made the vote for him much more important. So he was elected the first black commissioner ever in Lexington. Maybe during Reconstruction there were some black people, but certainly in my lifetime.

Then later Harry and I ran together. We ran on the same ticket in 1967 for the city commission. We ran with a candidate for mayor named Charlie Wiley. During that campaign in '67, there was still some resentment about black folks being elected officials. Harry said,

"If you all feel I'm going to hurt you, we won't campaign together in some of these white neighborhoods." Charlie Wiley said, "Oh no," he said, "We're all going to campaign together." So we'd go out in these neighborhoods—there were five of us: four commissioners and mayor candidate. We'd each get out and go in a different direction handing out our brochure. Well, what we found out is that the people were absolutely taken with Harry Sykes because he was a former basketball player, very tall, very likeable. So it turned out that Harry was really the most popular member of the team. So he got the most votes.

Joe Graves, Lexington

My husband was the first on the city council, I guess it was about '67 or '68. He won overwhelmingly, with more votes than any of the others. His name was Matthew L. Brooks. I feel like that there was a time when some of Simpson County realized some of the things that should have been done and could have been done. They had a slate of offices, and he was a representative on that slate. You could vote for the whole slate, or you could vote for that one person. But there were two blacks that ran at that time. He was the only one elected. The other guy, I think he was kept as a fifth person on the list. However, Brooks died before his term was over, and the other guy finished out his term.

Lucille Brooks, Franklin

The first black on the school board here, after integration, was a fellow named Doctor Brooks, in the early '70s. Now the way we got Doctor Brooks, we got all of our people to vote just for Doctor Brooks. See, you can vote for all five, but we told them to single-shot, so in all the precincts—we had four precincts in which the black vote was predominant—every one of those precincts didn't vote for the whole five, they just voted for Doctor Brooks. In those days, we had that type of organization, that get-that-togetherness.

F. E. Whitney, Hopkinsville

There had been a number of men to run for the city commission. They had a lot of political rallies and things like that, but nobody could ever get elected. The reason why that nobody could ever get elected was because they only campaigned in black neighborhoods and there were not enough black people to elect them. I couldn't figure out why anybody would campaign just in black neighborhoods when it was a city-wide election. There was no wards, no districts, so you were going to be a commissioner, if elected, by all the people in Paducah. So in 1968 I started to campaign and I said, "The first thing I am going to do is"—we had twenty-four, twenty-four districts at that time, twenty-four precincts at that time—I said, "I am going to cover all of them. I'm not just going to campaign where black people are."

So I went to Buckner Lane, which was one of the, probably, most famous Caucasian places at that particular time. There was a huge house, I can't remember the name of the people or anything at all, but it was wealthy people. I went there and knocked on the front door. A black woman came to the door. She said, "What you want?" I said, "I want to talk to the man of the house or the lady of house. I'm campaigning for commissioner." She said, "You go around to the back door." [*Laughs.*] I went around to the back door. She brought the lady to the back door. She was standing there behind her. Lady opened the door, and asked me who I was, what I wanted, and everything. I told her, "I'm Reverend W. G. Harvey, pastor of Harrison Street Baptist Church. I'm running for city commissioner and I'd just like to let her know a little about my platform." She said, "Come right on in, Reverend." I went on in the house and she carried me right on up to the den. We sat there and got acquainted and talked. "You know," she said, "You're the first black person that ever came and asked me to vote for them." I said, "Well, I probably am aware of that. I heard that most of them campaigned in black neighborhoods." She was just as nice as could be, and she called that black woman and told her, said, "Bring us some coffee." Boy, she rolled her eyes at me and looked all funny. She went and got coffee and brought it in there. And I drank coffee. I didn't even want coffee, but I drank coffee. [*Laughs.*] We sat there and talked probably a half an hour. When I got ready to go, I remember distinctly, she called that lady and said, "You let him out the front door. If he ever comes here again, don't you never take him to the back door."

I missed being elected. A white man by the name of Bill Fellows just barely beat me. He was the most outgoing, friendliest fellow you ever saw in your life when he talked to me. I found out when he was campaigning in white neighborhoods, he would tell them, "If you elect that nigger we are going to really be in serious trouble. We cannot afford to elect a black man." So he only beat me by that narrow margin, after indoctrinating Caucasian people with all that. I had told my church at that time, before the election, I said, "I'm going to be the next commissioner. I'm going to be the first black commissioner to be elected. I can tell by the attitudes of the people that I campaigned with in white communities."

After the election, Bill Fellows got seriously sick, this was before the swearing in and everything. So they sent Bill Fellows to the University of Kentucky Hospital. They had an exploratory operation, and Bill Fellows died at UK. He had not been sworn in as commissioner. So Robert Cherry was the mayor at that particular time. A large number of black and white people, they went to city hall and they said, "We believe that you ought to appoint Reverend W. G. Harvey, because he was the next man in line for votes and Bill Fellows just barely beat him." At that time, Robert Cherry was just a little reluctant to do this. The law is that the mayor has to make the appointment, and the city commission has to ratify it. I think it is the same law that is used when people are appointed to a board. The mayor makes an appointment, and the city commissioners ratify it. So anyway, reluctantly Bob Cherry made the appointment and it was ratified.

After so many days, there has to be a runoff election. So a man by the name of James Lynn, a white man who worked for an insurance company here, he filed to run against me. Bob Cherry thought I was going to be all right after those ninety days working with me. They begged him to not run against me, so I would automatically have that seat. He said, "No, I'm going to run against the nigger anyway." He ran. When he ran, I beat him three to one. So, that was really my first election. The first ninety days, it was appointment.

Wardelle G. Harvey, Paducah

I ran for the board of education and served eight years. . . . I was the first black elected to public office but somehow it was maneuvered so that I was not publicly sworn in. They had me sworn in in chambers. The person who was elected along with me was not even there. They don't change the board all the same so when I went in they elected two, and the next time they were going to elect three. When they were elected, the first night here comes the judge out in his robe and swore them in and presented them with a certificate. I sat there, I never felt so much like crying in my life. I said, "I didn't get a certificate when I was sworn in." He said, "I'll issue you one." He came out here himself and went through it again. But you see, that was the difference. They got pictures all in the paper and didn't even give me a certificate.

Thelma Johnson, Henderson

The same people who ran that place right after the Civil War, who took power right after the Civil War, they're still running [Russellville] now. Those same families are running it today. When I first came to Russellville, they thought I was some wild character. Where did this character come from? It was almost like going back, organizing again in Alabama and Mississippi, in terms of people's attitudes and the way they thought. What happened was they set me up as this wild, radical, crazy guy here. I said, "To dispel this, I'm going to run for political office." The only reason I ran was to get a chance to knock on everybody's door and introduce myself. I got a legitimate chance to knock on everybody's door in the town, so you don't have to hear what somebody said and all this kind of thing. You can meet me. It surprised a lot of people who met me and we sat and we talked. We sat and we talked and you see some strange looks on people's faces—this is not the guy I've heard about. I told them what position that I was taking and what I thought that needed to be done to help out the community. This was in 1975. I just got there. I almost won a seat and that blew everybody's mind. Then again, I ran again for city council and I almost won. But then I ran for magistrate in 1989. And I won. . . .

Some of the white community accused me of buying votes, electioneering. A whole list of things that I was charged with. They had an investigation by the State Police, were going to have a grand jury. Whatever evidence they had, they said they had some pictures. They just came up with any number of things. I went to the commonwealth attorney. I was kind of worried about him, because he used to work with J. Edgar Hoover. I know the experiences I had with J. Edgar Hoover and his boys. I told one of his little lawyer friends, who was a good guy, "This guy worked for J. Edgar Hoover and you know what kind of person Hoover was." Apparently he went back and told him. And this is the first time this guy ever even spoke to me. He told me that he felt like everything would be all right.

After they conceded I won [the primary], one of the ladies who ran against me turned around and ran again as a write-in candidate. I said, "Now wait a minute." How it works in Kentucky, everybody was a Democrat, right? So, if you win the primary, you've won the general election. But the thing is, she turned around and she ran as a write-in candidate for the general election. I said, "What is this? This is the first time in the history of Kentucky that anybody's ever had to run for the same seat twice. Had to beat the same person twice." I said, "I'm running against the same person." I said, "Something about this doesn't seem fair to me." "It's unfair. I don't know whether it's legal or not. It's not a point whether it is legal or not. It is unfair." I won by a landslide next time. People said, "This is wrong. The guy won fair and square. If he won, he won. He won fair and square."

I think that did a lot, in terms of the black community, to see me go through that whole process and see the things that can be thrown against you and you keep on. The way you handle it and you go ahead on and you win, I think it did a lot for the community. That's what it was all about, really, to help try to break off those shackles that people have that they don't realize they have, that bind you.

Charles Neblett, Russellville

Black Political Power in the Wake of the Movement

In the late 1960s and beyond, black political power in Kentucky increased as more African Americans ran for a wider variety of offices and as others organized to support their campaigns. In the first of these narratives, civil rights advocates recall the influence of the first electoral victories on black communities as well as strategies used by organizations to promote black leadership in the state. The rest, often centered on an individual's career and choices, reveal the broader context of political activity in the black community, the gains in black power in the state, but also the continuing restrictions on access to that power.

* * *

So one of the things my victory did was convinced blacks that they could run for political office. Because the only people who had run for political office there before were the people that the powers that be said, "Hey, we want you to be here." In fact, no one had been initially elected. What they'd done, they'd been appointed to a position and they kept them there. They re-elect them. I was the first black who initially ran for office and was elected to that office. In reality, there's no black from Logan County has ever been elected to political office there. We wanted to show that you could run for office. We're going to have to get some political strength here. Today, you've got people from Russellville, blacks, running for political office, determined that they are going to get into this process. These are the young people, who were there when I first came to Russellville, who worked with us; they are now running for political office, dealing with school boards. They are getting involved in a positive way in the community.

Charles Neblett, Russellville

One other thing that the Kentucky Commission on Human Rights did that was of significance was we held these seminars for black elected officials. We unquestionably succeeded in increasing the numbers of black elected officials in our time. These were really very good conferences. One of the stars of them was, of course, Luska J. Twyman, of Glasgow, who had been mayor. We had the people out of Hopkinsville, who came to those. . . . The reports that we did had a very emphatic result in terms of cities that noticed when we called it to their attention that they didn't have any black elected officials. When a vacancy occurred a lot of them would go looking for a black, and then they would appoint the black to the city council and then the guy or gal would get re-elected. That happened a lot of times. We really got swinging on them in the '70s, and that carried well up into the '80s.

Galen Martin, Frankfort

What happened was there was a group of young blacks that had decided they were going to run together as a unit in the Democratic primary. This was the Unity Slate. I think they were going to run people from different organizations all under thirty-five. I would guess it was Darryl Owens's idea, and Raoul Cunningham. There was a fellow by the name of Morris Jeff who was director of Plymouth Settlement House at the time. I think it might have been their brainchild. They were trying to show the power of the black community politically and get a bigger voice for blacks in political affairs. Over time I sort of had a split from the Black Unity slate. What happened was there was a difference in philosophy as to whether it was more important to make a statement or to get elected. Some felt that making a statement would be more advantageous, would garner more for the black community in the future than getting one person elected; I thought it was more important to get elected. We sort of had a friendly falling out and I ran on, I think it was Frank Burke's slate. [I was the only one to get elected.]

Neville Tucker, Louisville

I got heavily involved with that group and another group called PAC-10. It was a black political action committee in the early '80s. We formed that group and it was a powerful group. People like Joe Hammond, and Frank Clay and William Gatewood and Woodford Porter Jr. We formed that group of ten people, that's why they called it the PAC-10, so that we would raise our money and give to political candidates. That had not been done anywhere in the country by blacks before. We were responsible for a whole lot of people. Everybody who's been an elected official, Gerry Neal, Darryl Owens, Leonard Gray, all of them were members of PAC-10 and I was the president of that. We raised our money. We'd have chitlin suppers and dances and social affairs and fashion shows and all kinds of stuff that raised money. We put that money in and we then would go to the candidates and say, "Look, we'll give you so much money if you do this, this, this, and this."

So Darryl Owens got to be elected as C District Commissioner. I was his campaign chairman. In 1983 he became C District Commissioner. That was a great day there when we were able to take one-third of the county. We always had the chance to take one-third of the city with the four aldermen we had, but this was the first time that we got a black as county commissioner and I was the chairman of the committee. We had already won two or three others before that. The whites were still trying to control the aldermanic races and we got involved in that campaign and got Arthur Smith, who was a pastor at Portland Memorial Baptist Church, got him elected as tenth ward alderman against the white candidate. Harvey Sloane was playing games at that time, he was the mayor of the city. Several of the people on PAC-10's board were Sloane employees and the second time that they ran merger he threatened them with their jobs if they went out there [against] merger, and they did.[5] Charles Roberts left here, great political mind, and so that was the demise of PAC-10 because of the interference of Harvey Sloane and the people that he represented.

Joseph McMillan, Louisville

Reverend Harvey elected not to run for re-election in '73, I ran. Fortunately I won. I served '74 and '75. Then, in 1975 we began to experience a large number of complaints filed with the Kentucky Commission on Human Rights alleging police brutality here in the city of Paducah, Kentucky. They reached the volume where the Commission on Human Rights decided to send down an investigator. His name was Bill Holiday and he was out of Louisville, and he subsequently became a lawyer. I was in my second year of my first term. I was at home one evening and the doorbell rang. I went to the door and there stood a gentleman with a briefcase and an official I.D., and he said, "Mr. Coleman?" And I said, "Yes." He said "My name is Bill Holiday, I'm an investigator with the state Commission on Human Rights, may we speak?" "Yes sir, come on in." He said, "Mr. Coleman, the Kentucky Commission on Human Rights ha[s] received numerous complaints alleging police brutality here in Paducah, Kentucky, [and] has reached a level of concern where I have been assigned to investigate." He said, "I have a list of names and addresses here; I don't know anything about your city. I need to find these people. I need to talk to them, and what I need is someone as a guide to take me to these various people; and I have been told that you would do that for me."

Well, it doesn't take long before somebody says, "Something's going to be done, there was an investigator here and Commissioner Coleman brought him to my house." Well, the word leaked to the Police Department here, "Coleman has got an investigation going on." And they launched a smear campaign on me. I lost that election by less than a hundred votes. I would have won it, but the timing was such that I could not recover. The campaign was launched less than a week before the election, and that was my first term in office, I had not established full credibility. It turned out to be one of the best things that ever happened. . . . I was out for a two-year interval, and I came back for two successive elections. I ran number one out of the whole field of candidates. I was the mayor pro tem, and the only other interval I had in 1991. I elected to run for mayor, and I lost that election, so I, beginning in 1974, to the day, I had two intervals. Other than that I am in my twenty-third year.

Robert Coleman, Paducah

I decided that I needed to run for public office. I was the first black female, first black period, to run for city commission. There were some very, very strong candidates. There were more women than ever before in the history of Owensboro that ran. I survived the May primary and made the cut, and I almost won. That was in 1991 and that somewhat paved the way, because it let other blacks know that they could run and make a difference. Then after I lost, evidently someone felt that I had made quite an impact, and they felt that I needed to be in a position where that I could influence and even get the experience to run again. But not the next time. They said if you run twice and you lose the second time, you might as well forget it. That was when I was appointed as the first black to the powerful Utility Commission here, with assets in excess of five hundred million dollars. I served a record thirteen years on that commission. It was a very influential commission and they had no blacks employed. Before I left there we had made some dramatic changes in trying to get minorities hired as, in meaningful positions.

There's a lot of people that still remember. They say, "When are you going to run again?" "We voted for you." If I run again, I'm not going to run for city commission. I'm running for mayor. I'm going to the top. I mean, you've got to move up. We opened up the door. We have a black female city commissioner. I believe she's in her second term. And prior to that there was a black minister here in Owensboro, who was the first black elected. So we've accomplished that, but we've never had a black mayor, nor have we had a female mayor, so it's about time. Even Henderson, Kentucky, which is a smaller community, they have a female mayor. So it's time, it's Owensboro's time.

Daisy James, Owensboro

Joe Denning was elected to the school board in the 1980s. Right now we have a black school board member, but other than that, that's it. We have never had, and the black vote does not have, the power that it has in other communities. It just doesn't have the power here in Bowling Green. Here you would have to have white vote as well as black, so you'd have to be supported by both communities in order to win. The majority of them who run just simply would not be what you consider a leader or black people even consider. We haven't been a community which has rallied behind any concern. Those that would participate in community affairs left Bowling Green for better jobs elsewhere. So Bowling Green was drained of its potential leaders, or drained of people that would be community minded. It's been like that for a long time.

George Esters, Bowling Green

I ran for sheriff. I was the only candidate in there that had that law enforcement experience. And to show you how deep that racism is, those people in the Democratic Party, who could have endorsed my candidacy, they endorsed Melissa Mershon. Of course Melissa Mershon had no law enforcement experience, didn't even know how to shoot a gun, but you talk about running for the highest law enforcement position, well, sure! As a result the Republican candidate is the person who ran based on his law enforcement experience. Melissa Mershon won the Democratic primary. The Republican candidate ended up winning, and they hadn't had a Republican sheriff in there in I done forgot how many years. But rather than support the black, and that's the way I perceived it. I wasn't running as somebody unqualified, I knew that I was highly qualified for it over the other candidates that were running in that primary. But rather than the leadership there and these political leaders coming out and endorsing my candidacy, they end up supporting her candidacy and then she lost and the Republican guy got in there.

After that, I ran for the U.S. Congress against Dolores Delahanty. I ran in these primaries because the only opportunity an African American has is winning in the primary. The reality of it is you got to be running against more than one white candidate and then hopefully you'll get a lot of a big turnout from blacks and then you have a chance. If you win that primary, then either it's going to be racism or they're going to vote for the candidate of their party. I ran for those positions because I refused to be pigeonholed in this community. Blacks have been pigeonholed into running for what they say you run for. You run for alderman or you run for state rep, don't you run for positions where you can really effect change or where you have power. In other words, the sheriff is a power position because you have control over employment. The sheriff can employ over three hundred jobs. So what black people do is that our political people are alderman or state rep, they don't have no power to do nothing. . . . So then what happens when you run for [more powerful] positions, then the thing is, "He can't be that!" I didn't run for these things just to be running. Had I been able to raise the money, clearly I'd have won in the things. But you have to go to folks to beg money and that's the hardest thing for me to do. If I had the money to finance my own campaign I would run for office.

But anyway I ran for the U.S. Senate. I was running against Steve Beshear and Tom Barlow down in Paducah. Tom Barlow is a real nice guy. We even established some personal relationship that even exists now as result of me having run. We went all over the state of Kentucky. I went to places up in the mountains up there where the only thing black there was me. I've participated in the forums with folks. I've been out there in parts of southern Jefferson County where it is all white and then they attack me, and when I got through talking you could hear a rat pee on cotton because I'm talking the truth to them. I've had the same ones come up afterwards and shake my hand, and then when I go to some other meetings they're the first ones to tell other people, this is my friend Mr. Lanier. I was able to do the same thing in relating to people up there in Pike County and all up in the mountains up in there. The truth of it is that when I went back over the data after the election I got votes in every place I was able to go to, but I just couldn't raise the money necessary for that television stuff.

Shelby Lanier, Louisville

I ran for the state senate. Georgia was a candidate in that race—she was the incumbent—and so was Gerald Neal. I ran because there were some issues that I wanted to get out that I hadn't heard said. Then I ran for the alderman seat again here last year. I ran in the May primary against an incumbent, Paul Bather. There were two other folk in the race and we ran a heck of a race. I haven't won to be seated, but I think I won to get the issues out that affect poor working people regardless of what color they are. I let them know that there's not just one class of people that need to be heard. There are issues that're very pressing in the poor white community and also in the African American community.

Mattie Jones, Louisville

* * *

The most recent published study of black officeholders in Kentucky shows that as of 2001, there were sixty-two African Americans in elected positions in the commonwealth—accounting for less than 1 percent of such positions in the state. The great majority of those were in positions on city or county governing bodies.[6]

Conclusion

Remembered and Forgotten: What Kentuckians' Memories Teach Us about the U.S. Civil Rights Movement

In this volume, more than one hundred Kentuckians offer lessons about the conditions of life under Jim Crow and the persistence required to overcome discrimination in education, employment, and public life. Besides painting a vivid picture of dramatic moments, such as the March on Frankfort, these narratives also explain how collective action is organized. Oral history has long been recognized as valuable for providing these kinds of insights, which are rarely available in the same form from the written record. But more than merely providing new information, oral history can also shed light on how people think individually about the civil rights movement—what comprised it, when it was, and what were its results.

This collective portrait of memories of the civil rights years in Kentucky challenges what is commonly known about the movement. In particular, patterns of what is remembered and forgotten here raise questions about what people think of as activism and as significant in their own and their community's history. Most important, Kentuckians' memories direct our attention to individual acts of resistance in contrast to the mass nonviolent demonstrations that dominate the public perception of the movement, suggesting a new way to understand how change in the racial status quo comes about. The stories also break out of the traditional chronology of the movement, taking the saga of the struggle for racial equality well into the 1980s and 1990s. Finally, many of the Kentuckians who speak in this volume dispute the optimistic verdicts of civil rights success heard in public commemorations, and instead declare the job unfinished, implicitly encouraging us to rededicate ourselves collectively to creating a more racially just society.

While the memories presented in this volume were collected in private, one-on-one oral history interviews, every year in January and February there are occasions of more public remembering of the movement and particularly the role of Dr. Martin Luther King Jr. On the holiday in his honor and throughout African American History Month, communities across the country, and public and private institutions from churches to kindergarten classes, devote time to recalling and honoring the history of the struggle for racial equality. More permanent museums and exhibits, including for example the Birmingham Civil Rights Institute and the National Civil Rights Museum in Memphis, are also dedicated to preserving and presenting the memory of that struggle. Cultural expressions such as film and music have added their own interpretations, from the *Eyes on the Prize* series produced in 1987, to feature films such as *Long Walk Home* and (the wildly inaccurate) *Mississippi Burning,* as well as songs by the musical group Sweet Honey in the Rock and others. Finally, spokespeople for various political causes routinely invoke the memory of the movement to support arguments ranging from criminalization of abortion to education advocacy for the hearing impaired.

Recent scholars have examined the content of these portrayals and have argued that what emerges from them is a dominant public narrative that takes a very particular and, in the estimation of many, problematic shape. This narrative has at its core a focus on the life and work of the Reverend Martin Luther King Jr., emphasizing his nonviolence, integrationist goals, and vision of a beloved community wherein people would be judged by the "content of their character." Notably absent are his antiwar position and emphasis on economic justice, the very cause that took him to Memphis and to his death. The time line of the movement is set by King's career, stretching from "Montgomery to Memphis," or from the mid-1950s to the late 1960s, after which it disintegrates from internal dissension caused by Black

Power. Closely related to the emphasis on King is a more general conception of the movement as driven by male integrationist leaders who worked through the political system and in well-known national organizations to achieve their goals, thus erasing the day-to-day community organizing conducted more commonly by women. That widely understood overview has established a misconceived and over-simplified model for how and by whom change is achieved. To the extent that the dominant story moves away from King, it focuses on mass nonviolent direct action demonstrations—usually sit-ins—that persuaded public officials to adopt legislation guaranteeing equality. Once that legislation was passed, victory over racism was achieved. The picture that emerges from this memory is of a movement whose goal was tolerance and bringing people together, and whose success was the great liberal achievement of the twentieth century.[1]

While this shared public memory has at times led to simplification and complacency in public policy, it has also deeply influenced the stories that individuals tell and thus the content of oral histories like those collected here. The structure of an oral history project of course also shapes the content of personal narratives. All oral history is the product of a dialogue between two or more persons. The course of the conversation is directed in part by the agenda of the researcher, who comes in with specific questions, but it can be manipulated by the interviewee in his or her choice of how to answer. Moreover, each person brings to the conversation his or her own prior notions about what is important, and what is appropriate to share. To some extent, the latter will be conditioned by the rapport between the interviewer and interviewee, which is itself determined by the setting and a complex alchemy of personality, relative socioeconomic status, race and ethnicity, insider/outsider position, ideology, and relationship to the subject at hand. Any interpretation of the contents of the interview, then, must take into consideration the potential influence of these factors.

The issue raised by scholars that most directly bears on the nature of the interviews in the KCROHP is the complexity of cross-race interviewing. Specifically in this case, how might the results have been influenced by the fact that the primary interviewers in this project, with one exception, were white and approximately 75 percent of the interviewees were black? Scholars have noted dramatic differences in tone and content in interviews done by white and black interviews in perhaps the most famous oral history project on African American life, the WPA ex-slave narratives. Historians have discovered that some individuals were interviewed more than once, and in a few cases by both white and black interviewers. In their essay on the subject, James West Davidson and Mark Hamilton Lytle produce side-by-side transcripts to show that the narrator gave strikingly different versions of her story of life under slavery, emphasizing to the white visitor the kindness of her master but sharing stories of brutal whippings when speaking to an African American. Besides reminding historians to use their source material with care and to remember the audience, such evidence also raises questions about how a long-subjugated people will present their story to representatives of the oppressors. In a more recent set of interviews, Alessandro Portelli reports encountering at least one case of mistrust from a rural Kentucky African American informant, although the woman admitted her concerns only after several hours of telling her life story.[2] Other scholars have noted the potential misunderstandings that can arise when differences of race are compounded by a cultural divide, such as when white North Americans interview narrators from Africa, Latin America, or other non-Western settings.[3]

Certain factors mitigated some of the problems that might have arisen in the white interviewer/black interviewee situation in this project. First, the content of the project, including the topics for questions, was influenced by an advisory board that included many African American scholars. In addition, in the majority of interviews, the socioeconomic differences between the interviewers and the narrators were relatively small because so many of the latter had reached positions of high status and distinction in their careers. The interviewers also often expressed sympathy with the civil rights struggle, which our experience has taught us helps to lessen racial distance. Moreover, as a leading scholar of oral history and the civil rights movement in the Deep South has noted, and as we also observed, older African Americans often desire to make the usually younger white scholar truly understand how things were, which produces a sense of shared objective.[4] Finally, three of the researchers who did the majority of the interviews were from out of state and had little connection with local elites in Kentucky, a problem noted by historians in the WPA interviews.

On the other hand, the fact that the project was state-sponsored, and the way it was organized, may have created its own set of distortions. Many of the narrators had a connection to state or local government as employees of human rights or relations commissions or as elected officials. Others were recommended by such people. The primary researcher also selected people who were heads of organizations or prominent in news coverage. The result was an overrepresentation of leaders, the highly educated, and those who worked through the political and legislative system. It was perhaps more likely that these narrators would see value and success in working with the state, and might recall too rosy a picture. This tendency may also have been reinforced by the interviewer being viewed as a representative of the state. At the same time, individuals who viewed the state as part of the problem or had a more grassroots experience may have been overlooked altogether, or may have been unwilling to express themselves as openly.

Because we cannot know for sure how the narrators would have responded to a more independent interviewer or one of another race—there being no control group as there was in some of the WPA narratives—there is no way to conclude with certainty how these dynamics affected the interviews. There is some evidence of silences. There is a striking lack of testimony from those black militants who did not choose to turn toward working within the system, for example. In the case of the interviews on Louisville's Black Power movement, repeated efforts to find such individuals or convince them to be interviewed failed, which may have been due to a lack of trust on the part of potential interviewees. In the statewide project, the initial cut-off date of 1970 discouraged efforts to seek out Black Power advocates because in Kentucky much of that activity came later. In addition, there were a few interviewees who were relatively reluctant and unforthcoming. These were most commonly African American women from rural areas who were relatively older. It is impossible to say whether their resistance stemmed from an unwillingness to share with a white person or state representative, a feeling that their story did not "fit" the widely understood model of civil rights activity, a self-doubt as to the validity of their experiences, or a simple lack of detailed memories of long ago. In short, while we must be careful to consider the possible impacts of differences between the interviewer and narrator, we cannot be sure of how the many factors balanced out to affect the stories.

With these caveats in mind, it is possible to draw conclusions from the patterns that emerge from these interviews, in particular with regard to what is remembered and what is not. The interviewees in this project have much stronger, clearer memories of some of the significant campaigns of the period than of others. Stories about the early 1960s sit-ins in Louisville and Lexington were detailed, chronologically coherent, and dramatic. Participants very willingly agreed to be interviewed and to tell their story. In some cases, few questions were required to elicit an extensive tale. Moreover, narrators often connected these stories to broader national events—comparing to other places or talking about the inspiration of events elsewhere. Finally, these memoirs displayed the most collective spirit; that is, the narrators talked extensively about the activities of others and placed themselves into a group by discussing other participants and other grassroots involvement.

In comparison, narratives about open housing were more difficult to elicit and less coherent, with a few exceptions. To a great extent, of course, this is because only Louisville had major open housing demonstrations. But even there, although the campaign was harder fought, encountered more violent opposition, and thus might be considered more dramatic and memorable than the open accommodations battle, narrators were more resistant to discussing it. It was harder to find people who participated on a grassroots level who were willing to be interviewed—although, interestingly, white participants were more amenable than African Americans, due perhaps to the fact that for many of them it was their first foray into what was by then recognized as a national moral crusade. Nonetheless, the narratives of open housing were vaguer, shorter, and less chronologically coherent than the ones about open accommodations. Indeed, many of the details of the memories became confused with other periods or other campaigns. Meanwhile, narrators from other parts of the state answered questions about housing mostly by describing segregated conditions or telling stories of personal efforts to find a home. With prompting, a few gave short answers about how local ordinances were passed, but it was striking how few people raised the issue of housing on their own or connected it to a broader movement.

Even more forgotten, judging from interviews in this project, was collective agitation for equal economic opportunity. The written record of the civil rights era reveals a history of protest against employment discrimination that ran from the postwar era's union battles through enforcement of affirmative action in the 1980s and beyond. During that time both the NAACP and the Urban League led periodic community boycotts and pickets of particular firms. Meanwhile, individuals or short-lived coalitions inspired other actions, such as when the *Defender* led a protest against the Louisville phone company by encouraging customers to pay their bills in pennies. Memories of these types of actions are nearly absent from the narratives in this volume. There are a few stories specifically sought by the interviewers about the formation of the Black Workers' Coalition in Louisville or about enforcement of antidiscrimination legislation. One story arose spontaneously: the campaign to ensure that black workers were hired to complete the bridge over the Cumberland Gap, which occurred much later than the traditionally viewed period of the movement. Instead of a sense of collective struggle, what appear most commonly in these narratives are stories of individual struggles against job discrimination and efforts to overcome it.

Although narrators may have reasons for not telling certain stories, ranging from their personal priorities to a real lack of activity to simple forgetfulness, these incidents of memory and silence, taken as a group, point to the influence of the "grand narrative" of the civil rights movement on how individuals tell their stories. The young people who participated in the sit-ins of the early 1960s quite easily situated their own experience into the regional story of mass nonviolent direct action. Interestingly, even those few people—usually located in rural areas or smaller cities—who asserted that there was "no civil rights activity" in their community often went on to define that absence as a lack of demonstrations or sit-ins, revealing the extent to which those events have come to define the movement. Those whose stories are reinforced by the national narrative are more likely to remember it and be willing, even eager, to share it. This was more difficult for those who participated in open housing. Few cities in the country had open housing campaigns. Moreover, the Louisville open housing movement happened at a time when, according to the popular time line, mass demonstrations were dying. The struggle for open housing simply does not fit, and thus stories about it are shared less often. This is even clearer in the case of campaigns against job discrimination. The national "amnesia," as Vincent Harding put it, about Martin Luther King's commitment to economic equality extends to a broader forgetting that some of the most significant mass actions of the period, including the Birmingham demonstrations and March on Washington of 1963, were for open accommodations *and* jobs.[5] It is not surprising, then, that this silence would extend to stories about such actions in Kentucky.

A second factor accounting for the difference in how open accommodations, open housing, and antidiscrimination are remembered is the relative perceived success of each campaign. In public commemorations of the civil rights era, the movement is presented as a success because laws were passed and stores and restaurants did (by and large) open their doors and seats to all races. The participants in the sit-ins can point not only to local legislation in Louisville, Lexington, and elsewhere that resulted more or less directly from their efforts; they can place their story in the national narrative that ended with the March on Washington and the passage of the Civil Rights Act. Because the job discrimination component of the national and state legislation is relatively forgotten and certainly never met the hoped-for goal of full employment, it is harder to tie boycotts and protests for equal employment to that success. In the case of housing, the national legislation for fair housing in 1968 was passed at a time of rising racial tension and is rarely included in the heroic tale of upward progress. Moreover, countless studies attest to the fact that the success of that law is marginal.[6] Housing segregation still plagues American communities, just as economic inequality between blacks and whites remains. The narratives here suggest that when a campaign is perceived to have been a failure, people are less willing or less able to tell detailed stories about it.

Just as there are lessons in these narrators' silences and memory lapses, an examination of what they *do* talk about the most tells us something significant about the nature of the movement in the state. Outside of Louisville (where many told stories of collective action, especially in the open accommodations battle), what people talked about most often was personal struggles against racism. To some extent, this focus was shaped by the nature of the interview encounter and could be expected. An oral history interview, after all, typically elicits personal stories, and the interviewers here always began by asking for the narrator's individual biography and family background. And in many communities around the state, small African American populations simply could not generate the levels of mass action popularly associated with the movement. Even given those conditions, however, what is striking is the extent to which stories focus on the individual's actions without associating them with a larger movement. School desegregation is most often described not as the result of organized pressure but as the setting for individual students' or families' experiences. As described above, the fight for economic equality was almost exclusively remembered as a personal battle in a particular setting. In politics, voter registration campaigns and other community efforts are recalled only in relation to other issues—specifically the Louisville open accommodations and open housing campaigns. Instead narrators talk about how particular individuals, often themselves, got into office. The story focuses, then, on how individuals rather than communities accessed political power.

This pattern in the interviews sheds light on a significant aspect of Kentucky's civil rights struggle: the relative lack of importance, at least in the estimation and memory of people looking back upon it, of organizations, including the church. There were NAACP chapters in communities across Kentucky from a relatively early date. Some of these waxed and waned over the years, but the organization consistently made its presence felt through the state conference of branches. Likewise, the creation and subsequent campaigns of the Kentucky Commission on Human Rights (KCHR) are an integral part of this state's civil rights story. Other organizations arose over the years, including branches of national groups like the Urban League and the Congress of Racial Equality, and indigenous ones such as the West End Community Council or the Non-Partisan League. From the written record and from some of these interviews, it is clear that at times such groups provided a vital framework within which individuals worked against racial discrimination. But other than Galen Martin, whose career was long and intricately bound up with the KCHR, narrators spontaneously share memories of organizational activity only rarely. Even with prompting, stories about the NAACP, for example, are short and lack detail. The NAACP and CORE's importance in sparking major campaigns is evident insofar as leaders of those groups describe in their narratives how they organized demonstrations, for example. But rank-and-file participants in demonstrations rarely identify themselves with a particular organization. They situate themselves as part of a broader movement instead.

Similarly, the organization traditionally credited with guiding much of the southern civil rights movement—the church—played a relatively minor role in these narratives. When narrators listed local leaders, at times they mentioned individual churches and credited churches as meeting places during mass campaigns, especially in Louisville. But many Lexington leaders disputed the prominence of black ministers in the movement there. Elsewhere, people of other occupations—ranging from teachers to businessmen, miners, real estate agents, and others—were as often listed as equally significant players in local struggles. Although early histories of the movement placed black churches and ministers at the center of the action, based on the prominence of King and his organization's role in the region, more recent historians have challenged this view. The more complex picture emerging from scholarship is that although some black ministers were very important, as were their churches, others held back—a pattern repeated among other professions.[7] Kentucky's experience provides further evidence for this view.

While this observation adds to our understanding of the movement in Kentucky, the emphasis on personal stories of struggle also prompts some rethinking of the civil rights movement more broadly —in particular, the nature of civil rights activity in small communities and when, even *if*, it ended. In 1994, historian Robin D. G. Kelley argued that individual acts of resistance by African Americans in the period leading up to and including World War II were precursors to the civil rights movement.[8] The memories of these Kentuckians, however, suggest that the civil rights movement was not only a series of mass demonstrations and campaigns, but was the sum of ongoing individual struggles, including the mother who sent her child to a white school, the veteran who refused to give up when denied a job, and the volunteer election worker who decided to run for office herself. These personal battles take on greater significance in a state like Kentucky, where the population of African Americans in many places was not enough to reach the critical mass necessary for larger scale actions. Blacks in small-town Kentucky often had to become, as Paducah's Gladman Humbles described his appointment to the local fire department, a "fly in the milk" in order to make change. Cumulatively and over time, these grassroots, personal struggles in small towns and rural areas helped to bring about change in African Americans' daily lives not only for the individual but for his or her community.

The persistence of such individual struggles forces a re-periodization of when significant civil rights activity took place. This project was initiated with the official aim of covering 1930–1970, reflecting scholarship that reached back in time before Montgomery, *Brown*, or even World War II to find the movement's origins.[9] Yet most interviewers focused their questions on the period after 1954, again reflecting, perhaps, the power of the grand narrative. Narrators brought their own ideas into the interview as well. Regardless of questions or the stated time frame, they insisted on breaking out of the stated chronology with stories of actions long after 1970, into the 1980s and 1990s. In politics, several speakers remembered their own campaigns or those of other first elected officials in the early 1980s. In addition, those who focused on enforcement of laws described actions taken long after the laws were passed. It thus becomes very clear from this collection that in personal memory the civil rights movement persisted long after the "grand narrative" declares it ended.

Indeed, according to most narrators, the movement is not over still. When asked specifically when the movement ended, narrators gave answers such as, "We've been in this struggle forever, always the struggle continues," or "The fight to keep your civil rights, to exercise your civil rights will never end." They demonstrated this point of view by including stories that touched on contemporary debates. In part this dynamic reflects the fact that many of the interviewees were still engaged in human rights activity, whether through state agencies, civil rights organizations, or on their own. There were at times internal contradictions in the interviews. One woman, for example, insisted that after King's assassination, things "just kind of stopped. I can't remember anything that occurred." Yet a few minutes later she remarked that any story of the movement would have to go through the 1990s. These contradictions may again reflect the influence of the national narrative. Large-scale civil rights demonstrations in Kentucky—with a few exceptions—did cease after 1968, and thus what people perceive as movement activity could be said to have ended. Yet people also remember the ongoing smaller-scale but still-vibrant struggles that persist today. These observations challenge the whole question of "when the movement ended" and redirect our attention to what the movement became and how it continues in people's lives.

Implicit in the assertion that the movement is not over is the critique of its results and a call to further action. In popular commemorations of the civil rights era, especially those supported by government institutions, the story ends on a note of success; after being challenged by Martin Luther King Jr. and his nonviolent followers, Americans roused themselves to defeat racism through civil rights laws. In contrast to this optimistic conclusion, many of the Kentuckians interviewed for this project spontaneously pointed out the lack of results from those laws. "We're not there yet," said one interviewee, summing up a sentiment shared by many. Others specifically pointed out the lack of real political power in a system in which economic inequalities stemming from racial discrimination continue, housing segregation persists, and real or potential resegregation of schools threatens access to educational resources that is already racially uneven. In short, individuals, because they see so much evidence of continued inequality, voice a much less optimistic view of history than the one so prevalent in the national narrative.

The insights from these civil rights oral histories help us to place Kentucky's story into the larger sweep of movement history, and by doing so expand the popular understanding of that history. In both scholarly examinations and the public imagination, for example, the story of 1950s school desegregation in the South has been dominated by the dramatic events associated with massive resistance, especially the confrontations in Little Rock and New Orleans. Kentucky experienced some of that extreme reaction in Sturgis, Henderson, and Clay. But Kentucky's story of the response to *Brown* can more generally be described as an example of quiet reluctance. While leaders gave lip service to endorsing integration, school boards moved slowly and adopted plans meant to ensure that the movement of African Americans into "white" schools was as minimal and as slow as possible. As a result, although the state won national acclaim for the relatively rapid integration of the Louisville schools in 1956, many districts remained largely segregated until the 1960s or later. More important, the oral history evidence shifts attention away from questions of when and how schools integrated and toward what that process meant in the black community. Many of the narrators' memories of desegregation focus on the experience of students once they entered the schools or on the losses the black community suffered when their schools closed. Several scholars have documented the benefits of all-black schools, and evidence for those claims arises in these interviews. Others, however, have challenged this view, criticizing it as a class-biased perspective that privileges the memories of middle-class African Americans, who had access to urban and thus better schools, and erases the reality of poor conditions for the majority of black students. Moreover, as Barbara Shircliffe and others have pointed out, such oral history accounts stem from interviews conducted in the light of the failure of integration fifty years after the fact and are infused with nostalgia for a time prior to that development.[10] In any case, these narratives prompt us to shift the story of integration away from implementation or resistance policies and toward what actually went on inside the schools.

As this account moves into the period commonly understood as the peak of the civil rights era—the 1960s—we can see how Kentucky's story complements or diverges from the regional history, and adds detail to the picture. We learn, for example, how one of the state's major newspapers bent journalistic standards to near breaking to deny the Lexington movement coverage—an act that made journalism history in 2004 when the paper issued a civil rights retrospective that acknowledged its mistake and provided compensatory, if terribly belated, coverage.[11]

Although Kentucky cities with large concentrations of African Americans participated in the movement in ways that resembled activism elsewhere, where the story becomes more distinctive is in the smaller communities with smaller black populations. Most of the scholarly attention to the civil rights movement in rural areas has focused on the Deep South, where voter registration drives brought volunteers from regional and national organizations into sharecropping areas to give poor black farmers access to the vote. Kentucky did not become part of that movement. African Americans here had the vote, though the small concentrations of population left them relatively unable to translate it into power. Those small numbers also made their hometowns less interesting as places for organizing, from the point of view of national civil rights leaders. So what emerges in Kentucky is the story of how blacks organized as a small electoral minority to get candidates elected, which in some places did not happen until the 1990s. Meanwhile, smaller communities had their own forms of movement against Jim Crow, too. Narrators there share stories of spontaneous sit-ins by a few people caught up in the spirit of the time—people who, as one person put it, "felt in their heads they had to challenge the system" even though they had no organization or broad campaign to help them do it. Nevertheless, the results were a slow opening—often long after legislation was passed—of public space.

Besides offering insight into life under segregation and the civil rights movement in Kentucky, these stories also broaden our understanding of the regional and national movement. We know that whether opposition to school integration took the form of massive resistance or quiet reluctance, the result for African American students and their communities was much the same. We learn that having access to the vote does not translate into political power without the determination of a few individuals to challenge themselves, and their communities, by seeking office. These stories demonstrate that the civil rights movement could take the form of large collective actions, but also could be the sum of persistent personal struggles by an individual or a few people working together for change without much outside support. Finally, these stories remind us that a social justice movement does not end when laws are passed or the crowds dwindle, but continues as long as people experience inequality and act against it.

Appendix

Narrators

Many of the interviewees chose not to give their birth dates. We are respecting that decision here. The town or towns most associated with a narrator's story are listed, followed in parentheses by the county, at first reference to each town. At the end of each biography is a citation to the interview, which includes the interviewer, date, and location of the tape or transcript. We would like to thank the archivists at these institutions for their help in locating interviews for this book. Abbreviations for the locations are:

KOHC   Kentucky Oral History Commission Collection,
            Kentucky History Center, Frankfort, Kentucky
OHC   Oral History Collection, University of Louisville
            Archives and Records Center, Louisville, Kentucky
UK   Louie B. Nunn Center for Oral History, University
            of Kentucky, Lexington, Kentucky

Wesley Acton, Owensboro (Daviess): Acton was born to a sharecropping family on a Hartford, Kentucky, farm in 1937. He attended Brescia College in Owensboro, then taught high school in Knoxville, Tennessee, and middle school in Daviess County schools, his career in the latter spanning thirty years. President of his local NAACP chapter's youth group, Acton then headed the Owensboro NAACP as a young man. He was involved in local sit-ins and was a founder in 1963 of the Owensboro Human Relations Commission. Interview by Betsy Brinson, May 5, 1999 (KOHC).

Bill Allison, Louisville (Jefferson): Born and raised in Louisville, Allison graduated from the University of Kentucky law school in 1968 and became a lawyer for the activist organization Southern Conference Educational Fund (SCEF). He served on the legal team defending first the Black Six (1968–

1970) and then the Louisville Black Panthers (1971). Continuing to be civically active, he was later involved in politics, serving on the Louisville Board of Aldermen. Interview by Tracy E. K'Meyer, September 21, 2001 (OHC).

Harold T. Alston Sr., Paducah (McCracken): Born in 1920 in Paducah, Alston began work at age twelve to help support his family. After high school he worked as an agent for the Louisville-based Mammoth Life Insurance, then became an electronic technician. Alston served as part of the 332nd fighting group in World War II and studied radar. Repeated postwar encounters with discrimination in the private sector led Alston to the Paducah NAACP. He worked for the postal service for twenty-seven years and became Paducah's first black mail carrier. Interview by Betsy Brinson, August 16, 2000 (KOHC).

Mervin Aubespin, Louisville: Aubespin was born in Louisiana in 1937 and moved to Louisville after graduating from the Tuskegee Institute. He became a teacher at Duvalle Junior High and later a journalist for the *Courier-Journal.* He was active in the open accommodations struggle in Louisville as well as in the Louisville Art Workshop, a group of artists inspired by the Black Arts Movement. Interview by Tracy E. K'Meyer, September 14, 1999 (OHC).

Howard Bailey, Middlesboro (Bell): Bailey is a native of Middlesboro, a small coal-mining town where schools were integrated in 1964, a full decade after *Brown.* Bailey finished high school in 1966 and became part of the first mass influx of African Americans to enroll at Western Kentucky University. At the time of the interview he was Dean of Students and Associate Vice President for Student Affairs at Western Kentucky University. Interview by Maxine Ray, December 13, 2000 (KOHC).

Anna Beason, Bowling Green (Warren): A native of Henderson born in 1947, Beason experienced school desegregation there before moving to Bowling Green as a teenager, where she went through it again, more turbulently this time. Influenced by her mother, who had been a poll worker and always stressed the importance of voting rights, Beason became an NAACP member herself. She later worked as an assembler at the General Motors Corvette Plant. Interview by Maxine Ray, March 20, 2001 (KOHC).

Joyce Hamilton Berry, Lexington (Fayette): Born in 1937 and reared in Lexington, Berry attended Hampton Institute in Virginia, graduating in 1958. During the height of the civil rights movement in the 1960s, as a married woman with children, she earned first a master's degree and later a doctorate in psychology (1970) from the University of Kentucky, where she was one of a small minority of black graduate students. After serving on the faculty of Kentucky State University, Dr. Berry relocated to the Washington, D.C., area, where she still lived and worked at the time of this interview. Interview by Betsy Brinson, March 31, 2000 (KOHC).

Anne McCarty Braden, Louisville: Born in 1924 in Louisville but raised in Alabama, Anne McCarty returned to Kentucky in 1947 as an education reporter for the *Louisville Times,* where she met and married labor activist Carl Braden. She spearheaded the Interracial Hospital Movement in 1950 and found infamy during the Cold War as a suspected communist for her radical interracial activism. Later a leader in many local as well as regional civil rights drives, Braden was one of the South's most outspoken white activists for racial justice until her death in 2006. Interview by Ruth Pfisterer, January 5, 1981 (OHC); interviews by Tracy E. K'Meyer, June 7, 2001, and September 18, 2001 (OHC).

Theodore Braun, Henderson (Henderson): Born in Missouri in 1927, Braun came from a long line of clergy—including both his parents—in the Evangelical Reform Church denomination (later United Church of Christ), which was involved in racial reconciliation. He completed Eden Seminary in St. Louis and went on for a master's degree from Yale Divinity School. In 1953 Braun accepted a pastorate in Henderson, where he promoted integration and cross-racial communication and was instrumental in averting violence during the desegregation of the schools. Braun left Kentucky in 1958. Interview by Ethel White, September 19, 2001 (KOHC).

Governor Edward Thompson Breathitt, Frankfort (Franklin): Born in Hopkinsville, Breathitt grew up acutely aware of both abolitionists and Confederates in his family's Civil War past. Breathitt received his bachelor's degree from the University of Kentucky in 1948 and his law degree in 1950. He became a legislator representing Christian County in the 1950s and from 1963 to 1967 Breathitt served as governor of Kentucky—at age thirty nine, the nation's youngest. At President Lyndon Johnson's request he sat on the presidential commission to implement the 1964 Civil Rights Act. In 1966 Breathitt supported and signed the South's first state civil rights act into law. Interview by Betsy Brinson, February 24, 2000 (KOHC).

Lucille Brooks, Franklin (Simpson): Brooks was born in 1922 and grew up on a farm in Simpson County. She graduated from Kentucky State University and became a high school teacher. She was one of the few blacks who kept her job, and was transferred during school desegregation to a majority-white high school. An NAACP member, she was also the wife of Matthew

L. Brooks, who served on the local school board and became the first African American elected to Franklin's city council. Interview by Betsy Brinson, June 6, 2000 (KOHC).

Ruth Bryant, Louisville: Bryant was raised in Detroit and moved to Louisville with her husband, Dr. Roscoe Bryant. She became involved in civic activities and worked with the West End Community Council during the War on Poverty and in the open housing movement. After supporting the work of the Black Unity League of Kentucky, Bryant was accused of plotting racial violence as part of the "Black Six" conspiracy. Interview by Tracy E. K'Meyer, September 27, 1999 (OHC).

Anne Butler, Stanford (Lincoln) and Richmond (Madison): Butler was born in 1948 and raised in Stanford. She enrolled in 1966 at Eastern Kentucky University, where she was active in the first Black Student Union on campus. After graduation she went on to an academic career, first in Kansas and later at the Center of Excellence for the Study of Kentucky African Americans at Kentucky State University. Interview by Betsy Brinson, January 7, 2000 (KOHC).

Selvin Butts, Bowling Green: A native of Bowling Green born in 1933, Butts has been civically active for decades in his union, the International Association of Machinists; in the local human rights commission; and in many leadership capacities of his local NAACP, starting with the youth chapter in high school. He cofounded a grassroots group, Black Concerned Citizens, and was involved in passage of local open housing and anti-mask (Ku Klux Klan–related) ordinances in Bowling Green. Interview by Maxine Ray, March 21, 2001 (KOHC).

Ken Clay, Louisville: Clay was born and raised in Louisville, where he graduated from Bellarmine College in 1960. When the War on Poverty was launched, he was hired as a research associate in the program division. In the late 1960s he started his own business, the Corner of Jazz, a shop specializing in African American and African art and culture. As a businessman, in the 1970s he also participated in efforts to increase African American economic opportunity. Interview by Tracy E. K'Meyer, February 19, 2001 (OHC).

Robert A. Coleman, Paducah: Coleman was born in Hopkinsville in 1932. After returning from the Air Force in the mid-1950s, he attended the recently desegregated Paducah Junior College. He served as city commissioner from his election in 1973 into the twenty-first century with only two interruptions, and worked to get more African Americans into local politics and civic leadership. Interview by Betsy Brinson, August 18, 2000 (KOHC).

Esther Costner, Middlesboro: Costner grew up in a coal-mining community and married a coal miner. She was active during the War on Poverty with a Community Action Project. Later she got involved with the Black Mountain Improvement Association and the Democracy Resource Center. Interview by Betsy Brinson, March 18, 1999 (KOHC).

Julia Cowans, Cardinal (Bell) and Evarts (Harlan): Born and reared in an eastern Kentucky coal camp in the 1920s, Cowans ultimately married a trade union activist, Hugh Cowans, and got active in both the labor and civil rights movements in Harlan County. Later in life they moved to Lexington. Interviews by Alessandro Portelli, 1983 and 1988 (transcripts in Catherine Fosl's possession and on file at KOHC); follow-up interview by Betsy Brinson, April 2, 2002 (KOHC).

Jesse Crenshaw, Knob Lick environs (Barren/Metcalfe) and Lexington: Crenshaw grew up mostly on his grandfather's tobacco farm near tiny Knob Lick, where he attended segregated schools in the larger town of Glasgow, but held some local stature because his family owned land. He graduated from Kentucky State University, earned his law degree at the University of Kentucky, and became active in local politics, becoming a state representative for Fayette County in 1993, a position he still held in the twenty-first century. Interview by Catherine Fosl, February 9, 2001 (KOHC).

Bob Cunningham, Louisville: Born in Cadiz in 1934, Cunningham moved to Louisville at age eight. After a tour of duty in the military and a few years living in California in the early 1960s, he returned to Louisville. Influenced by the Black Power movement, Cunningham helped to found the Black Workers' Coalition. He later was involved in the pro-integration response to the busing crisis of 1975–1976, and remained active into the twenty-first century. Interview by Tracy E. K'Meyer, September 1, 1999 (OHC).

Raoul Cunningham, Louisville: Cunningham was born in Louisville in 1934. He joined the NAACP Youth Council in high school and was one of the initiators and leaders of the 1961 sit-in campaign. He later worked on Georgia Davis Powers's election campaign and in Democratic Party politics, remaining active in black political action and later the NAACP for decades. Interview by Tracy E. K'Meyer, June 19, 1996 (OHC); interview by Betsy Brinson, May 28, 2002 (KOHC).

Robert "Bob" Douglass, Louisville: Douglass was born in 1934 in Louisville. He graduated from the University of Louisville in 1963 with a degree in fine art. He became a community organizer for the War on Poverty in the

West End of Louisville, and then was one of the founders of the Louisville Art Workshop, a group of artists inspired by the Black Arts Movement. He earned his Ph.D. in 1983 and joined the Pan-African Studies faculty at the University of Louisville in 1985. Interviews by Tracy E. K'Meyer, October 28, 1996, and September 19, 1999 (OHC).

Amanda Cooper Elliott, Lexington: Born in 1921, Amanda Cooper grew up in segregated Lexington's Kincaidtown. As a young woman in World War II, she worked at Wright Field while her new husband served in the armed forces. After the war, she held a variety of part-time jobs amid raising two children. Interview by Betsy Adler, April 15, 1993 (UK).

Constance Ellison, Benham (Harlan): Ellison was born in the 1920s in Georgia, where she lived until enrolling in the Tuskegee Institute in Alabama. During World War II, Ellison accepted an offer to teach home economics at an all-black school in Benham, where she later experienced desegregation of the schools. Ellison earned her master's degree at Cornell University and taught in eastern Kentucky for thirty-eight years. Interview by Betsy Brinson, March 23, 1999 (KOHC).

James Embry, Lexington: Embry was born in 1949 in Richmond. In 1967 he enrolled at the University of Kentucky and became involved in black student politics, first through the group Orgena and then the Black Student Union. He was involved in unrest at the university in the late 1960s, but later returned to campus as an official with the Office of Minority Student Affairs. Interview by Doris Weathers, July 12, 1987; interview by John Jason Peter, November 14, 1978 (UK).

George Esters, Bowling Green: Born in Bowling Green in 1941, Esters attended Arkansas University on a football scholarship. He returned home and taught high school history in the final year before school desegregation. After one year in mixed classrooms, he secured a directorship in adult education and mentored black students. Esters later became a Baptist minister. Interview by Betsy Brinson, June 6, 2000 (KOHC).

Robert "Bob" Estill, Lexington: Born in Lexington in 1927, Estill received his undergraduate education at the University of Kentucky and his divinity degree from the Episcopal Divinity School at Harvard University. He returned to Kentucky as a pastor, first in Middlesboro, then in the mid-1950s at his home church, Christ Church in Lexington. He worked on behalf of civil rights through the church, CORE, as first chairman of the Kentucky Commission on Human Rights, and by founding an Urban League local in

Lexington in 1963. He left the state for a pastorate in Washington, D.C., later in the decade, but returned to Lexington for retirement. Interview by Betsy Brinson, March 23, 2000 (KOHC).

Helen Fisher Frye, Danville (Boyle): Frye was born in 1918 in Danville. She graduated from Kentucky State University and became a teacher. A church, civic, and NAACP leader, Frye became the first African American to attend Centre College. Interview by Betsy Brinson, January 6, 1999 (KOHC).

Betty Gabehart, Campbellsville (Taylor): Gabehart was born in Campbellsville in 1935 but in her youth moved to Lexington, where she graduated from an all-white high school and then the University of Kentucky. Gabehart became involved in civil rights causes through her work with the YWCA. She later studied theology at Yale Divinity School. She worked on voter registration projects across the country and as a YWCA staff member, later retiring in Lexington. Interview by Betsy Brinson, April 26, 1999 (KOHC).

James F. Gordon, Madisonville (Hopkins): Gordon was born in 1918. He graduated from the University of Kentucky law school in 1941. After completing military service in World War II in 1945, he returned to Kentucky to practice law. Appointed by President Lyndon Johnson as a federal judge, Gordon served on the U.S. District Court for the Western District of Kentucky from August 1964 until his retirement for disability in May of 1984. In 1975, at the direction of the federal court of appeals in Cincinnati, Gordon ordered the integration of the Louisville-Jefferson County school system by system-wide busing. Multiple interviews by Ethel White, June 22–August 14, 1987 (OHC).

Joe Graves, Lexington: Graves, born in Lexington in 1930, graduated from Transylvania University and went to work for the family business, Graves-Cox and Company, a men's specialty store. Graves used his position to desegregate his staff and clientele and to urge other businesses to do the same. He became cochair of the Lexington Human Rights Commission in 1960 and in 1963 cochaired Kentuckians for Public Accommodations legislation, which fought to integrate public accommodations in the state. Interview by Betsy Brinson, March 16, 2000 (KOHC).

Audrey Grevious, Lexington: Grevious was born in 1930 and attended segregated schools, where she was inspired to become a teacher. She also became president of the Lexington chapter of the NAACP, and worked closely with Julia Lewis, president of the Congress on Racial Equality. Together the two built a strong coalition in the early 1960s, organizing many campaigns for civil rights. Interview by Betsy Brinson, April 13, 1999 (KOHC).

Ann Beard Grundy, Berea (Madison): Grundy was born in Birmingham, Alabama, in 1945. She was recruited to attend high school at New York's Liberty Central, a majority Jewish school, from which she graduated in 1964. Her father was a minister at Sixteenth Street Baptist Church when four little girls were killed in the infamous bombing there in 1963. She attended Berea College and helped organize the first Black Student Union there, then served as a field representative for the state Human Rights Commission in Louisville from 1969–1970. She later became youth director of Plymouth Settlement House, working with people in poverty. Interviews by Betsy Brinson, February 9, 1999, February 17, 1999, and June 23, 1999 (KOHC).

Chester Grundy, Lexington: Grundy was born in Louisville in 1947, and graduated from an integrated Male High School in 1965. He attended the University of Kentucky, where he organized Orgena, a social club for blacks and forerunner of what became the Black Student Union in 1965. He and his wife, Ann Beard Grundy, traveled through Africa and Europe, where their Pan-African views were solidified. The Grundys have for years organized Lexington's Martin Luther King Day commemorations and have long been outspoken advocates for black history and African heritage. Interview by Betsy Brinson, June 23, 1999 (KOHC).

Cheri Bryant Hamilton, Louisville: Hamilton is the daughter of Ruth Bryant, a civic and open housing activist in Louisville. She joined the open housing demonstrations as a teenager and went on to a career in local government, serving on first the board of aldermen and then the metro council. Interview by Tracy E. K'Meyer, October 23, 1999 (OHC).

Iola Willhite Harding, Yosemite (Casey): Born in 1931, Harding was the oldest child of her tiny farming town's only remaining African American family. Therefore, her father had to drive her and her siblings twelve miles to school each day. She became the first in her family to pursue higher education, attending Kentucky State University. She and her husband, Robert Harding, completed graduate study in the mid-1950s at the University of Kentucky—he in law, she in education. She then earned her Ed.D. from the University of New Mexico, and has lived much of her adult life in Albuquerque. Interview by Betsy Brinson, April 8, 2000 (KOHC).

Wardelle G. Harvey, Paducah: Harvey was born in 1926 in Booneville, Indiana, where he attended a one-room, all-black elementary school and then an integrated high school. He went on to earn a bachelor's degree in theology from Tri-State Baptist College in Evansville. In 1962, he took up responsibilities as a pastor in Paducah, Kentucky, where he also founded the Non-Partisan League, a civil rights group instrumental in integrating Paducah's public facilities. In the 1970s he served as Paducah city commissioner, as well as serving a brief stint as mayor pro tem. Interview by Betsy Brinson, August 16, 2000 (KOHC).

John Wesley Hatch, Lexington: Hatch was born in Louisville, but because his father was an African Methodist preacher, the family moved often. In 1948 he began taking law classes at Kentucky State taught by University of Kentucky law faculty. Once the University of Kentucky campus desegregated, Hatch attended there briefly, but disheartened by his treatment, he moved to Arkansas, where his parents by then lived. Never returning to Kentucky or to the study of law, he went on for a master's degree from Atlanta University and a doctorate in public health from the University of North Carolina, where he taught for many years. Interview by Lauretta Byers and Terry Birdwhistell, May 1, 1994 (UK).

Gustava Hayden, Owensboro: Hayden was born in 1912 in Owensboro. She joined the NAACP during World War II. Over the course of her life, she witnessed many episodes of discrimination. Interview by Betsy Brinson, May 6, 1999 (KOHC).

Tony Heitzman, Louisville: Heitzman was born in 1931 and raised in Louisville. He attended St. Meinard Seminary in Indiana to fulfill a lifetime dream of becoming a priest and then became a teacher at Louisville's Trinity High School. In 1967 he worked for the War on Poverty, coordinating programs in the West End. Interview by Tracy E. K'Meyer, May 26, 2000 (OHC).

Ruth Higgins, Louisville: Higgins was the white principal of the Morris Elementary School in Louisville during the 1956 school desegregation, which was featured in the media along with the formerly black Douglass Elementary School as an example of successful integration. Interview by Darlene Eakin, August 1, 1973 (OHC).

Jean Higgs, Owensboro: Jean Higgs was born in 1937 in Arkansas and graduated from an integrated parochial school in Chicago in the 1950s. Though they themselves were active in civil rights marches, Higgs's mother and aunt refused to let her participate, out of fear for her safety. In 1966 Higgs moved to Owensboro, her husband's hometown, to get away from Chicago's race riots. In Owensboro, Higgs worked for the previously all-white telephone company and served on the school board from 1979–1981. Interview by Betsy Brinson, May 6, 1999 (KOHC).

Morton Holbrook, Owensboro: Holbrook was born in Daviess County in 1914 to a Scotch-Irish family with deep roots in Kentucky. He attended the University of Kentucky, the National Institute of Public Affairs in Washington, D.C., and Harvard Law School. Holbrook served in World War II and returned to Owensboro to practice law, serving as attorney to the Daviess County School Board for twenty-five years, including the years of school desegregation. Interview by Betsy Brinson, June 9, 2000 (KOHC).

James Howard, Sturgis (Union): A native of Sturgis, Howard wanted to attend the all-white school six blocks from his house instead of the all-black school miles away in Morganfield. In 1956 he enrolled in Sturgis High School and found himself in the middle of an uproar over desegregation. Forced out by the school board later that fall, Howard subsequently returned to Sturgis High to graduate, going on to a career as an educator and school principal outside Kentucky. Interview by Betsy Brinson, n.d. [2001] (KOHC).

J. Blaine Hudson, Louisville: Born in 1949 and raised in Louisville among an extended family of educators, Hudson graduated from Male High School as a National Merit Scholar. Attending the University of Louisville, he became a prominent leader of the Black Student Union and was suspended from school after a campus occupation. Hudson returned for his degree. He later became first a professor, then a dean at the University of Louisville. Interview with Betsy Brinson, August 23, 2000 (KOHC).

Gladman Humbles, Paducah: Humbles was born in 1930 and grew up in Paducah, where he graduated from an all-black school. After being denied service at a laundromat in 1957, Humbles decided to open his own, catering to the black community and thus forcing white owners to integrate their laundries. Later, he worked with the NAACP and became the first black member of the Paducah Fire Department. Humbles has written extensively on black history and published articles in the *Paducah Sun*. Interview by Betsy Brinson, August 15, 2000 (KOHC).

Jerome Hutchinson Sr., Louisville: Hutchinson was born in Louisville in 1931 and graduated from Louisville Municipal College in 1951, after having served in World War II. He worked for both the federal Small Business Administration and then a local program called Economic Development Now to promote business ownership and economic opportunity for African Americans. Interview by Tracy E. K'Meyer, October 19, 1999 (OHC).

Evelyn Jackson, Louisville: Born in Louisville, Jackson graduated from Central High School in 1927 and became a teacher in 1929. At the time of the 1956 desegregation of the Louisville schools she was principal of Douglass Elementary, which was featured in the national media as an example of successful desegregation in the city. Interview by Tracy E. K'Meyer, December 3, 1999 (OHC).

Daisy James, Owensboro: Daisy James was born in Owensboro in 1939 and has lived there almost all of her life. Graduating from all-black Western High School around 1960, James was forced to forego further educational opportunities in order to support her family. However, she worked for a community action group as its equal employment officer and later for the Health Department. In the 1970s, James worked with the NAACP, particularly on issues of police brutality. She ran as a candidate for city commissioner in 1991, and was the first black appointed to the Utility Commission. Interview by Betsy Brinson, May 5, 1999 (KOHC).

Robert Jefferson, Lexington: Born in 1932 in Lexington, Jefferson attended segregated schools there with his sister Audrey Grevious. He then went to college in Providence, Rhode Island, and served in the U.S. Army in the late 1940s, during the time it desegregated. Returning to Lexington, he became involved in the Urban League, eventually serving as its chairman. He was also a longtime officer of the Lexington-Fayette Human Rights Commission. In 1971, on behalf of his children, he became a plaintiff in *Jefferson et al. v. the Fayette County Board of Education,* which led to a major desegregation and reorganization of the schools. Jefferson was later elected to the urban county council. Interview by Edward Owens, June 5, 1978 (UK).

Lyman Johnson, Louisville: Johnson was born in 1906 in Columbia, Tennessee, and earned degrees from Virginia Union University and the University of Michigan before settling in Louisville as a history teacher at Central High School. He was the plaintiff in the lawsuit that desegregated the University of Kentucky as well as a later suit that led to court-ordered busing in the Louisville and Jefferson County public schools. He was also a longtime leader of the Louisville NAACP. Johnson died in 1997. Interview by Catherine Fosl, June 24, 1991 (UK).

Nancy Johnson, Baxter (Harlan): Nancy Johnson was born in Harlan County in 1931. She graduated from the Washington (D.C.) Bible Institute, where she decided to become a missionary. Johnson then worked for a previously all-white mission in Harlan County for thirteen years, ministering to students in black schools and working with the NAACP and the local PTA. She also worked as a community organizer for the Harlan County Planning and Development Association, and later as a teacher. Interview by Betsy Brinson, March 19, 1999 (KOHC).

Thelma Johnson, Henderson: Thelma Johnson was born in Georgia in 1909 but has lived in Henderson and Daviess counties since 1946. As a home economist hired by the University of Kentucky, she worked with low-income families while suffering many instances of blatant racism and discrimination on the job. She also served as the chairman of the local human rights commission. Interview by Maxine Ray, October 21, 2000 (KOHC).

Loyal Jones, Berea: Loyal Jones was born in 1928 in North Carolina to a poor white family. Jones began college at Berea in 1950, around the same time it was reintegrated after invalidation of the Day Law. Later, Jones became involved with rural organizing through the Council of the Southern Mountains, Appalachian Volunteers, and the Highlander Folk School. He was also heavily involved in Berea's local human rights commission. Interview by Betsy Brinson, December 8, 1999 (KOHC).

Mary Jones, Lexington: Jones was born in Lawrenceburg. Her husband, the Reverend W. H. Jones, who was pastor of Lexington's Pleasant Green Baptist Church for twenty-eight years, worked closely with CORE during the civil rights movement. The Jones family participated in the 1960s sit-ins and protests in many capacities. Interview by Edward Owens, January 19, 1979 (UK).

Mattie Jones, Louisville: Jones was born in Memphis, Tennessee, in 1933 and moved to Louisville at age six. She attended the University of Louisville in the 1950s and later was a part of the 1964 March on Frankfort and the two-day sit-in and hunger strike in the legislature. Later she worked through the Black Workers' Coalition and Justice Resource Center against economic and racial inequality. Interview by Betsy Brinson, February 5, 1999 (KOHC).

Eleanor Jordan, Louisville: Jordan was born in Louisville in 1953 and graduated from Central High School in 1971. She grew up on the edge of the civil rights struggle, recalling her brother's involvement in the riots of 1968, and went on to a career in Democratic Party politics and state government. In 2008 she became director of the Kentucky Commission on Women. Interview by Betsy Brinson, February 3, 1999 (KOHC).

Mae (Jones) Street Kidd, Millersburg (Bourbon) and Simpsonville (Shelby): Born a light-skinned biracial child in 1904 in Millersburg, Mae Jones spent her childhood there, then attended the Lincoln Institute in Shelby County, an African American teacher-training school established in 1912 as a result of the Day Law. She spent most of her adult life in Louisville, where she championed equal rights for women and minorities and founded the Louisville Urban League Guild. Kidd was elected as a representative to the legislature in 1967. She died in 1999. Interview by Kenneth Chumbley, n.d. [1978] (OHC).

James Kiphart, Louisville: Kiphart was born in 1933 in Eminence, and moved to Louisville in 1952 after graduating high school. In the late 1960s he worked against employment discrimination through the West End Community Council and Black Workers' Coalition, which he helped to found. He was one of a group of employees who filed a complaint against Louisville Gas and Electric with the Kentucky Commission on Human Rights. Interview by Tracy E. K'Meyer, September 29, 1999 (OHC).

Shelby Lanier, Louisville: Lanier was born in 1936 in Louisville. After serving in the military he returned to the city and became a police officer. He was a pioneer on the force, serving as the first black officer in a number of divisions. Responding to discrimination he witnessed within the police department, he helped to form the Louisville Black Police Officers' Organization, which fought racism on the force and in police/community relations. Interview by Tracy E. K'Meyer, September 29, 1999 (OHC).

Ronald "Ron" Lewis, Bowling Green: Born in 1948 in Bardstown, Lewis came to Bowling Green to attend Western Kentucky University in 1966, along with Howard Bailey and the school's largest group of African Americans at that time. Upon graduating, he became a junior high teacher in Bowling Green. He later served as chairman, then president of a rejuvenated Bowling Green/Warren County NAACP, working on issues related to housing and local implementation of affirmative action. Interview by Maxine Ray, June 20, 2001 (KOHC).

Ken Litchfield, Hopkinsville (Christian): Litchfield grew up on a farm in Christian County and graduated from Singing Fork High. He served in the Korean War, then received his undergraduate degree from the University of Kentucky and attained his master's degree at Ohio State University. He worked as a reporter during desegregation and the open housing struggle in Louisville. Interview by Ethel White, February 15, 2001 (KOHC).

George Logan, Lexington: George Logan was born in Stanford in 1929 and studied at Kentucky State College. He then attended graduate school at the University of Kentucky, where he encountered harsh racism from fellow students. Logan served in the integrated Air Force in the early 1950s and returned to Kentucky to teach in the Fayette County Public Schools, where he fought to include black history in the curriculum. Interview by Betsy Brinson, March 14, 2001 (KOHC).

Norbert Logsdon, Louisville: Logsdon was born in 1929 in the West End of Louisville. When the neighborhood began to shift from majority white to black, Logsdon, who was white, and his family refused to move. He joined the West End Community Council and participated in its community-building efforts to keep the West End integrated. Interview by Tracy E. K'Meyer, October 25, 1999 (OHC).

Abby Marlatt, Lexington: Marlatt was born in 1916 in Kansas to an educated, white family with deep roots in the abolitionist movement. She attended Kansas State University, and went on to complete a certificate in dietetics and later a doctorate at the University of California-Berkeley. In 1956, Marlatt accepted a position as Director of the School of Home Economics at the University of Kentucky. In Lexington, Marlatt worked with the YWCA and helped found the local CORE chapter, with which she was very active until the emergence of Black Power in 1968. She was a controversial figure on the campus for that activism and for her involvement in antiwar and women's causes. Interview by Betsy Brinson, February 2, 1999 (KOHC).

Galen Martin, Louisville: Martin was born in 1927 in West Virginia. He first came to Kentucky to attend Berea College, then left for graduate school and to work in Washington, D.C. He returned to the commonwealth in the mid-1950s to head the Kentucky Council on Human Relations. He was executive director of the Kentucky Commission on Human Rights from its formation in 1960 until 1989, remaining active as a white ally to racial justice causes until his death in 2006. Interview by Betsy Brinson, November 4, 1999 (KOHC).

Clarence Matthews, Louisville: Matthews was born in 1929 in Alabama and grew up in Detroit, Michigan. In 1956, after graduating from Wayne State University, he moved to Louisville. He secured a job as a reporter for the *Defender,* and in that position covered black life and politics around the state. Interview by Ethel White, May 10, 2000 (KOHC).

Loraine Mathis, Paducah: Loraine Mathis was born around 1918 in Bolivar, Tennessee, but moved to Paducah very soon afterward. Mathis graduated from an all-black school and Paducah Community College. She worked in voter registration for the NAACP and later for the Council of Organizations, an umbrella civil rights group. Interview by Betsy Brinson, August 16, 2000 (KOHC).

Michelle McCrary, Richmond: Born in Louisville in 1950, McCrary attended desegregated schools in the mass civil rights movement years, and graduated from Male High School. She went to Eastern Kentucky University in 1968, part of the largest influx of African Americans to attend. She was a leader in the Black Student Union there and became the first African American member of the drill team. McCrary had a son and dropped out for a decade, then returned to finish. Interview by Betsy Brinson, April 2, 2002 (KOHC).

Joseph "Joe" McMillan, Louisville: McMillan was born in 1929 in Louisville and graduated from Louisville Municipal College. While a student he made his first foray into politics, campaigning for Progressive Party candidate Henry Wallace in 1948. Though he left Kentucky in 1951, when he returned in 1976 he reentered the political arena, raising money for and supporting black candidates for office. Interview by Tracy E. K'Meyer, November 23, 1999 (OHC).

Don Mills, Lexington: Raised in Hickman County in the western end of the state, Mills began mimeographing and distributing his own newspaper in high school in the 1940s. He later studied journalism at the University of Kentucky, where he wrote for the *Kernel.* Mills, a liberal-minded writer, served as press secretary for Governor Breathitt. In 1968 he became editor of the *Lexington Herald,* under general management at the time of Fred Wachs, who was known for his hostility to covering civil rights. Mills pushed the paper toward more balanced coverage and hired African American reporters. Interview by Ethel White, December 1, 2000 (KOHC).

Louis Mudd, Louisville: Born in Louisville in 1943, Mudd was one of the generation of young people who went through the 1956 school integration process. He transferred to Male High School and experienced ongoing discrimination there. He also joined his fellow African American students at Male and Central High Schools in leading the 1961 sit-in demonstrations. Interview by Tracy E. K'Meyer, August 28, 2000 (OHC).

Sterling Neal Jr., Louisville: Neal was born and raised in Louisville, the son of activist parents. After earning his degree in social work, he worked for the War on Poverty program in Louisville's West End. Influenced by the Black Power movement, he became the leader of a number of nationalist organizations, focusing on fighting the rise of drug use in the black community. Neal remained a community activist until his 2006 death. Interview by Tracy E. K'Meyer, April 21, 2000 (OHC).

Charles Neblett, Russellville (Logan): Charles Neblett was born in Robinson County, Tennessee, in 1941, and grew up in Simpson County, Kentucky. He attended Southern Illinois University, where he engaged in activism and did not graduate. Soon after, he became involved in SNCC and helped form the SNCC Freedom Singers, coming to realize the power of music as an organizing tool. He worked as an organizer in Missouri, Chicago, Mississippi, and Tennessee. After Neblett settled in Russellville, he ran for public office and was elected magistrate. He also continued musical human rights activism. Interview by Genie Potter and Betsy Brinson, June 26, 2002 (KOHC).

Mary Northington, Covington (Kenton): Northington was born in 1929 in Addison, Alabama, and moved to Covington in 1933. She returned to Alabama to attend Talladega College, graduating in 1949. Her mother, Jane Roberta Summers, was a leader in the Covington NAACP and for twenty-five years managed the Jacob Price Homes, a public housing project established initially for blacks. Northington moved back to Covington in 1989 and has since been involved in the Northern Kentucky African American Heritage Task Force. Interview by Betsy Brinson, April 10, 1999 (KOHC).

Don Offutt, Bowling Green: Offutt was born in Bowling Green in 1947. His ancestors were slaves in Warren County on the Offutt Plantation. He was in the last graduating class before his high school, High Street, was closed down when desegregation occurred. He attended Kentucky State University, then transferred a year later to Western Kentucky University, where he was responsible for starting the first black fraternity, Omega Si Phi, on campus. He was also a founder of the Black Student Union. Interview by Betsy Brinson, January 6, 2001 (KOHC).

Howard Owens, Louisville: Owens was born in 1948 in Arkansas and moved to Louisville at age five. He graduated high school in 1966. After attending Wilberforce University, he returned to Louisville in 1971 to become a school teacher. Influenced by the Black Power movement, he became part of the collective response to the racism engendered by the antibusing movement in Jefferson County and remained active in the community for decades. Interview by Tracy E. K'Meyer, February 28, 2000 (OHC).

Porter G. Peeples, Lynch (Harlan) and Lexington: Born in Lynch, a small coal-mining town where the majority of men—black and white—worked in the mines, Peeples was involved in the Baptist church growing up and served as a junior deacon. In the tradition of other eastern Kentucky black families, Peeples spent his summers with relatives in northern cities, working. He attended Cumberland Community College and then the University of Kentucky. There he studied special education and became the first black president of the Student Council for Special Education. He has long been director of the Lexington Urban League. Interview by Betsy Brinson, October 5, 2000 (KOHC).

H. Foster Petit, Lexington: Born in Lexington in 1930, Petit grew up there but attended boarding school in Virginia, then the University of Virginia. His military and law school experience expanded his awareness of being white amid racial discrimination. He practiced law in Louisville and Lexington, and served three terms in the legislature and two terms as mayor of Lexington at the time of the city-county governments' merger. Interview by Betsy Brinson, March 15, 2000 (KOHC).

David Pettie, Sturgis: The son of a coal miner who became a miner himself, Pettie was born in 1925 in Earlington but moved to Sturgis as a young man. At nineteen, he joined the United Mine Workers, and later became a mine foreman, a minister, and the first African American in Union County to be certified as an emergency medical technician. He battled considerable white resistance when his daughter Mary desegregated Sturgis High, but she graduated from there. Pettie then became active in his local NAACP. Interview by Betsy Brinson, August 16, 2001 (KOHC).

Nancy Pollock, Louisville: Pollock was born in Springfield, Kentucky, and moved to Louisville at age two. As a young teenager she participated in the open accommodations struggle, and then left the state to work with the Student Nonviolent Coordinating Committee. In the late 1960s she joined the Black Panther Party and came to Louisville to help organize a local unit. Interview by Tracy E. K'Meyer, September 9, 1999 (OHC).

Woodford Porter Jr., Louisville: Porter was the son of one of the founders of the Lincoln Independent Party. After attending Indiana University and serving in the Navy, he returned to Louisville to run the family funeral parlor business. He was involved in the NAACP throughout the movement era, and was the first African American elected to the Louisville Board of Education. Interview by Tracy E. K'Meyer, September 9, 1999 (OHC).

Suzy Post, Louisville: Post was born in 1933 and raised in Louisville. While a student at Indiana University she joined a student branch of the NAACP. Returning to Louisville after years away, married now with five young children, she joined the Kentucky Civil Liberties Union, which she revitalized and later directed. She was involved in the open housing movement and was one of the plaintiffs in the suit that led to court-ordered busing in the Jefferson County Public Schools. Post remained committed to civil rights and was also a leader in fair housing, women's rights, and antiwar drives. Interview by Tracy E. K'Meyer, April 3, 2000 (OHC).

Georgia Davis Powers, Louisville: Powers was born in Springfield and moved to Louisville as a child. She worked for the Allied Organizations for Civil Rights organizing the March on Frankfort and then joined the Louisville open housing movement. In 1967 she was elected as the first woman and first African American in the Kentucky Senate, a position she used to secure the Kentucky Fair Housing Act in 1968. Powers remained an outspoken human rights advocate. Interview by Betsy Brinson, n.d. [2002] (KOHC).

Gertrude Ridgel, Frankfort: Born in Charleston, West Virginia, in the 1920s, Gertrude Ridgel graduated from West Virginia State College and received her doctorate in zoology at the University of Wisconsin. Ridgel moved to Frankfort in the summer of 1960, where she and her husband became professors at Kentucky State. They were immediately recruited to the local NAACP chapter, helped make the local arrangements for the March on Frankfort, and participated in CORE training workshops to conduct sit-ins throughout the city. Interview by Betsy Brinson, April 27, 1999 (KOHC).

Sanford T. Roach, Danville: Born in Frankfort in 1916 while his parents attended Kentucky State Normal Institute (the future Kentucky State University), Roach soon moved with his family to Danville and graduated from the all-black Bate High School in 1933. His father was a dentist and his mother a teacher. After attending Kentucky State, Roach returned to Bate to teach. In 1938, he moved to Lexington to work at the Paul S. Dunbar High School, where he taught science and coached basketball and football. Roach became an important figure in desegregating basketball in Kentucky high school athletics. Interview by Betsy Brinson, October 23, 1999 (KOHC).

Runette Robinson, Louisville: Robinson was born in Tennessee and moved to Louisville with her family when she was a small child. In 1961 she joined her fellow Central High School students in the sit-in campaign for open accommodations. She later worked for Head Start and had a career as an educator. Interview by Tracy E. K'Meyer, September 9, 2000 (OHC).

Ken Rowland, Louisville: Rowland was born in Kansas and attended Kansas State University and the National Academy of Broadcasting in Washington,

D.C. He moved to Louisville in 1956 and after a short absence returned in 1958 to a career in broadcast journalism. Interview by Ethel White, June 30, 2001 (KOHC).

Wilfred Taylor Seals, Lexington: Seals was born in Lexington in 1934. He worked for the state parks department in 1953 after returning from the Army, and witnessed the use and changes in the parks before, during, and after integration. Interview by Boyd Shearer and Harold Barker, March 25, 1997 (UK).

Ben Shobe, Louisville: Shobe was born in Bowling Green and raised in communities around the state. He graduated from the Lincoln Institute, Kentucky State College, and the University of Michigan Law School before moving to Louisville to establish a practice. In the postwar era he was an attorney for the NAACP on a number of desegregation cases. He later became assistant commonwealth attorney and later a judge. Interview by Tracy E. K'Meyer, July 22, 1996 (OHC).

Ricardo Sisney, Henderson and Bowling Green: Sisney was born in Henderson in 1939. He attended Kentucky State on a music scholarship, graduating with a degree in science. He taught initially in Bowling Green schools, witnessing their integration in 1965. After some years of teaching teachers at Western Kentucky University, Sisney served as an assistant principal in the Bowling Green school system for twenty-seven years. He was long active in the local commission on human rights and served as a hearing examiner throughout western Kentucky. Interview by Betsy Brinson, June 5, 2000 (KOHC).

Charles Tachau, Louisville: Tachau was born in 1922 and raised in Louisville. He was first a lawyer and a juvenile court judge, then became an Episcopal priest. Assigned to a pastorate in the West End of Louisville, Tachau became interested in neighborhood issues and joined the open housing movement. He went on to be a leader in the West End Community Council. Interview by Tracy E. K'Meyer, August 16, 1999 (OHC).

Newton Thomas, Horse Cave (Hart): Thomas was born in 1912 in Georgetown. He attended Kentucky State College and immediately after graduation became the principal of the black high school in Horse Cave. After the University of Kentucky opened its doors to African Americans he received his master's degree in education administration and management. When he returned to Horse Cave he worked with a committee to organize the integration of the local schools, and then became a science teacher in the newly mixed high school. Interview by Betsy Brinson, May 28, 2002 (KOHC).

Neville Tucker, Louisville: Tucker, the son of civil rights activist Bishop C. Eubank Tucker, was born in Louisville in 1933. He was an attorney who defended activists in many local campaigns, and also helped to lead the open accommodations and open housing movements. He ran for office in 1969 on the Black Unity Slate, and was elected as the first African American police court judge in Louisville. Interview by Tracy E. K'Meyer, September 10, 2001 (OHC).

William Turner, Hopkinsville: William Turner came from a family of farmers who had been in Hopkinsville since 1827. He graduated from segregated Austin-Peay College in 1963 and then received his master's degree in a more integrated Murray State in 1969. He was an advocate for civil rights throughout his life. Interview by Betsy Brinson, June 8, 2000 (KOHC).

Luska J. Twyman, Glasgow (Barren): Twyman was born in 1918 in Hiseville, Kentucky. He graduated from Kentucky State College in 1939 and served in World War II. Returning to Glasgow, he served as principal of the Ralph Bunche School. In 1968 he became Kentucky's first African American mayor. He was also the first African American to serve on the U.S. Commission of Human Rights. Interview by Lynwood Montell, August 5, 1977 (Western Kentucky University).

Andrew Wade, Louisville: Born in the 1920s, Wade grew up in Louisville. After serving in World War II, he returned to the city to work with his father's electrical business and became active in postwar civil rights campaigns. In 1954 he and his wife, Charlotte, with the help of Anne and Carl Braden, bought a home in an all-white suburb, triggering a wave of hostility that culminated in the dynamiting of the home and the sedition trial of the Bradens and a group of white associates. The Wades were never able to return to their home or see the bombers prosecuted, and they returned to the city's West End to live. Wade died in 2005. Interview by Catherine Fosl, November 8, 1989 (UK).

Hal Warheim, Louisville: Warheim was born and raised in Pennsylvania. After receiving a divinity degree from Eden Seminary in St. Louis and a Ph.D. from Columbia University, he moved to Louisville to teach at the Louisville Presbyterian Seminary. He joined the Kentucky Civil Liberties Union and through that organization became a white ally in the open housing struggle. Interview by Tracy E. K'Meyer, August 6, 1999 (OHC).

Charles Whitehead, Ashland (Boyd): Whitehead was born a sharecropper's son in 1937 in Mississippi, but moved with his family to Ohio when he was four years old. He first came to Kentucky in 1963 to work for Ashland Oil, and after a brief period back in Ohio, returned as the company's director of equal opportunity affairs. He used that position to work with community groups to secure equal access to housing for African Americans in Ashland. Interviews by Betsy Brinson, November 18, 1999, and January 10, 2000 (KOHC).

F. E. Whitney, Hopkinsville: Whitney was born in Hopkinsville in 1916. His father, who passed the bar but did not practice law, became one of the first black mail carriers in the county. Whitney attended Kentucky State College and graduated with a degree in education. Because of the Depression, he was pushed into accepting a job at a black insurance agency in Louisville. A World War II veteran, Whitney was elected in 1953 to the Hopkinsville City Council. Interview by Betsy Brinson, July 7, 2000 (KOHC).

Alice Wilson, Mayfield (Graves): Wilson was born in 1941. After the *Brown* decision, she and nine friends decided to enroll in all-white Mayfield High School. With the support of their families, the ten ninth graders successfully began school integration. Wilson later enrolled in Hampton University and has for many years taught music in the New Jersey public school system. Interview by Betsy Brinson, August 17, 2000 (KOHC).

Jennie Wilson, Mayfield: Wilson was born in 1900, into a family of share-croppers. She was the daughter of former slaves and her father was a veteran of the Civil War. Growing up in Mayfield, she witnessed several lynchings of black men. She was Alice Wilson's mother. Interview by Betsy Brinson, August 17, 2000 (KOHC).

Jesse Zander, Berea: Zander was born in a small coal-mining town in western Virginia in 1932. She was recruited to attend Berea College and became the first black student to graduate after the Day Law was set aside. After teaching in eastern Kentucky and other Appalachian schools throughout the 1950s, Zander moved with her husband to Arizona, where she spent thirty years as an educator specializing in intercultural relations. Zander returned to Berea briefly in the 1990s to teach, and remained active in its Alumni Council. Interview by Betsy Brinson, June 2, 1999 (KOHC).

Notes

Introduction

1. Kenneth Stampp, *The Peculiar Institution: Slavery in the Antebellum South* (New York: Knopf, 1956; revised edition, Vintage, 1989), 86.

2. George C. Wright, *Racial Violence in Kentucky, 1865–1940: Lynchings, Mob Rule, and "Legal Lynchings"* (Baton Rouge: Louisiana State Univ. Press, 1990), 1.

3. Ibid., 4.

4. George C. Wright coined this phrase in *Life behind a Veil: Blacks in Louisville, Kentucky, 1865–1930* (Baton Rouge: Louisiana State Univ. Press, 1985), 1.

5. Some of this information is drawn from a 1997 report prepared by the Kentucky Advisory Committee to the U.S. Commission on Civil Rights, entitled "Bias and Bigotry in Kentucky," p. 3, www.law.umaryland.edu/marshall /usccr/documents/cr12b472z.pdf (accessed on November 18, 2008).

6. That statistic enlarges to 7.7 percent if one considers the African American population to incorporate those of mixed race origin including African American. Data is from U.S. Census Bureau, Census 2000 Summary File 1, Matrices P7 and P9, http://factfinder.census.gov/servlet/ QTTable?_bm=y&-geo_id=04000US21&-qr_name=DEC_2000_SF1_U_ QTP5&-ds_name=DEC_2000_SF1_U&-_lang=en&-_sse=on (accessed on November 18, 2008).

7. A groundbreaking thesis was put forward by Charles Payne, "Men Led, But Women Organized: Movement Participation of Women in the Mississippi Delta," in *Women in the Civil Rights Movement: Trailblazers and Torchbearers, 1941–1965*, ed. Vicki Crawford, Jacqueline Rouse, and Barbara Woods (Brooklyn, N.Y.: Carlson, 1988), 1–12. This anthology was the product of a 1988 conference of the same title, held in Atlanta, which more or less launched the much wider exploration of women's contributions that followed. Payne's thesis has since been substantially refined and expanded.

8. Steven F. Lawson and Charles Payne, *Debating the Civil Rights Movement, 1945–1968* (Lanham, Md.: Rowman and Littlefield, 1998), 99.

9. For a discussion of how the "grand narrative" of the civil rights move-ment has influenced subsequent historiography, see Kathryn Nasstrom, "'Talking for a Purpose': Storytelling and Activism in the Life of Fran-ces Freeborn Pauley," in *Everybody's Grandmother and Nobody's Fool: Frances Freeborn Pauley and the Struggle for Social Justice* (Ithaca: Cornell Univ. Press, 2000), 146–94. An overview of the debate surrounding the origins and pe-riodization of the civil rights movement can be found in Patricia Sullivan, "Southern Reformers, the New Deal, and the Movement's Foundations," in *New Directions in Civil Rights Studies*, ed. Armistead Robinson and Patricia Sullivan (Charlottesville: Univ. Press of Virginia, 1991), 81–104. On the Long Civil Rights Movement, see Jacquelyn Hall, "The Long Civil Rights Movement and the Political Uses of the Past," *Journal of American History* 91 (March 2005): 1233–63.

10. A fuller discussion of this dynamic appears in this book's concluding es-say, including a number of oral history–related sources. For a bracing argument on this topic with respect to literature, see Bob Shacochis, "The Enemies of Imagination," *Harper's* (November 1995), 13–15. Various writers address the debates surrounding voice and "other-ness" in *MultiAmerica: Essays on Cultural Wars and Cultural Peace*, ed. Ishmael Reed (New York: Penguin, 1997).

11. At times we combined two sentences containing redundancies into one for clearer understanding. Using excerpts also required omissions of large explanatory portions of some interviews, so that what appears here omits some topics that a given narrator used as transitions among her thoughts. Such omissions occasionally (although not often) required that the sequence of a narrator's thoughts be altered, meaning that a discussion that preceded another discussion in the original interview now follows it in the excerpt.

12. Martin Luther King Jr., "The Rising Tide of Racial Consciousness (1960)," in *I Have a Dream: Writings and Speeches That Changed the World*, ed. James Melvin Washington (San Francisco: HarperSanFrancisco, 1992), 67.

1. Life under Segregation

1. Leon F. Litwack, "Jim Crow Blues," *OAH Magazine of History* 18 (January 2004): 7. For a fuller account of this history, see Robert C. Toll, *Blacking Up: The Minstrel Show in Nineteenth-Century America* (New York: Oxford Univ. Press, 1974), 28.

2. Wright's *Life behind the Veil* is the source of this phrase, but Wright himself borrowed the "veil" concept from W.E.B. DuBois's 1903 classic, *The Souls of Black Folk*.

3. For Harlan's words, see p. 1 of http://en.wikipedia.org/wiki/Equal_protection_clause (accessed on November 19, 2008).

4. On Reconstruction, see Eric Foner, *Reconstruction, 1863–1877* (New

York: Harper and Row, 1988). On the origins of Jim Crow, see C. Vann Woodward, *The Strange Career of Jim Crow* (New York: Oxford Univ. Press, 1974), and Joel Williamson, *Crucible of Race: Black/White Relations in the American South since Emancipation* (New York: Oxford Univ. Press, 1984).

5. Wright, *Life behind a Veil*, 1.

6. See interview with James Jones by Boyd Shearer and Harold Barker, December 19, 1997, in Louie B. Nunn Center for Oral History collection, University of Kentucky, Lexington, Kentucky.

7. Robin D. G. Kelley, *Race Rebels: Culture, Politics, and the Black Working Class* (New York: Free Press, 1994); Tera Hunter, *To 'Joy My Freedom: Southern Women's Lives and Labors after the Civil War* (Cambridge: Harvard Univ. Press, 1997).

8. For more on this mixed-race group whose origins continue to be debated and who are located predominantly in southern Appalachia, see, for example, Wayne Winkler, *Walking toward the Sunset: The Melungeons of Appalachia* (Macon, Ga.: Mercer Univ. Press, 2005).

9. The date was August 14, 1936. Details of Rainey Bethea's execution (known among African Americans and their allies as a "legal lynching" because the public punishment was the result of a trial rather than without benefit of one, as it so often had been in the nineteenth century) can be found in *The Kentucky Encyclopedia*, ed. John Kleber et al. (Lexington: Univ. Press of Kentucky, 1992), 74 (entry by Lee A. Dew).

10. Although many texts agree with this assertion, in fact, there were later "legal lynchings" that were also race-related. Willie McGee, for instance, was executed in Laurel, Mississippi, in 1951 by public hanging for the rape of a white woman who was rumored to have been his mistress for years prior to his being charged. See, for example, Catherine Fosl, *Subversive Southerner: Anne Braden and the Struggle for Racial Justice in the Cold War South* (Lexington: Univ. Press of Kentucky, 2006), 123–24.

Profile: Jesse Crenshaw

1. Franklin Kleckley was a law professor from a university in West Virginia, and Hardy did pursue hiring him, but Kleckley declined in favor of another job offer.

2. In 1978 the University of Kentucky did hire a second African American law professor.

2. Desegregation in Education

1. Bonnie J. Burns, "The Sturgis Incident—Desegregation of Public Schools in Union County, Kentucky" (Master's thesis, Murray State University, 1969), 3.

2. For a survey of school desegregation after *Brown*, see James T. Patterson, *Brown v. Board of Education: A Civil Rights Milestone and Its Troubled Legacy* (New York: Oxford Univ. Press, 2001). For a sample of recent scholarship on various aspects of the *Brown* decision and its legacy, see "Round Table: *Brown v. Board of Education*, Fifty Years After," *Journal of American History* 91 (June 2004): 19–118. On massive resistance to school desegregation, see Michael J. Klarman, "Why Massive Resistance," in *Massive Resistance: Southern Opposition to the Second Reconstruction*, ed. Clive Webb (New York: Oxford Univ. Press, 2005), and Numan V. Bartley, *The Rise of Massive Resistance: Race and Politics in the South during the 1950s* (Baton Rouge: Louisiana State Univ. Press, 1969). For more on the connection between anticommunism and the defense of segregation, see Fosl, *Subversive Southerner*, especially chapter 8, and Jeff Woods, *Black Struggle, Red Scare: Segregation and Anticommunism in the South, 1948–1968* (Baton Rouge: Louisiana State Univ. Press, 2003).

3. Hugh Morris, "Decision Voids State's Day Law," *Courier-Journal*, May 18, 1954; Omer Carmichael and Weldon James, *The Louisville Story* (New York: Simon and Schuster, 1957), 46; Wright, *A History of Blacks in Kentucky*, 197–99.

4. David Wolfford, "Resistance on the Border: School Desegregation in Western Kentucky, 1954–1964," *Ohio Valley History* 4, no. 2 (summer 2004): 41.

5. Ibid. The entire article unpacks this resistance more fully, and the historian referred to here is Wolfford, who defines western Kentucky as areas west of and including Bowling Green and Owensboro, encompassing portions of the following Kentucky regions: Jackson Purchase, Western Coal Fields, and Pennyrile.

6. Burns, "The Sturgis Incident," 36 (information taken from Kentucky Writers' Project of the Works Progress Administration, *Union County, Past and Present*, American Guide Series [Louisville: Schumann Printing Company, 1941], 60).

7. More details on the Gordon story are available in Box 27, Folder 3, of the Carl and Anne Braden Papers, State Historical Society of Wisconsin.

8. Details about the lawsuits and Crumlin are drawn from David Wolfford, "Kentucky after *Brown*," *Kentucky Humanities Magazine* 2 (2003), 11–20. A compelling account of one of the more repressive consequences for African Americans stemming from freedom-of-choice school desegregation policies—and the case based upon which they were ruled unconstitutional—is found in Constance Curry, *Silver Rights* (New York: Algonquin, 1994).

9. Wolfford, "Resistance on the Border," 41.

10. For a review of the suit, see Robert A. Sedler, "The Louisville-Jefferson County School Desegregation Case: A Lawyer's Retrospective," *Register of the Kentucky Historical Society* 105 (winter 2001): 3–32.

11. For comparison to busing and antibusing crises in other communities, see Nicholaus Mills, ed., *Busing U.S.A.* (New York: Teachers College Press, 1979); Matthew D. Lassiter, *The Silent Majority: Suburban Politics in the Sunbelt South* (Princeton: Princeton Univ. Press, 2006); and Richard A. Pride and J. David Woodard, *The Burden of Busing: The Politics of Desegregation in Nashville* (Knoxville: Univ. of Tennessee Press, 1985).

12. For details, see "Federal Court Applies University of Michigan Ruling to Affirm Voluntary School Integration Plan in Louisville, KY," NAACP Legal Defense Fund statement, June 30, 2004, available at www.naacpldf.org/content.aspx?article=318. More on recent school desegregation findings and the results of the Harvard Report mentioned here are found in E. Wayne Ross, "School Segregation Redux," *Z Magazine*, March 2003, online at http://www.zmag.org/zmag/viewArticle/14011 (accessed on November 18, 2008).

3. Opening Public Accommodations

1. On the 1960–1961 sit-ins and the rise of the Student Nonviolent Coordinating Committee, see Clayborne Carson, *In Struggle: SNCC and the Black Awakening of the 1960s* (Cambridge: Harvard Univ. Press, 1981), and Martin Oppenheimer, *The Sit-In Movement of 1960* (Brooklyn, N.Y.: Carlson, 1989). For an example of how the sit-ins affected one community, see William H. Chafe, *Civilities and Civil Rights: Greensboro, North Carolina, and the Black Struggle for Freedom* (New York: Oxford Univ. Press, 1980).

2. *Kentucky's Black Heritage: The Role of the Black People in the History of Kentucky from Pioneer Days to the Present* (Frankfort: Kentucky Commission on Human Rights, 1971), 113. Note: The one park not reserved for whites was restricted to African Americans only.

3. The historian George C. Wright has written extensively on the tensions and interplay between Louisville's racial image and the realities of life for its African American citizenry. See, for example, his essay "Desegregation of Public Accommodations in Louisville," in *Southern Businessmen and Desegregation*, ed. Elizabeth Jacoway and David Colburn (Baton Rouge: Louisiana State Univ. Press, 1982), 191–210.

4. In *Race and Rumors of Race* (Chapel Hill: Univ. of North Carolina Press, 1943), sociologist Howard Odum documents how commonly racial conflicts occurred in those two walks of life in the WWII South, as well as the paranoid fear of change that began to grip white southerners during this time. For more on the impact of World War II on race relations and the civil rights struggle, see Patricia Sullivan, *Days of Hope: Race and Democracy in the New Deal Era* (Chapel Hill: Univ. of North Carolina Press, 1996); Harvard Sitkoff, "African American Militancy in the World War II South: Another Perspective," in *Remaking Dixie: The Impact of World War II on the Ameri-*

can South, ed. Neil R. McMillen (Jackson: Univ. of Mississippi Press, 1997): 70–92; Kelley, *Race Rebels,* 55–75.

5. *Kentucky's Black Heritage,* 93.

6. Fosl, *Subversive Southerner,* 122. This postwar era has been called by some historians a "window of opportunity" for real change in the racial status quo brought about by a left/labor/civil rights coalition. For descriptions of this era, see John Egerton, *Speak Now against the Day: The Generation before the Civil Rights Movement in the South* (Chapel Hill: Univ. of North Carolina Press, 1994), and Robert Korstad, *Civil Rights Unionism: Tobacco Workers and the Struggle for Democracy in the Mid-Twentieth Century South* (Chapel Hill: Univ. of North Carolina Press, 2003).

7. Wright, "Desegregation of Public Accommodations," 195. On the development of local direct action organizing in this late 1950s period, see Aldon D. Morris, *The Origins of the Civil Rights Movement: Black Communities Organizing for Change* (New York: Free Press, 1986).

8. Patrick S. McElhone, "The Civil Rights Activities of the Louisville Branch of the National Association for the Advancement of Colored Persons, 1914–1960" (Master's thesis, University of Louisville, 1976), 155–56.

9. This history received coverage in the *Lexington Herald-Leader,* July 4, 2004, p. A8. The UK protests in 1959 were also explained by Abby Marlatt in her KCROHP interview.

10. Oppenheimer, *The Sit-In Movement,* 42–43.

11. Some of the preceding data on CORE in Kentucky is drawn from August Meier and Elliot Rudwick, *CORE: A Study in the Civil Rights Movement, 1942–1968* (New York: Oxford Univ. Press, 1973). The story of CORE in Cincinnati is found in Roger C. Hansen, "Pioneers in Nonviolent Action: The Congress of Racial Equality in Cincinnati, 1946–1955," *Queen City Heritage* 52, no. 3 (1994), 23–35.

12. Gerald L. Smith, *A Black Educator in the Segregated South* (Lexington: Univ. Press of Kentucky, 2002), 151–62.

13. *Kentucky's Black Heritage,* 113–14.

14. For the story of Louisville's public accommodation battle, see Wright, "Desegregation of Public Accommodations," 199–203; Tracy E. K'Meyer, "'The Gateway to the South': Regional Identity and the Louisville Civil Rights Movement," *Ohio Valley History* 4 (spring 2004): 43–60; and Tracy E. K'Meyer, *Civil Rights in the Gateway to the South: Louisville, Kentucky, 1945–1980* (Lexington: Univ. Press of Kentucky, 2009).

15. The description of Wachs's view is from his son, Fred Wachs Jr., quoted in "Dramatic Stories, Little Coverage," on page 8A of the July 4, 2004, *Lexington Herald-Leader.* This article and others surrounding it also offer more background on this lack of coverage.

16. Meier and Rudwick, *CORE,* 120. Background on the Lexington move-

ment comes from Gerald L. Smith, "Blacks in Lexington, Kentucky: The Struggle for Civil Rights, 1945–1980" (Master's thesis, Univ. of Kentucky, 1983). On the Freedom Rides, Raymond Arsenault, *Freedom Riders: 1961 and the Struggle for Racial Justice* (New York: Oxford Univ. Press, 2006).

17. This remark was made by Robert Estill, chairman of the Kentucky Commission on Human Rights, in testimony at the first annual Mayors' Meeting on civil rights, in April 1962. See news clipping (n.a., n.d.) and Estill journal notes in Robert Estill folder, subject files, Kentucky Civil Rights Oral History Project files, Kentucky Oral History Commission, Frankfort.

18. "Civil Rights in Kentucky since 1863," published pamphlet, n.a., n.d. (Commonwealth of Kentucky, circa 1963), in authors' possession, pp. 16–19.

19. The material in this paragraph is drawn mostly from *Kentucky's Black Heritage*, 118–21.

20. Ridgel's implication here is that her husband was not sufficiently non-violent when attacked.

21. Of a local population of seven thousand, 12 percent were African American.

22. Although the correct name is the Kentucky Commission on Human Rights, we did not correct it when narrators used a different form of the name.

4. Open Housing

1. Wright, *A History of Blacks in Kentucky*, 58.

2. *Kentucky's Black Heritage*, 61.

3. Wright, *A History of Blacks in Kentucky*, 59; Winona L. Fletcher and Sheila Mason Burton, *Community Memories: A Glimpse of African American Life in Frankfort, Kentucky* (Frankfort: Kentucky Historical Society, 2003), 3–4.

4. For explanations of how housing segregation developed in the post-war era, see Kenneth T. Jackson, *Crabgrass Frontier: The Suburbanization of the United States* (New York: Oxford Univ. Press, 1985), and Steven Grant Meyer, *As Long As They Don't Move Next Door: Segregation and Racial Conflict in American Neighborhoods* (New York: Rowman and Littlefield, 2000).

5. For the story of the Wade house incident and the prosecution of Carl Braden and others, see Anne Braden, *The Wall Between* (Knoxville: Univ. of Tennessee Press, 1999), and Fosl, *Subversive Southerner*. On southern anti-communism and its impact on the civil rights movement, see Woods, *Black Struggle, Red Scare*, and George Lewis, *The White South and the Red Menace: Segregationists, Anti-Communism, and Massive Resistance, 1945–1965* (Gainesville: Univ. Press of Florida, 2003).

6. On the national open housing movement during this period, see Juliet Saltman, *Open Housing: Dynamics of a Social Movement* (New York: Praeger, 1978).

7. *Kentucky's Black Heritage*, 127–28. For Powers's retrospective account of her role in the passage of the fair housing law, see Georgia Powers, *I Shared the Dream: The Pride, Passion and Politics of the First Black Woman Senator from Kentucky* (Far Hills, N.J.: New Horizon Press, 1995).

8. For statistics on white/black segregation in Kentucky cities, see www.censusscope.org, produced by the Social Science Data Analysis Network of the University of Michigan.

9. Here Logsdon refers to the effort to get him to join the homeowner association's attempt to deny the home to African Americans.

10. William Warner was the safety director for the city of Louisville during the open housing movement. As safety director he had authority over the police and fire departments. Warheim refers to the marches as "illegal" because by that point there had been an injunction against demonstrations after dark.

11. "Children's Center" was the colloquial name for the Juvenile Detention Center.

12. The Fayette Fiscal Court prohibited housing discrimination in Lexington in 1967 before the adoption of the state open housing law. "History of Blacks in Lexington," *Lexington Herald-Leader*, February 21, 1988.

5. Economic Opportunity

1. Wright, *A History of Blacks in Kentucky*, 3–5.

2. Ibid., 6, 11–12.

3. Ibid., 17–24.

4. Ibid., 6, 14–16, 25; *Kentucky's Black Heritage*, 75–76. For a survey of the relationship between African Americans and organized labor in industry, see Robert H. Zieger, *For Jobs and Freedom: Race and Labor in America since 1865* (Lexington: Univ. Press of Kentucky, 2007). For a survey of the role of African Americans in the coal industry, see Ronald L. Lewis, *Black Coal Miners in America: Race, Class, and Community Conflict* (Lexington: Univ. Press of Kentucky, 1987).

5. On the Farm Equipment Workers, see Toni Gilpin, "Left by Themselves: A History of the United Farm Equipment and Metal Workers Union, 1938–1955" (Ph.D. diss., Yale University, 1992). For examples of postwar jobs campaigns in Louisville, see Tracy E. K'Meyer, "Building Interracial Democracy: Stories of the Early Civil Rights Movement in Louisville, Kentucky, 1941–1956," in *Time Longer Than Rope*, ed. Charles Payne and Adam Green (New York: New York Univ. Press, 2003), 411–39. For a study of the

fate of civil rights and labor postwar partnerships, see Robert Korstad and Nelson Lichtenstein, "Opportunities Lost and Found: Labor, Radicals, and the Early Civil Rights Movement," *Journal of American History* 75 (December 1988): 786–811.

6. For a survey of the War on Poverty, see Irwin Unger, *The Best of Intentions: The Triumphs and Failures of the Great Society under Kennedy, Johnson, and Nixon* (New York: Doubleday, 1996). For examples of scholarship that link the War on Poverty and the civil rights movement, see Annelise Orleck, *Storming Caesar's Palace: How Black Mothers Fought Their Own War on Poverty* (Boston: Beacon Press, 2005), and Rhonda Y. Williams, *The Politics of Public Housing: Black Women's Struggles against Urban Inequality* (New York: Oxford Univ. Press, 2004).

7. *Kentucky's Black Heritage*, 118–21.

8. Ibid., 122.

9. For a study of how African Americans and other minority groups pushed for the enforcement of antidiscrimination laws, see Nancy Maclean, *Freedom Is Not Enough: The Opening of the American Workplace* (New York: Russell Sage Foundation, 2006).

Profile: Julia Cowans

1. For more on the history of African Americans in Appalachia, see William H. Turner and Edward J. Cabbell, eds., *Blacks in Appalachia* (Lexington: Univ. Press of Kentucky, 1985).

2. Creating a profile of Julia Cowans from Portelli's lengthy conversations with her and her husband together required considerably more editing, condensing, and rearranging than was the case with the other interviews used in this collection. The narrative that appears here is consequently more a condensed compilation of multiple conversations than is true of any other profile in this book, and we are grateful to Portelli for allowing us to include it in a volume whose aims are quite different than his were in doing the interviews and writing about them later. We constructed this vignette by (a) selecting and reorganizing portions of Portelli's interviews with Julia and Hugh Cowans in 1983 and 1988, and (b) interspersing a few clarifying comments taken from Betsy Brinson's follow-up interview with Julia Cowans, done as part of the KCROHP in 2002. Portelli's comments here are from his *The Battle of Valle Giulia: Oral History and the Art of Dialogue* (Madison: Univ. of Wisconsin Press, 1997), 26. This book also gives more information on and comments by the Cowans.

3. "Scrip" refers to currency that was generated by the company in order to pay workers in something other than cash. Scrip could be used only to purchase goods from the company store and was worth nothing outside the

coal camp. "Ax" is a form of "ask" used widely by both African Americans and whites in Appalachia.

4. By "tinhorns," Cowans means National Guardsmen. "Scab" is a term for a replacement worker who is brought in to work when the long-term workforce is on strike.

5. The period Cowans refers to here took place much later than the organizing drives she observed as a child in the 1930s. The women's activities she recounts here took place during the Brookside Strike in 1973.

6. Black Consciousness, Black Power

1. For more on Black Power, see Peniel E. Joseph, *Waiting 'til the Midnight Hour: A Narrative History of Black Power in America* (New York: Henry Holt, 2006).

2. For an introduction to the repression of Black Power advocates and others in the late 1960s and early 1970s, see Nelson Blackstock, *COINTEL-PRO: The FBI's Secret War on Political Freedom* (New York: Anchor Foundation, 1988).

3. On black student activism, see Peniel E. Joseph, "Black Studies, Student Activism, and the Black Power Movement," *The Black Power Movement: Rethinking the Civil Rights–Black Power Era*, ed. Peniel E. Joseph (New York: Routledge, 2006), 255–71.

4. SCEF was the Southern Conference Educational Fund, a regional civil rights organization Braden and her husband had worked for since 1957. In the 1960s, they moved its headquarters to Louisville. Until its decline in 1974 it was a hub of movement activism on West Broadway.

5. KCLC was the Kentucky Christian Leadership Conference, the state affiliate of King's Southern Christian Leadership Conference, headquartered in Atlanta.

7. Black Political Power

1. This story is told in Nancy J. Weiss, *Farewell to the Party of Lincoln: Black Politics in the Age of FDR* (Princeton: Princeton Univ. Press, 1983).

2. For the story of how African Americans across the South fought for the vote and to use it for political power, see Steven F. Lawson, *Black Ballots: Voting Rights in the South, 1944–1969* (New York: Columbia Univ. Press, 1976), and Steven F. Lawson, *In Pursuit of Power: Southern Blacks and Electoral Politics, 1965–1982* (New York: Columbia Univ. Press, 1985).

3. On black political activity in Kentucky, see *Kentucky's Black Heritage*, 44–49; Wright, *A History of Blacks in Kentucky*, 92–102; 158–60; Alice Allison Dunnigan, *The Fascinating Story of Black Kentuckians: Their Heritage and*

Traditions (Washington, D.C.: Association for the Study of Afro-American Life and History, 1982), 349–96.

4. The story of this election is told in Allen Yarnell, *Democrats and Progressives: The 1948 Presidential Election as a Test of Postwar Liberalism* (Berkeley: Univ. of California Press, 1974).

5. Here, "merger" refers to the campaign in 1982 to merge the city of Louisville and Jefferson County governments, which Sloane supported, but which failed at the time at the polls.

6. David A. Bositis, *Black Elected Officials: A Statistical Summary, 2000* (Washington, D.C.: Joint Center for Political and Economic Studies, 2001), 18.

Conclusion

1. For a sample of the scholarship on the theme of the civil rights movement in popular memory, see Brian Ward, "Forgotten Wails and Master Narratives: Media, Culture, and Memories of the Modern African American Freedom Struggle," in *Media, Culture and the Modern African American Freedom Struggle*, ed. Brian Ward (Gainesville: Univ. Press of Florida, 2001), 1–15, and Renee C. Romano and Leigh Raiford, eds., *The Civil Rights Movement in American Memory* (Athens: Univ. of Georgia Press, 2006). On the memory of King, see Vincent Gordon Harding, "Beyond Amnesia: Martin Luther King, Jr., and the Future of America," *Journal of American History* 74 (September 1987): 468–76. On women's absence from the popular memory of the movement, see Kathryn L. Nasstrom, "Down to Now: Memory, Narrative, and Women's Leadership in the Civil Rights Movement in Atlanta," *Gender and History* 11 (April 1999): 113–44.

2. George P. Rawick, "General Introduction," *The American Slave: A Composite Autobiography: Supplement, Series 1*, vol. 6: *Mississippi Narratives, Part 1* (Westport, Conn.: Greenwood Press, 1977); James West Davidson and Mark Hamilton Lytle, *After the Fact: The Art of Historical Detection*, 5th ed. (New York: McGraw-Hill, 2005), 179–206. The Portelli exchange is recounted in Paul Thompson, *The Voice of the Past: Oral History*, 3rd ed. (New York: Oxford Univ. Press, 2000), 242.

3. For examples, see Warren Anderson, "Oral History and Migrant Wage Labor: Sources of Narrative Distortion," *Oral History Review* 28 (summer/fall 2001): 1–20; Yvette J. Kopijn, "The Oral History Interview in a Cross-Cultural Setting," in *Narrative and Genre: Contexts and Types of Communication*, ed. Mary Chamberlain and Paul Thompson (New Brunswick: Transaction Publishers, 2004), 142–59; Tamara Giles-Vernick, "Lives, Histories, and Sites of Recollection," in *African Words, African Voices: Critical Practices in Oral History*, ed. Louise White et al. (Bloomington: Indiana Univ. Press, 2001).

4. Kim Lacy Rogers, "Memory, Struggle, and Power: On Interviewing Political Activists," *Oral History Review* 15 (spring 1987), 165–84.

5. Harding, "Beyond Amnesia."

6. See, for example, Douglas S. Massey and Nancy A. Denton, *American Apartheid: Segregation and the Making of the Underclass* (Cambridge, Mass.: Harvard Univ. Press, 1993).

7. For an example of a critique of emphasis on the church and SCLC, see Charles Payne, "Bibliographic Essay," in *I've Got the Light of Freedom: The Organizing Tradition and the Mississippi Freedom Struggle* (Berkeley: Univ. of California Press, 1995), 413–42.

8. Kelley, *Race Rebels.*

9. For examples, see Adam Fairclough, *Race and Democracy: The Civil Rights Struggle in Louisiana, 1915–1972* (Athens: Univ. of Georgia Press, 1995); John Dittmer, *Local People: The Struggle for Civil Rights in Mississippi* (Urbana: Univ. of Illinois Press, 1995); Patricia Sullivan, *Days of Hope: Race and Democracy in the New Deal Era* (Chapel Hill: Univ. of North Carolina Press, 1996); and the review of the literature in Jacquelyn Dowd Hall, "The Long Civil Rights Movement and the Political Uses of the Past," *Journal of American History* 91 (March 2005): 1233–63.

10. On black schools under segregation, see, for example, David S. Cecelski, *Along Freedom Road: Hyde County, North Carolina, and the Fate of Black Schools in the South* (Chapel Hill: Univ. of North Carolina Press, 1994); Sonya Yvette Ramsey, *Reading, Writing and Segregation: A Century of Black Women Teachers in Nashville* (Urbana: Univ. of Illinois Press, 2007); Vanessa S. Walker, *Their Highest Potential: An African American School Community in the Segregated South* (Chapel Hill: Univ. of North Carolina Press, 1997). For a critique of the positive portrayal of schools under segregation, see Gary Orfield and Susan E. Easton, *Dismantling Desegregation: The Quiet Reversal of Brown v. Board of Education* (New York: New Press, 1996). For reviews of the role of nostalgia in this research and critique of it, see Jack Dougherty, "From Anecdote to Analysis: Oral Interviews and New Scholarship in Education History," *Journal of American History* 86 (September 1999): 712–23, and Barbara Shircliffe, "'We Got the Best of That World': A Case for the Study of Nostalgia in the Oral History of School Segregation," *Oral History Review* 28 (summer/fall 2001): 59–84.

11. See Don Mills's narrative in this volume; the newspaper's acknowledgment was commented on by a variety of national media outlets, but see especially "Front-Page News, Back-Page Coverage," *Lexington Herald-Leader,* July 4, 2004, pp. 1A and 8–9A. One consequence of this news blackout was a lack of archival photos, and we are grateful to Calvert McCann, who shot the protests as a teen and who shared some of his work for the 2004 *Herald-Leader* piece and for this volume.

Index

CPSIA information can be obtained at www.ICGtesting.com
Printed in the USA
BVOW05s1351270115

385165BV00001B/73/P